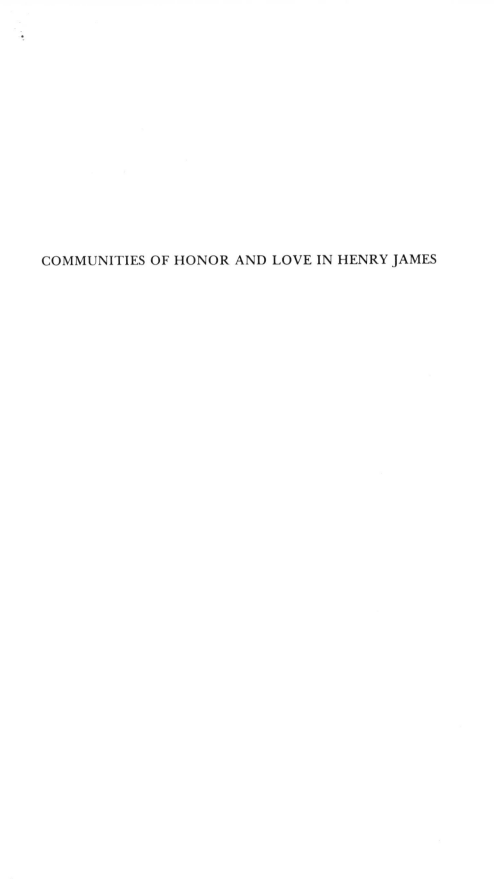

COMMUNITIES OF HONOR AND LOVE IN HENRY JAMES

COMMUNITIES
OF HONOR AND LOVE
IN HENRY JAMES

Manfred Mackenzie

Harvard University Press
Cambridge, Massachusetts
and
London, England
1976

Library of Congress Cataloging in Publication Data
Mackenzie, Manfred, 1934-
   Communities of honor and love in Henry James.
   Includes bibliographical references and index.
   1. James, Henry, 1843-1916 — Criticism and interpretation.   I. Title.
PS2124.M265   813'.4   75-17756
ISBN 0-674-15160-7

Publication of this book has been aided by a grant
from the Andrew W. Mellon Foundation

Preface

The first part of this book is concerned with James's social imagination. Assuming, at least, his acute and omnivorous social sensibility, I have begun by asking what kind of society it is that he regularly portrays. Are there any social "structures" to which he returns? More specifically, I have asked why, on the one occasion when James sets out to write a novel of society of the big mid-Victorian kind, he should produce a story that seems unequivocally to uphold established or manifest society and yet centers imaginatively upon a revolutionary conspiracy dedicated to pulling down that society. Supposing for the moment that *The Princess Casamassima* were a Jamesian norm, is it that society in his work is characteristically "secret"? In fact, the reader will see, society is secret throughout James (and no less so in an American work like *The Bostonians* than in the international stories). If the society for which James's hero would qualify is likely to withhold itself from him, this hero may in turn resort to cabal and conspiracy as the only way open to him of knowing the real, established, civilized thing.

The question of James's social imagination leads to a consideration of the psychology of his characters. This seems an obvious enough step: the Jamesian civil alien who stands on the hither side of an exclusive society may well feel himself divested of social identity. Voluntarily yet also involuntarily deracinated, he may be left only with his character (as *The Portrait of a Lady* calls it). Accordingly, my second chapter rewrites my broad conclusions about James's social imagination as much as possible in complementary, psychological terms. I try to develop, by way of examples drawn mainly from the early and middle periods, a series of formulas that will both cope with the many aspects of James's work and amount to a coherent theory of his psychology.

For a start, it seems plain that secrecy or the use of secrecy in conspiracy is a reaction to the experience of exposure, an experience to be found everywhere in James. In turn, exposure in him is closely related to shock (understood as a drastic loss of identity). And in their turn, exposure and shock regularly give rise in him to the emotion of shame. In short, the psychological novelist in James writes along what a social scientist might call a shame axis of experience. James's psychological subject is the ordeal of self-consciousness.

Within this second chapter I have argued that James's protagonist is committed to a quest. If exposure, shock, and shame seem to be of the mysterious nature of things, then this hero must set out either to acquire or simply to recover identity. If he has been exposed to the extent of "dying of shame" and feels that he only lives posthumously as his own ghost, or if in the extremity of his self-consciousness he is visited by another self who seems to make off with all the identity, then he must commit himself correspondingly to the goal of sufficiency or decent pride or freedom or honor. On the other hand, should he fail in this quest for identity, he may literally die of shame, of suicidally punitive self-rejection.

Morally speaking, I argue here, the Jamesian hero's ordeal of self-consciousness is in itself neutral. Its manner and consequences, however, are definitely evaluable. Thus if the hero does not bear with his loss of identity, and if on the contrary he feels compelled to deny this loss absolutely, he will want merely to extort his value from society. In time, he may feel compelled to contrive an act of resentment which, being based in the first place upon an extraordinary sense of weakness, will also be an ambiguous one; revenge-feeling in James typically flowers into the use of secrecy described by the formula "secret revenge for secret injury." At this point of course the hero's shame has become morally critical. Indeed, this hero stands on the brink of the Jamesian immoral, ready to commit himself to a left-handed version of the quest for identity, a revenge cycle.

As I say, the first half of this book concerns itself mainly with that plane of experience on which identity and honor are sought, won, or lost. As James always recognized, however, and especially during the later nineties, identity and honor cannot ultimately be sustained on their own terms. They are entirely ambiguous, too much the other aspect of shame, self-doubt, and the compulsion that initiates revenge cycles not to end in disastrous dehumanization. Even the familiar ethic of renunciation, which is designed to avert all cycles of irony and falsification, can but aggravate this ambiguity when it appeals to no higher plane of experience. As a result, it becomes vital for James to find, or perhaps to restate in purer form, an ideal that will transcend the insufficient plane on which one wins or loses sufficiency, but that, while so doing, will redeem and sustain it. Finally James appeals to a spiritual value that will constitute the ground of identity and honor.

Accordingly I argue in the second half of this book that another, higher plane of experience steadily emerges in James, that of love as manifested in the capacity to sacrifice the claim to identity and honor. If "love remains" at the end of *The Portrait of a Lady* or at the end of *The Princess Casamassima* — it has always moved James's passionate pilgrims — it emerges still more unequivocally in the later work. It is this "prodigious spirit," as James himself put it, that informs the wonderful beginning of James's "second go," *What Maisie Knew*. And it is this that "swelled accordingly even in her abasement," as Maggie Verver puts it, right through the major novels that follow. In Henry James, it turns out, a saintly love is above identity and honor while there is nothing above saintly love.

Finally, I should say that I have tried to express my sense of the relation in James of the ambiguous claims of identity and honor and the unequivocal presence of love by dividing this book thematically into two halves. (Perhaps inevitably, this organization slights, in the first two chapters, some of the positive side of James.) At the same time, a one-two organization does generally express the development of James's career, which, relatively speaking, seems almost to have broken down during the early nineties. I should also like to think that it will serve to remind the reader of James's own characteristic binary form and its ruefully misplaced middle.

I wish to thank the American Council of Learned Societies for the generous assistance which allowed me to begin this book. I also wish to thank Edwin Honig both for his intellectual example and for his active interest over the years; Rosemary Sweetapple for Jamesian "germs" that stimulated thoughts on boxes and doubles; Antonio Regalado for revolutionary conversations on revengers and their cycles; Thea Astley for so vividly explaining acolytes; and my wife, Janet, for all her support.

Permission to quote from Erik H. Erikson, *Childhood and Society*, second edition, revised, was granted by W. W. Norton & Company, Inc. (Copyright 1950, © 1963 by W. W. Norton & Company, Inc.), British rights by permission of The Hogarth Press, Ltd. The quotation from William Empson, *Some Versions of Pastoral*, is reprinted by

permission of New Directions Publishing Corporation (Copyright ©
1974 by William Empson; all rights reserved), British rights by permission of Chatto and Windus, Ltd. I also acknowledge with thanks
permission to use material from my articles "Communities of Knowledge: Secret Society in Henry James," *ELH,* 39 (March 1972), 147-168,
© 1972 The Johns Hopkins University Press, and "A Theory of Henry
James's Psychology," *Yale Review,* 62 (Spring 1974), 347-371. Chapter
two contains a slightly revised version of "The Lapse and Accumulation of Time in Henry James," an essay in *American Studies Down
Under: Pacific Circle 3,* ed. Norman Harper, University of Queens-
land Press, 1975.

Sydney, N.S.W.   M.M.
April 1975

Contents

I have used the Macmillan Collected Edition (London, 1921-1923) when referring to James's novels and prefaces and *The Complete Tales of Henry James,* ed. Leon Edel (Philadelphia and New York, 1961-1964), when referring to his short stories.

I. Communities of Knowledge:
Secret Society in Henry James

No State, in the European sense of the word, and indeed barely a specific national name. No sovereign, no court, no personal loyalty, no aristocracy, no church, no clergy, no army, no diplomatic service, no country gentlemen, no palaces, no castles, nor manors, nor old country-houses, nor parsonages, nor thatched cottages, nor ivied ruins; no cathedrals, nor abbeys, nor little Norman churches; no great Universities, nor public schools—no Oxford, nor Eton, nor Harrow; no literature, no novels, no museums, no pictures, no political society, no sporting class—no Epsom nor Ascot! Some such list as that might be drawn up of the absent things in American life—especially in the American life of forty years ago, the effect of which, upon an English or a French imagination, would probably as a general thing be appalling. The natural remark, in the almost lurid light of such an indictment, would be that if these things are left out, everything is left out. The American knows that a good deal remains; what it is that remains—that is his secret, his joke, as one may say.

Henry James, Hawthorne

Although the supersensible social pilgrim in Henry James is familiar to us, criticism seems never to have asked what *kind* of society it is that James typically imagines. Are there any social "structures" implicit in his comparative international situations?

We might invent a Jamesian scenario—hopefully an unexceptionable one—in order to answer these questions. In this, the hero will abjure American society more or less on the grounds that it is insufficient for him, or he for it, and that he can best complete, best civilize himself in Europe; his is something of a social apostasy. Should he now succeed in his quest for social completion, his story will end with his marriage: in the international comedy, he marries in Europe, is married to Europe (Europe understood as a civilized quality or style of life). Even at best, however, the Jamesian apostate hero in Europe will have met a complex fate. As Van Wyck Brooks long ago showed,[1] he will, exactly on account of his craving completion, have risked and perhaps forfeited altogether American social possibilities—life-feeling, identity, and power—without necessarily becoming eligible to earn any corresponding social identity in Europe. Because of his prior or primary American association he cannot participate in any conventional modes of European social power, only in "seeing," or "knowledge," or "consciousness." Indeed, all that he can claim to be is what one might call a social aesthete: "not the fruit of experience but experience itself is the end" (Pater).[2] But then, on account of this voluntary aestheticism in Europe, he will have forfeited still further whatever social claims he might have laid in America, becoming that much more the involuntary social aesthete. The international hero has proved to be merely an interstitial one. After all, he is not "more"; neither a civilized man nor a good barbarian, he is *not*.

One can describe this hero's deracination in another way. While his own society would seem to preclude him from all but what *Roderick Hudson* calls a "light ornamental" identity, James's apostate has gone on to claim a compensatory social identity in Europe. It now turns out, however, that Europe is only apparently accessible to him. In fact, James's claimant encounters in Europe a kind of sphere of protection, a graduated secrecy, around an innermost social substance or essence. Even when he succeeds with mediators, he finds that they function ultimately to confirm this sphere of protection. What is complex about his social fate is that he is initiated exoterically, but never esoterically, into a group that takes on something of the character of a secret society, "not a formal association, nor a secret society — still less a 'dangerous gang' or an organization for any definite end. We're simply a collection of natural affinities . . . governed at any rate by Mrs. Brook, in our mysterious ebbs and flows, very much as the tides are governed by the moon" (*The Awkward Age*, 109-110).

At first the claimant's situation may be no more than awkward. It may be merely that he is neither one thing nor another, neither flesh nor fowl, a kind of civil barbarian. But if he has indeed been admitted to a social group only the more gallingly to be precluded, he will eventually find himself threatened with the total forfeit of a social personality that, while incomplete, has up until now at least been reliably so, and that might well have deserved to be completed. He finds himself occupying an untenable position. Precluded from a secret to which he has considered himself to be admitted, he is left with a sense of being exposed and tricked, of being mortally pretentious. He himself appears to have no secret whatsoever. He may as well not be.

At this point we may distinguish a further phase in the transaction to which the Jamesian claimant has submitted himself. Out of an inevitable resentment, a resentment that he may have suppressed during his social probation, he now looks for compensation. He would react by possessing a comparable secret of his own, even if he has forcibly to dispossess those who preclude him of their secret. He may be compelled not only to possess himself of a secret but also to make use of this secret in order to assert himself. And if he cannot exactly expropriate for his own use a secret of real substance, he will adopt the appearances and technique of secrecy; he will simply use secrecy.[3] Whatever his reaction, the hero will eventually resort to conspiracy. He will involve himself in a cabal, a schismatic, secret association — "communities of knowledge," as a phrase from "The Jolly Corner" puts it. Only by this reactionary means, it appears, can this civil alien know anything of social essence.

In the final phase of this situation, James's hero either accommodates himself to his complex fate on the grounds that he *has* sufficiently known the real, established thing or, failing to accept himself, persists in extorting compensation for *not* knowing it. The social and ethical crisis of the international story shows the hero confronted with a difficult choice of false positions: either he renounces all reaction in favor of a morally superior but minor social standing or he commits himself further to what is essentially a revenge cycle, barbarously imposing himself upon an alien order.

[4]

A good early example of this paradigm situation in James would be the short story "Adina." In this fable two passionate pilgrims, a lover of the picturesque and his "disbyronized" friend Sam Scrope, surprise a young Italian peasant sleeping on the Roman Campagna. Identifying a jewel that the peasant has only just discovered as being potentially of great value, Scrope immediately bargains unscrupulously for it and is contemptuous of the ignorant Beati into the bargain. The latter, dishonored, now plots his revenge, and takes it eventually by persuading Scrope's American fiancée Adina to leave Scrope and marry himself. It is a case of an eye for an eye, in fact a "pearl" (as Beati styles Adina) for a topaz. In the end Beati's honor is satisfied while Scrope, throwing the disputed jewel into the Tiber, renounces any further claim on Adina.

Like so much of James's fiction, "Adina" develops according to an injury-resentment psychology. We are told that the passionate American claimant looks "common" in a society where "almost everything has, to the outer sense, what artists call style" (213). Suddenly the situation has him confronted with the European other self he would claim for his own, a nobly self-sufficient "rustic Endymion" (214), a "young Hercules" (215); and inevitably it is as if the man who in all points completes him also competes all too successfully with him. Indeed, this competitor seems, in his extraordinary being-unto-self, to rob the claimant of all precious identity; one might say that Beati completes Scrope only to deplete him. Even in his unready, exposed, and disadvantaged attitude on the Campagna the European becomes an injury to the hero, a revelation of Scrope's own unready and disadvantaged self.

The advent of the hero's double means that his anxious secret life, his barbarian's secret that he may in fact have no secret or valuable being-unto-self, is out. Exposed all around, subject to a sudden ordeal of self-consciousness, he now reacts resentfully and compulsively to conceal himself, not least from himself. And he best conceals himself from himself by being other than his exposed self, indeed by trying to be the other self, by displacing the man who has had the power to displace him: he wrests Beati's jewel from him — it is of course the "jewel" of his social identity or honor. In other words, the hero, whose apostasy in itself constitutes a revenge upon himself, now commits himself to a compensation or revenge cycle. The upshot of his encounter with the double is that he carries off the jewel, subsequently to make an esoteric cult of it: he will have a "secret." And in fact it turns out that he has expropriated a Roman stone that bespeaks social power and quintessence in an emblematic way, a way that makes it more than it appears:

> I [the narrator] saw the surface of the stone was worked in elaborate intaglio, but I was not prepared for the portentous character of image and legend. In the centre was a full-length naked figure, which I supposed at first to be a pagan deity. Then I saw the orb of sovereignty in one out-stretched hand, the chiselled imperial sceptre in the other, and the laurel-crown on the low-browed head. All round the face of the stone, near the edges, ran a chain of carven figures — warriors, and horses, and chariots, and young men and women interlaced in elaborate confusion. Over the head of the image, within this concave frieze, stood the inscription: DIVUS TIBERIUS CAESAR TOTIUS ORBIS IMPERATOR (222).

To adorn himself with this portentous dynastic spoil is to convert his mere having into a quality of his being. On account of its virtue, he feels compensated and complete, valuable, "more."

Here is a thoroughly Jamesian range of experience. One hero, the rather ghostly narrator, is content that his civil inheritance be the European picturesque; he can accept his social aestheticism. James's other claimant, however, unable to rest with such a ghostly minority, seeks to press his claim further. If Scrope cannot *be* his European double, he can compensate himself by trying to be more, to be major, in his enforced aestheticism. He can aggrandize himself — always, if merely, in aesthetic terms — by adorning himself with a stylized or formal symbol of Europe's social vitality, for such a locus of social power as the dynastic jewel can, by its very nature, bestow on him a personal quantity that cannot readily be estimated, a superfluity that is in principle limitless. It is without price, a more-than-appearance, universal. And yet he is its master.[4]

The reactive American social aesthete would, then, either adorn himself with a social secret, or expropriate from Europe a secret, a knowledge or consciousness of social quintessence, that will serve to adorn him. Thereby, he dreams, he comes into his inheritance of all the ages:

> "Don't you think it was worth while getting up to shake hands with the Emperor Tiberius?" cried Scrope, after observing my surprise. "Shabby Nineteenth Century Yankees, as we are, we are having our audience. Down on your knees, barbarian, we're in a tremendous presence! Haven't I

worked all these days and nights, with my little rags and files, to some purpose? I've annulled the centuries — I've resuscitated a *totius orbis imperator*. Do you conceive, do you apprehend, does your heart thump against your ribs? Not as it should, evidently. This is where Caesar wore it, dull modern — here, on his breast, near the shoulder, framed in chiselled gold, circled about with pearls as big as plums, clasping together the two sides of his gold-stiffened mantle. It was the agraffe of the imperial purple. Tremble, sir!" and he took up the splendid jewel, and held it against my breast. "No doubts — no objections — no reflections — or we're mortal enemies. How do I know it — where's my warrant? It simply must be! It's too precious to have been anything else. It's the finest intaglio in the world. It has told me its secret; it has lain whispering classic Latin to me by the hour all this week past . . . It has told me everything — more than I can tell you now" (223).

His compulsive reaction is such that he not only dispossesses the European other self of his secret, he must then make use of this secret. He makes a kind of secret secret of it that will affect and even provoke all the characters concerned:

> "Yes, surely," I said, "it's the finest of known intaglios."
> Scrope was silent a while. "Say of unknown," he answered at last. "No one shall ever know it. You I hereby hold pledged to secrecy. I shall show it to no one else — except to my mistress, if I ever have one" (224).

In James's fable there is now a cabal, a reactionary secret society, the mysteriously potent head of which is DIVUS TIBERIUS CAESAR, lying alongside the manifest society Angelo Beati represents, a society whose innermost essence is likewise DIVUS TIBERIUS CAESAR. This cabal is consummated with a pledge or vow.

The second half of this story of an eye for an eye is concerned with the lifetime of this community of knowledge. Being falsely based, being willed and reactive rather than spontaneous and organic, it can necessarily have but an interim life. Thus Scrope's reaction provokes — as perhaps it is secretly intended that it should — a dangerous counterreaction. The injured Beati subsequently conspires to persuade his American adversary's fiancée to marry himself. Confronted with this counterreaction, Scrope presumably has the choice either of renouncing altogether the dangerously intensifying revenge cycle or of further committing himself to it. Instructed perhaps by Adina's obscurely self-sacrificial part in Beati's conspiracy, but recognizing also

[7]

the powerful presence of the real thing, he chooses to renounce both Adina and his claim to the grand topaz.

Not of course that the American claimant is not in a false position at the end; it is just that he has freed himself and the others from a false, barbarous reaction to this position. Socially speaking, indeed, James's story reaches a remarkably equivocal resolution. For all the noble realism of his renunciation, the American hero remains a relative nobody of an outside-insider. Henceforth his identity will lie merely in what he knows. Meanwhile, for all that they are married, Adina and the European Beati are only ambiguously "happy, happy, happy" (253), parties to something as much like a conspiratorial liaison as any authentic relationship. It amounts, probably, to an honorable settlement: the American hero will honorably refrain from giving the lie to the international marriage-lie. In James, it turns out that the community of the civilized is also something of a secret society.

The Princess Casamassima opens with an epochal "little boy lost" episode, Hyacinth Robinson's encounter in London's Millbank prison with his dying and dishonored mother. It is as if this hero were born of shock, of a premature jarring that means no less than that he may not have lived. At one stroke Hyacinth loses his trust both in Lomax Place and in his aristocratic pretensions. Not only this, he knows by his association with "a French impropriety" (I, 32) the fever-chill of the Jamesian interstice. From now on Hyacinth will stand, a yearning social sensibility, on the hither side of an impregnable society. With him, everything has to be authenticated.

By adult life Hyacinth seems to have forfeited any direct claim upon social place. Holding true to his stigmatized self, he entertains the idea of marriage to Millicent Henning only to put it out of mind. "She [Amanda Pynsent] was always in a fearful 'funk' about their getting hold of him and persuading him to make a marriage beneath his station. His station!—poor Hyacinth had often asked himself and inquired of Miss Pynsent what it could possibly be. He had thought of it bitterly enough, wondering how in the world he could marry 'beneath' it" (I, 71). The matter of "place" has become a bitter point of honor. If he occupies an apparently irremediable false position to begin with, any claim to place on his part can only be falsely based and falsely pursued. Offered only a choice of false positions, then, a probable social insufficiency or a probably false sufficiency through marriage, Hyacinth renounces marriage almost as a kind of dishonor: "He would never marry at all — to that his mind was absolutely made up; he would never hand on to another the burden that had made his own young spirit so intolerably sore, the inheritance that had darkened the whole threshold of his manhood" (I, 71-72).

Given the pervasiveness of Hyacinth's sense of stigma, however, one must ask whether this vow *not* to vow is not something of a counter-reaction. Is this finely honorable hero "imprisoned" in some ambiguity of honor? Whatever the case, Hyacinth's renunciation results in a vital privation that, in turn, urgently requires a compensation: "All the more reason why he should have his compensation; why, if the soft society of women was to be enjoyed on other terms, he should cultivate it with a bold free mind" (I, 72). Thus even his "bold free" relationship with Millicent — a kind of honorable liaison — is potentially another false position tainted with reactionary spirit. In spite of, but also on account of, his best efforts to be authentic, Hyacinth Robinson has entered an elaborate cycle. His terrible pathos is that he has been initiated in childhood into relationship and place and life-feeling only to be effectively precluded from "the good things of life" (II, 54). And he has been precluded from these goods of life only to find himself at least eligible to claim them. And now he lays his compensatory claim to them only to find himself in all probability precluded.

It is the social aesthete's complex fate. In fact, so aesthetic is Hyacinth's station that James regards him as "a true artist" (II, 139). The anomaly of Lomax Place, the potential *deraciné* who looks "for all the world like a little plastered-up Frenchman" (I, 67) is almost necessarily theatrical: "he didn't care for fancy costumes, he wished to go through life in his own character; but he checked himself with the reflexion that this was exactly what he was apparently destined not to do. His own character? He was to cover that up as carefully as possible; he was to go through life in a mask, in a borrowed mantle; he was to be every day and every hour an actor" (I, 77). From his childhood Hyacinth has lived as if in a prison. From childhood, too, he has stood as if exposed to a theater of a myriad eyes. The hero is imprisoned in theater.

If he must be the social aesthete, he yet cannot remain the social aesthete. So much "in" as to be — grotesquely enough — too much "out," Hyacinth can only be expected to try reactively for his tribalization. If he cannot confidently know social reality, he will seek initiation into a community of knowledge. In Eustache Poupin's *"intérieur"* (I,

92), therefore, he volunteers to serve the social question and "the great revenge" (I, 96). It is as if the little bookbinder *exists*; he might be an *"interne"* (I, 103). He qualifies, anyway, to meet another initiate in Paul Muniment:

> "What do you mean by force that will shake the globe?" the young man [Muniment] inquired . . .
>
> " '89 was an irresistible force," said M. Poupin . . .
>
> "And so was the entrance of the Versaillais, which sent you over here ten years ago," the young man returned . . . The young man burst out laughing; whereupon his host declared with a dignity which even his recumbent position didn't abate that it was really frivolous of him to ask such questions as that, knowing as he did — what he did know.
>
> "Yes, I know — I know," said the young man good-naturedly . . . "And do you know too?"
>
> "Do I know what?" asked Hyacinth in wonder.
>
> "Oh, if you did you would!" the young man exclaimed and laughed again (I, 98-100).

A force that will shake the globe — force so irresistible as to sweep a "prison" aside? One remembers an earlier, comparably disadvantaged claimant standing in his dream of Caesarism, in presence of DIVUS TIBERIUS CAESAR TOTIUS ORBIS IMPERATOR.

Hyacinth Robinson dreams likewise. At least, as a social aesthete he stands extraordinarily open to the illusion of social quintessence, to the reactionary transformations of it that a fellow reactionary might offer. What fascinates him in the conspirators is not so much social or ideological substance; Paul Muniment, who will get over any ideas he may have, can own only to a "poverty of programme" (I, 203) and understands only what he ostensibly denounces, "a fine, stiff conservative" (II, 205). Hyacinth, rather, would claim community with a certain style of secrecy. If he can be recruited by Poupin's conspiratorial histrionics, still more can he be seduced by the laconic Muniment, whose "knowledge" takes the form of a masterful irony or other-speaking. Hyacinth Robinson, the finely honorable man who so fears his own imposture, is the more for being with an ironist who ridicules and cannot easily be ridiculed.

But what finally draws him to the conspirators is their use of secrecy, at least secrecy understood as the suppression of revenge-feeling. Paul Muniment is a master of irony, and a potential master by means of this irony, on account of a prior, almost anomalous equanimity: "In his own imagination he [Hyacinth] associated bitterness with the revolutionary passion; but the young chemical expert, at the same time that he was planning far ahead, seemed capable of turning revolutionists themselves into ridicule even for the entertainment of the revolutionists" (I, 117). "For a loyal servant," Hyacinth notices, "an effective agent, he was so extraordinarily candid — bitterness and denunciation so rarely sat on his lips. The criticism of everything — since, everything *was* wrong — took so little of his time" (II, 122). Just as the aesthetic Hyacinth works as a journeyman artist, so the equable conspirator is a scientist given to the "humanitarian" understatement of statistics: "the most that he did in the way of expatiation on the woes of humanity was occasionally to allude to certain statistics" (II, 122-123). Paul Muniment's impersonal equanimity, one imagines, is deeply imbued with vengefulness. If this particular careerist cannot be genuinely benevolent, then it must be that he is so essentially subversive as to have no need to exert himself towards specific subversion; one thinks here of Max Scheler's notion of "organic mendacity," according to which the individual ridden with the desire for revenge may become so false in his being as to *be* a lie, and as to have no need to lie.[5] On this view of him, Muniment the Master simply evinces a greater capacity for self-concealment than other more exoteric men.

Of course Hyacinth, supersensible and yearning, is a genuine reactionary, never a false one. Still, if he cannot know himself by any direct initiation, he will know what he is by way of what he is not. He has need of the conspirators, however superior he may be to them morally. It is even likely that they embody both his aspirations and his impulse to reject himself. Thus Hyacinth instinctively claims community with Paul Muniment as the double who will complete him by virtue of an initiate knowledge, but who also repudiates himself on account of his invalid and invalidating sister ("Her life and mine are all one," II, 263), altogether represses the sense of an injury that, seemingly, is life itself — injury incarnate.

While the yearningly susceptible Hyacinth knows through Paul Muniment what it might be to master, he knows through Muniment's sister what it might be to be a Duke. Precluded from ordinary vitality, yet managing to seem extraordinarily vital, Rosy has become obsessed with "the sense of . . . differences" (as the Princess Casamassima describes "the English religion," I, 256). It is as if the most feeble epiphyte were trying to turn forcible parasite: social "differences" so gall her in her unbearable abjection that she would revenge herself on the aristocracy "up there" (I, 130); but then, simply because she so craves to be "other" and "different," she cannot bring herself to renounce all existential comparison. Eventually Rosy bears a wholly equivocal attitude towards "differences"; she needs them to revenge herself on them, and she revenges herself on them because she so depends on them. On the one hand she will support the English religion: "You'll make a tremendous mistake if you try to turn everything round. There ought to be differences, and high and low, and there always will be, true as ever I lie here. I think it's against everything, pulling down them that's above" (I, 117). But then there is the characteristically Jamesian non sequitur: while ostensibly snubbing the timid Lady Aurora as an exemplar of differences, Rosy herself becomes a perverse exploiter of them. "They'll trample on her just the same as on the others, and they'll say she has got to pay for her title and her grand relations and her fine appearance" (I, 120). And, because this is a tormented reactive cycle, the further non sequitur: "Therefore I advise her not to waste her good-nature in trying to let herself down. When you're up so high as that you've got to stay there; and if the powers above have made you a lady the best thing you can do is to hold up your head. I can promise your ladyship *I* would!" (I, 120). In her artist's imagination Rosy is other, conclusively different.

But Rosy's ghastly cycle of suicidal vitality seems unending, for she no sooner *is* Lady Aurora Langrish than she has to recognize that she should either have been born again or born differently.[6] And this recognition of her "illegitimacy" in turn leads to the secret revenge of spite. James's Jenny Wren knows social quintessence:

> "Oh yes, everything's a joke!" cried the irrepressible invalid — "everything except my state of health; that's admitted to be serious. When her ladyship sends me five shillings' worth of coals it's only a joke; and when she brings me a bottle of the finest port, that's another; and when she climbs up seventy-seven stairs (there are seventy-seven, I know perfectly, though I never go up or down) to spend the evening with me at the height of the London season, that's the best of all. I know all about the London season though I never go out, and I appreciate what her ladyship gives up. She's very jocular indeed, but fortunately I know how to take it. You can see it wouldn't do for me to be touchy, can't you, Miss Pynsent?" (I, 210-211).

It is this unabated, ever infiltrating malice that earns for Rosy Paul's remark that she is "the deepest of the lot" (II, 259).

[*12*]

For Hyacinth, the community of knowledge at Audley Court would seem to hold out a valuable secret, a sense of mastery, and "a suggestion of race" (I, 114). But like all James's reactionaries, whether more or less genuine or false, Hyacinth has on the basis of one false position worked himself into another, even less tenable one. Having earned his internship in part in reaction to his feeling of insufficiency with Millicent, he now finds that he must actually forfeit relationship with her, the careerist who instinctively upholds society. The greater his need to taste through her London's vitality, the more aesthetic he becomes with her, and the more like some Anglo-French hour she becomes for him: "Having the history of the French Revolution at his fingers' ends, Hyacinth could easily see her (if there should ever be barricades in the streets of London) with a red cap of liberty on her head and her white throat bared so that she should be able to shout the louder the Marseillaise of that hour" (I, 146). It is an almost insolent irony. Hyacinth dreams an infinite dream, yet he dreams compulsively and as though in "prison": "He wanted to drive in every carriage, to mount on every horse, to feel on his arm the hand of every pretty woman in the place. . . . There were individuals whom he followed with his eyes, with his thoughts, sometimes even with his steps; they seemed to tell him what it was to be the flower of a high civilization" (I, 150-151). The social aesthete *sees*. "The itching, prurient, knowing, imagining eye, I am cursed with it, I am hampered up in it" (*The Plumed Serpent*).

He sees because he is always James's all too visible man, too much his own performer to his own audience. He has qualified for a community of knowledge only to find himself that much the more "out." Appropriately enough, then, Hyacinth's next station of reaction is the theater in which he meets the Princess Casamassima. It is all theater. The hero's born theatricality qualifies him for another, and a fantastic internship: the Princess Casamassima herself treats him as if he were possessed of a true and significant secret. While his value for Millicent has lain in his theatrical pretensions to "society," he now finds that he has his value insofar as he plays the conspirator against this society.

It is of course with the formation of this new community of knowledge that James comes upon the imaginative center of his story. It is as if the expatriate writer of the early eighties were rediscovering, even while creating his reactionary London society, an early situation the ironic subject of which is the barbarian's dream of Europe's civilization. If the Princess Casamassima's newest *tour de force* is nothing less than "another go" (I, 312) on her part, a comprehensive rehearsal of and reaction to her Roman career in *Roderick Hudson, The Princess Casamassima* itself is no less than a second go on James's—a critical one: James would reflect on previous quests for the civil ideal and yet look forward in the hope of resolving the irony that attends these roads to Rome.

During her remarkable first go—we ourselves may reflect—Christina Light is an ambiguous *deracinée* who has been hawked about Europe by an expatriate American mother. Depending upon fashionable society's admiration, yet so abjectly dependent upon it as to want to punish both it and her own "light" self, she has learned to inflict a kind of piteous-provocative theater upon the eyes of the world: "she *looked like* some immaculate saint of legend being led to martyrdom" (156, my italics). As her name suggests, Christina Light is at once a kind of martyr to social scandal and a sophisticated scandalmonger. This is the force of James's imagining her in the Coliseum—always a scene in him for ordeals of self-consciousness—dispossessing Roderick Hudson of his secret:

"... you're simply as weak as any other *petit jeune homme*. I'm so sorry! I hoped—I really believed—you were strong . . . Is it written then that I shall really never know what I've so often dreamed of . . . A man whom I can have the luxury of respecting . . . I'm a poor weak woman; I've no strength myself, and I can give no strength . . . I'm all that, and yet I believe I have one merit. I should know a great character when I saw it . . . For a man who should really give me a certain feeling—I have never had it, but I should know it when it came—I would send Prince Casamassima and his millions to perdition" (227-228).

The *deracinée* would both honor bold American authority and ambiguously revenge herself upon it as being, in the Rome of a Prince Casamassima, unreliably "scant."

Christine's tragedy is to be light, theatrical, subjective, when she might otherwise have been exquisitely fitted to claim authentic European place. Consequently, when Roderick Hudson fails in her theater she turns to his sponsor Rowland Mallet, who functions as a kind of withheld side of the too susceptible Roderick (in the Coliseum scene, Mallet is a voyeur in the wings); Mallet's esteem is the secret of which she would possess herself. And when she fails to dispossess Mallet, and when she finally learns of her illegitimacy—she is in shocking truth a scandal—she once again reacts, this time violently, by making a brilliant marriage to the Prince Casamassima. In James's elaborate context, it is another ambiguous *coup de théâtre* and a compulsive self-concealment: "the proudest girl in the world, deeply wounded in her pride and not stopping to calculate possibilities, but muffling her wound with an almost sensuous relief in a splendour that stood within her grasp and would cover everything" (369). First it is as if some final honesty in Christine has provoked and even welcomed the news of her illegitimacy, and then as if she revenges herself on herself and her tormentors by collapsing into the other extreme of careerism. And finally it is as if she manages to resolve herself between her better and her worse selves, or at least to vow herself to a life of secrecy; at the end she seems to give out, with a kind of sinister dignity, that she may yet revenge herself upon the husband whose princeliness she has so craved. She might equally be the too passionate acolyte, or a slavishly superstitious reactionary, in presence of DIVUS TIBERIUS CAESAR: does the civil ideal really exist outside the dream of that least person, the barbarian?

It is the troubling secrecy of this career that *The Princess Casamassima* would rehearse. James discovers that Christine Light is going one further, taking an ambiguous compensation for an earlier, failure-haunted compensation. As Mme Grandoni explains her, "She regards her doing so [marrying the Prince Casamassima] as such a horrible piece of frivolity that she can't for the rest of her days be serious enough to make up for it" (I, 271). Where before she has been tragically "subjective," now she cries out for ideology. "I don't want to teach," she tells Hyacinth, "I want to learn; and above all I want to know *à quoi m'en tenir.*" So much would she know that she would provide the state itself with its reactionary imitation, the secret society: "Are we on the eve of great changes or are we not? Is everything that's gathering force underground, in the dark, in the night, in little hidden rooms, out of sight of governments or policemen and idiotic 'statesmen'—heaven save them!—is all this going to burst forth some fine morning and set the world on fire?" (I, 195). But new ideology is old subjectivity. At bottom her incendiary revolutionism is an ambiguous revenge upon people, the cleverest way of humiliating a Prince of unthinking, almost primitive Romanitas.

The Princess Casamassima in no way redeems Christine Light, she only revamps her. Thus during her earlier go, Christine is drawn first to Roderick Hudson as the fiancé of the American girl Mary Garland

and then to Rowland Mallet as a man possessing an unavowed secret, his own esteem for Mary Garland. In other words Christine grows aware through the tandem heroes of another possible social identity, an American one; the enviable Mary Garland seems both to complete her in her own social inanition and to compete with her for identity, avowedly as regards Roderick, unknowingly as regards Rowland. Now, in *The Princess Casamassima*, this double situation duplicates itself. Through Hyacinth, the princess encounters her English social double, Lady Aurora Langrish. Although Lady Aurora is something of a class apostate and impostor, at once someone "animated by a vengeful irony" (I, 223) against aristocracy and a dubious saint or charity worker, she is, as an aristocrat in the first place, nevertheless a kind of genuine impostor. As this other self, therefore, she constitutes a real source of envy for the princess. "I don't know that there's anyone in the world I envy so much," she acknowledges. "Better than anyone I've ever met she has solved the problem — which if we are wise we all try to solve, don't we? — of getting out of herself. She has got out of herself more perfectly than anyone I've ever known. She has merged herself in the passion of doing something for others. That's why I envy her" (II, 199-200). But then, at a successive turn of her emotional cycle, the princess recognizes in Lady Aurora a humiliating double. For all that the latter may be "one of the caprices of an aristocracy" (I, 114), she can still show the princess up as a thoroughly false impostor, a *"capricciosa"* (II, 9). On any odious comparison, the princess is again only the *"princesse de théâtre"* (221) of Roman days. In consequence, by a further compulsive turn of her cycle, the princess competes with Lady Aurora in order to dispossess her of *her* secret. She determines upon a liaison with Paul Muniment (the Rowland Mallet of this second go) thus ideologically to spite and provoke Prince Casamassima.

But while reflecting on the complex fate of spectacular barbarians, James might yet be looking towards another, a kind of "little" go in the guise of his hero. Hyacinth Robinson may yet glimpse the ideal of Europe, if only in a perverse embodiment: "Hyacinth, on the opposite side of the fire, felt at times almost as if he were married to his hostess, so many things were taken for granted between them" (II, 241). Not that James fails to see the complexity even of this modest fate, for once Hyacinth has been superseded with Millicent by Sholto, cosmopolite philanderer, he has sharply brought home to him the fact of yet another community of knowledge, a liaison in relation to which he himself might be a duped and ridiculous voyeur. Confronted unexpectedly by Sholto and Millicent, Hyacinth once again stands in the inimical chill of the interstice. If he is the voyeurist aesthete with an increasingly ambiguous Millicent, what can he be with the bewilderingly secret princess? He is nobody, this little bookbinder.

Not surprisingly, Hyacinth again reacts feverishly. Extraordinarily exposed, the hero would possess himself of being-unto-self. All too visible in a vast cockpit of "a million of spectators" (I, 307), he will *see* "the real thing" (I, 319). Abjectly subjective, he would serve non-personal force. Accordingly, Hyacinth volunteers as an instrument of conspiracy, thus to pass into the presence of the Master himself. Committing himself formally to Hoffendahl—who, since this is a story of society qua secret society, necessarily remains unknown[7]—he might at last be "more." He *is*. It is a pathetic and terrible autonomy that James expresses by a remarkable withdrawal; for a moment it is as if there were no story. How can a nobody, who in the effort to give himself a story only depersonalizes himself, quite have a story?

The hero's first go brings him to a Jamesian halfway mark; like other reactionaries in James, he will never be better than this. Hyacinth has now qualified supremely for community with the princess, a community that seems the whole point of his lifelong history of reaction. Initiated into "the innermost sanctuary . . . the holy of holies" (II, 44), he embodies in his turn all the fascination of the secret: "she was listening to him as she had never listened before" (II, 50). Hyacinth might be "more—more—more" (II, 33); he could not be better adorned than this for the princess' theater. So depersonalized is he by virtue of his sacred-secret vow that he might be a pure instance, as well as an instrument, of irresistible force:

Hyacinth's little job was a very small part of what Hoffendahl had come to England for; he had in his hand innumerable other threads . . . He had exactly the same mastery of them that a great musician—that the Princess herself—had of the keyboard of the piano; he treated all things, persons, institutions, ideas, as so many notes in his great symphonic massacre. The day would come when—far down in the treble—one would feel one's self touched by the little finger of the composer, would grow generally audible (with a small sharp crack) for a second (II, 50).

Not only does Hyacinth know, he makes himself known to the beloved princess. Indeed the latter's greatest frisson occurs, presumably, just at this moment of avowal; knowledge of the secret of his illegitimacy could not, one imagines, fail to satisfy so "illegitimate" a pretender as herself. Not that the princess revenges herself in an obviously personal way upon Hyacinth: she would confess and dispossess him as she has already done Roderick Hudson, in the name of ideology.

But if Hyacinth's community with the beautiful barbarian who tastes of Rome is more of the real thing, his long history of reaction is only the more unreal. It is as if Hyacinth has won his precious secret only to have given himself away to a strikingly careless princess: he is as illegitimate as ever. A little nobody of a reactionary needs therefore to consolidate his second go — since it indeed seems that he has embarked upon one. (Earlier on Paul Muniment has advised him "to make it your supreme duty, make it your religion, to lie close and keep yourself for another go," I, 311-312). He becomes, in his next episode, his own counterreactionary. He formally avows himself to the princess and the civilized ideal:

> "The monuments and treasures of art, the great palaces and properties, the conquests of learning and taste, the general fabric of civilization as we know it, based if you will upon all the despotisms, the cruelties, the exclusions, the monopolies and the rapacities of the past, but thanks to which, all the same, this world is less of a 'bloody sell' and life more of a lark — our friend Hoffendahl seems to me to hold them too cheap and to wish to substitute for them something in which I can't somehow believe as I do in things with which the yearnings and the tears of generations have been mixed" (II, 130).

Standing on ground native to the Prince Casamassima, however, Hyacinth might be standing not a little grotesquely on his head. His social aestheticism has now been exalted into an ideology. The social passion of the reactionary turns out to be deeply aristocratic in cast. Aesthetic and cultural values are superior, vital values inferior. As in art, "differences" are eternally true, and equality eternally untrue. And while an aristocratically ordered civilization should be conserved, democracy — Muniment's and Hoffendahl's and, until lately, his own — is no more than a subjective, barbarian critique of this order. Indeed, to this newly avowed social aesthete, revolutionary action now represents a kind of vengeful disfigurement of culture. A Hoffendahl, says Hyacinth, will but mutilate in restitution for his own "mutilated hand" (I, 314): "He would cut up the ceilings of the Veronese into strips, so that everyone might have a little piece. I don't want everyone to have a little piece of anything, and I've a great horror of that kind of invidious jealousy which is at the bottom of the idea of a redistribution" (II, 130). Back in England, he discerns a mere avenger even in the apparently generous Eustache Poupin: "Everywhere, everywhere he saw the ulcer of envy — the greed of a party hanging together only that it might despoil another to its disadvantage" (II, 142). James, it appears, can splendidly imagine a revolutionary conspiracy, but then cannot imagine this secret society developing into a legitimate orthodoxy based on alternative, authentic values.[8] Hyacinth's, at least, is the externe's revolutionism and, correspondingly, conservatism.

James's equivocal story has reached its crisis. It is faced with a choice of false positions. On the one hand there is the tortuous career of the subjective men who would be truly ideological. This has been Hyacinth's reactionary way, as it is still the way of the conspirators, Muniment and Hoffendahl and the self-acknowledged barbarian, the princess. On the other hand, there is the newly avowed creed of a man who would abjure all subjectivity as an "odious stain upon my soul" (II, 131). This is but ideology, not only because it seems so incomplete an answer to the human suffering experienced in the story, and not only because it sums up the unmoving conservatism, ostensibly denounced but secretly craved, of more ruthless reactionaries than Hyacinth. Given the tenuousness of Hyacinth's foothold in life, it cannot but be tainted with counterreactive spirit. It has to be a disavowal as much as it is an avowal.

But while Hyacinth's begins to look like another, failure-haunted go, the second half of *The Princess Casamassima* nevertheless constitutes a remarkable second go on James's own part. As I have said, James is rehearsing here the long-standing, perhaps the long-deferred, ambiguities of his quest for the civilized identity. Let us say that he rewrites *Roderick Hudson,* or at least all the stories that it typifies, in order to show that the barbarian *can* convert to and affirm the civil ideal — provided that he pays for this new life with nothing less than his reactionary and his counterreactionary life.

Thus the ethical resolution of this story lies not so much in the hero's renouncing either his reaction or his counterreaction as in his recognizing that he must sacrifice himself altogether. If he does not really live except in equivocal reactive and counterreactive terms, to give up all reaction means to give up, for love of the ideal, his claim to life itself. Thus although Hyacinth's pacific, renunciatory heroism is in no way spiritually identical with a suicidal self-rejection, it yet amounts to one. Upon avowing himself to the princess he inevitably forfeits his community — even if it is only a community of knowledge — with her and with the other conspirators. In fact, no sooner does he give himself away at Medley Hall than he stands known and expendable; and the arrival immediately afterwards of the superseded Sholto seems almost a bringing in of a grim verdict against him, for Sholto — it is his ambiguous revenge on the little bookbinder who has succeeded him as well perhaps as a settling of scores with the contemptuous princess — Sholto has not only displaced Hyacinth with Millicent, he would contrive to have the powerful Paul Muniment displace him from the princess' favor. Subsequently, in a marvellously poignant scene of shock, the hero who knows no place stands shoulder to shoulder with the man of an ancient *Romanitas*: "At this moment a part of the agitation that possessed the Princess's unhappy husband seemed to pass into his own blood . . . 'What does he say? what does *she* say?' hissed the Prince; and . . . our stricken youth felt a voice given to his own sharpest thought" (II, 288-289). Neither Hyacinth nor the prince are privy to the knowledge of this provocatively ambiguous community. A kind of passive, renunciatory version of the prince, who has been reduced to a voyeurist and prurient *seeing*, Hyacinth simply sees. He loves, but he does not really live.

After such recognition, Hyacinth's taking up again with Millicent Henning can result only in "the perpetual, sore shock of the rebound" (II, 237). Unreal as a reactionary, he is no more real as a social and sexual aesthete, certainly a counterreactive one. With Millicent, too, Millicent now respectably at church, all is theater: "yet now that she treated him to the severer spectacle it struck him for the moment as really grand sport, a kind of magnification of her rich vitality. She had her phases and caprices like the Princess herself" (II, 293). And just as he has been superseded in the princess' regard by Muniment, his masterful reactionary double, so now he is superseded by Sholto, his trivial, cosmopolitan gentleman competitor. The hero who loves yet does not live. If he can lay no real claim upon life, then he is for the mortal snubbing.

At this point Hyacinth is recalled to his unconditional vow to the master, Hoffendahl. It is now utterly false that he should continue living, whether as a reactionary against his social aestheticism or as a ghostly aesthete who would renounce reaction. As if making sure of his unworthiness for life, he visits Lady Aurora, the beloved princess, and

Millicent in turn. With Lady Aurora he experiences "an odd, occult community of suffering. A tacit confession passed and repassed, and each understood the situation of the other . . . What had each done but lose that which he or she had never so much as had?" But "they wouldn't speak of it" (II, 315), for the eccentric Lady Aurora has withdrawn into a scandalized aristocratic orthodoxy; and, if Hyacinth is not Paul Muniment, he may as well not be at all. In her turn the princess, still playing the ideological martyr to the amphitheater, stands on the brink of scandal. "The Princess looked grave, as if her old friend's [Mme Grandoni's] departure had been indeed a very awkward affair. 'You may imagine how I feel it! It leaves me completely alone; it makes, in the eyes of the world, an immense difference in my position. However, I don't consider the eyes of the world" (II, 356). The princess' sacrifice of herself to the conspirators amounts to a desperate eye for the eyes of the world, and always remains self-serving enough to save her chances with her European prince in the wings. And yet, as in his visit to Lady Aurora, Hyacinth and the princess wouldn't speak of it in any spirit of recrimination. "So much out of it now" (II, 358), Hyacinth finds himself excluded by still another community of knowledge. He comes across London's Millicent performing in the almost cruelly expert theater of Captain Sholto's eye. Never sexually right with Millicent, he is now a proven pretender, an extra and an encumbrance. Yet again, he goes quietly.

For love of the civil ideal, Hyacinth has himself become a cynosure of a kind of scandal of impotence. Indeed, should he consummate his lifelong reaction and assassinate the duke, he will actually reopen the scandal of his origins: "the horror of the public reappearance, in his person, of the imbrued hands of his mother . . . the idea of the personal stain made him horribly sick . . . It passed before him, or rather it stayed, like a blow dealt back at his mother, already so hideously disfigured; to suffer it to start out in the life of her son was in a manner to place her own forgotten, redeemed pollution again in the eye of the world" (II, 372). He will only have had another go — a "repetition" (II, 372), he will not have transcended a cycle of goes. Best, then, to give up altogether the claim to a life. Best, with what little life he has been able to claim for himself, to die for the communities of the suffering — to reclaim the Princess Casamassima, perhaps, before she destroys herself. Hyacinth Robinson, one can say, dies of a higher false position.

A degree of fantasy has always been evident in James — for instance, the ambiguous mixture of the marvellous and the Zolaesque in *The Princess Casamassima* has been seen as deriving from James's anxiety that what his hero knows is not social substance at all but all fantasy.[9] My own view, however, is that the presence of fantasy in him is still insufficiently recognized, and that a double, that is, fantasist situation like "Adina," probably underlies all of his international situations. After all, in his quest for a quintessential social reality that was also an alien reality, James must necessarily have found himself recoiling upon the merely psychological and even epistemological, the merely imaginative — upon fantasy.

Probably the most important example here would be the remarkable account of his Galerie d'Apollon nightmare. As he recounts in his autobiography, James had as a young man come upon quintessential European glory in the Louvre:

> It was as if they had gathered there into a vast deafening chorus; I shall never forget how — speaking, that is, for my own sense — they filled those vast halls with the influence rather of some complicated sound, diffused and reverberant, than of such visibilities as one could directly deal with. To distinguish among these, in the charged and coloured and confounding air, was difficult — it discouraged and defied; which was doubtless why my impression originally best entertained was that of those magnificent parts of the great gallery simply not inviting us to distinguish. They only arched over us in the wonder of their endless golden riot and relief, figured and flourished in perpetual revolution, breaking into great high-hung circles and symmetries of squandered picture, opening into deep outward embrasures that threw off the rest of monumental Paris somehow as a told story, a sort of wrought effect or bold ambiguity for a vista, and yet held it there, at every point, as a vast bright gage, even at moments a felt adventure, of experience. This comes to saying that in those beginnings I felt myself most happily cross that bridge over to Style constituted by the wondrous Galerie d'Apollon, drawn out for me as a long but assured initiation, and seeming to form with its supreme coved ceiling and inordinately shining parquet a prodigious tube or tunnel through which I inhaled little by little, that is again and again, a general sense of *glory*.[10]

James is not simply the social aesthete initiated into the picturesque; he is the passionate claimant of empire; one recalls here the dream of civilization on the parts of the hero of "Adina," of Christine and Mrs. Light in *Roderick Hudson* ("The Empress, certainly, was a pretty woman; but what's my Christina, pray? I've dreamt of it sometimes every night for a month," 222), of a Mme Merle who fails "to marry Caesar," of Hyacinth Robinson, lover of the Princess Casamassima, and of Adam Verver, collector of a Roman prince. "The glory," James continues, "meant ever so many things at once, not only beauty and art and supreme design, but history and fame and power, the world in fine raised to the richest and noblest expression. The world there was at the same time, by an odd extension or intensification, the local present fact, to my small imagination, of the Second Empire . . . " Here, standing at his transcultural point of vantage, he seems to have been almost violently freed as to his consciousness. He is here made initiate, made "more — more — more" in a way that all his international heroes — whether Roderick Hudson or Christopher Newman, or Isabel Archer or Hyacinth Robinson or Maggie Verver (not to mention his more negative characters) — are made initiate at some time or other.

In James, however, the freedom of the international interstice invariably has its false aspect. Recounting the nightmarish second go to which the epiphany in the Galerie d'Apollon gave rise many years later, James tells of a

> sudden pursuit, through an open door, along a huge high saloon, of a just, dimly-descried figure that retreated in terror before my rush and dash (a glare of inspired reaction from irresistible but shameful dread), out of the room I had a moment before been desperately, and all the more abjectly, defending by the push of my shoulder against hard pressure on lock and bar from the other side. The lucidity, not to say the sublimity, of the crisis had consisted of the great thought that I, in my appalled state, was probably still more appalling than the awful agent, creature or presence, whatever he was, whom I had guessed, in the suddenest wild start from sleep, the sleep within my sleep, to be making for my place of rest. The triumph of my impulse, perceived in a flash as I acted on it by myself at a bound, forcing the door outward, was the grand thing, but the great point of the whole was the wonder of my final recognition. Routed, dismayed, the tables turned upon him by my so surpassing him for straight aggression and dire intention, my visitant was already but a diminished spot in the long perspective, the tremendous, glorious hall, as I say, over the far-gleaming floor of which, cleared for the occasion of its great line of price-less *vitrines* down the middle, he sped for *his* life, while a great storm of thunder and lightning played through the deep embrasures of high windows at the right. The lightning that revealed the retreat revealed also

the wondrous place and, by the same amazing play, my young imaginative life in it of long before, the sense of which, deep within me, had kept it whole, preserved it to this thrilling use; for what in the world were the deep embrasures and the so polished floor but those of the Galerie d'Apollon of my childhood?[11]

Presumably this nightmare fantasy springs from James's anxiety that he has been initiated into European glory only aesthetically, initiated, but only to be threatened with preclusion from it. At any rate, far from being free, the ego-dreamer finds himself unexpectedly and extraordinarily oppressed by a hitherto unknown alter ego who, in being all but admitted, shows every intention of displacing the dreamer from himself, indeed "to be making for my place of rest": the inadmissible alter ego pretends to—knows, we might say—the dreamer's stead and right. But if the dreamer himself has been seeking admission to classic ground, then this alter ego has previously established himself as its guardian: it is the dreamer who is the false claimant to glory. What is more, this devastatingly mischievous invader of his consciousness may also be a barbarian twin to himself in his consciousness of glory. Whatever the case, the dreamer has no right to the glory of civilization. Shocking as this recognition may be, this scuffle of doubles may question even more terribly the ego-dreamer's identity, for if this overpowering other "half" is real, then he himself is only half alive. Does he in fact live, this mortally pretentious aesthete? Has he ever really lived? The great gallery has proved to be another galling Jamesian amphitheater or theater.

The scuffle-transaction takes a new turn. In a compulsive denial of the self that would seem to punish and falsify the self otherwise truly in possession, the ego-dreamer now dismays the alter ego with his own "straight aggression and dire intention," a knowledge that we may see as in part a fantasy condensation of the Jamesian reactionary cycle between competing and mutually depleting doubles, but in part as a proper denial of any falsely established selfhood. In this way the ego-dreamer reaffirms what James has previously called "that continuity of honour," that is, his own lifelong valuation on his youthful experience in the Louvre, for with his "shameful dread" receding, he discovers that he remains alone in expansive possession of nothing other than "the deep embrasures and the so polished floor . . . of the Galerie d'Apollon of my childhood." If Henry James cannot stand in any unquestioned possession of European glory—a full, pretentious, and hitherto secret "half" of himself has had to be more or less admitted before being discredited and expelled—he at least lays an honorable claim to it. This claim, the claim of a strict social aesthete, always has been honorable.

II. The Pandora Situation:
Shame, Honor, and Revenge in James

The box, the box, and nothing but the box! It seemed as if the box were bewitched, and as if the cottage were not big enough to hold it, without Pandora's continually stumbling over it, and making Epimetheus stumble over it likewise, and bruising all four of their shins.

Hawthorne, "The Paradise of Children"

I know no better word for it then ego integrity . . . It is the acceptance of one's one and only life cycle as something that had to be and that, by necessity, permitted of no substitutions: it thus means a new, a different love of one's parents . . . Although aware of the relativity of all the various life styles which have given meaning to human striving, the possessor of integrity is ready to defend his own style against all physical and economic threats. For he knows that an individual life is the accidental coincidence of but one life cycle with but one segment of history; and that for him all human integrity stands or falls with the one style of integrity of which he partakes. The style of integrity developed by his culture or civilization thus becomes the "patrimony of his soul," the seal of his moral paternity of himself (" . . . *pero el honor/Es patrimonio del alma*": Calderón). In such final consolidation, death loses its sting.

The lack or loss of this accrued ego integration is signified by fear of death: the one and only life cycle is not accepted as the ultimate of life.

Erik H. Erikson, Childhood and Society

We have seen that a cycle of exposure and reaction to exposure underlies James's social situations, certainly the international ones. I want now to consider the psychology of this experience of exposure and reaction, thereby to develop a theory of James's psychology as a whole. Of course, since any distinction between the social and the psychological must be a fluctuating one, some of what follows will be concerned with a middle ground.

The sense of exposure meets us everywhere in James but it is particularly well illustrated in "Pandora," a story which is almost a model of the international-interstitial situation. Here the hero, a young German diplomat, is embarking at Southampton for New York together with a boatload of German immigrants. About to forfeit something of his European social identity, he feels himself "lost in the inconsiderate crowd . . . neither in his own country nor in that to which he was in a manner accredited . . . reduced to his mere personality" (358). He begins to ready himself against his American exposure by reading "Daisy Miller," by Henry James, Jr. And when "The ship was passing the Needles — the beautiful outermost point of the Isle of Wight . . . Certain tall white cones of rock rose out of the purple sea; they flushed in the afternoon light, and their vague rosiness gave them a kind of human expression . . . " (361), the hero, as if feeling an unaccountable anxiety or embarrassment, moves to conceal the back of his sea-chair, which has his name and title emblazoned on it: "the blazonry was huge; the back of the chair was covered with enormous German characters" (361). Count Vogelstein would conceal himself in proportion to his feeling himself exposed.

A remarkable scene now ensues. Turning back to "Daisy Miller" from his view of the Needles, "the last note of a peopled world," Vogelstein is arrested by the entrance on deck of a young woman: "what attracted Vogelstein's attention was the fact that the young person appeared to have fixed her eyes on him . . . She passed near him again, and this time she almost stopped, with her eyes bent upon him attentively . . . At last it became evident to him that she was trying to look round a corner, as it were, trying to see what was written on the back of his chair" (362-363). Although the hero realizes that the girl may be no more than looking out for a sea-chair, for him the moment is a crisis of being looked at, not to say a sexual encounter with another forward Daisy Miller. Already socially self-conscious, he feels his sexual identity called sharply into question: " 'She wants to find out my name; she wants to see who I am!' " (363). Unexpectedly the hero is something of an involuntary performer, and the young woman something of an audience; they are both potentially aesthetic. Indeed, in this "air so tremendously 'open' " (368), both these characters are theatrical.

Vogelstein's exposure is a comprehensive one, and he feels himself revealed all around. In this awkward comedy of "the back of his chair" he has been made to feel hyperconscious of having a back as well as a front. Evidently, too, some resentment is associated with his exposure, a rage against the eyes of the outsider as well as his own eyes for their having seen an unready, and no doubt sexually anxious self. He would put out the eyes that see. Since he cannot do this, however, he insists instead on his being-unto-self, conceals himself both from himself and from his audience. He becomes other than himself. Involuntarily exposed, he now volunteers to expose himself—seemingly without sensibility to himself, unblushingly, even shamelessly. The hero would put a strong "front" on any vulnerable, Winterbourne "back"— affront "his invader" (363). Count Otto Vogelstein seizes his chair and, "turning it round, exhibited the superscription to the girl" (363). Meanwhile, having been made to seem a premature debutante before a critical audience, the affronted heroine reacts likewise:

> She coloured slightly, but she smiled and read his name . . . "I thought you had one of our chairs, and I didn't like to ask you. It looks exactly like one of ours; not so much now as when you sit in it. Please sit down again. I don't want to trouble you. We have lost one of ours, and I have been looking for it everywhere. They look so much alike; you can't tell till you see the back. Of course I see there will be no mistake about yours," the young lady went on, with a frank smile. "But we have such a small name—you can scarcely see it," she added, with the same friendly intention. "Our name is Day. If you see that on anything, I should be so obliged if you will tell me. It isn't for myself, it's for my mother; she is so dependent on her chair, and that one I am looking for pulls out so beautifully. Now that you sit down again and hide the lower part, it does look just like ours. Well, it must be somewhere. You must excuse me; I am much obliged to you" (363-364).

Just as the hero hides behind an exhibition of his social credentials, so the heroine conceals herself behind a display of putting her family through the trials of the voyage. In fact, this debutante might be her own chaperon putting herself through her ordeal in the marriage market by putting her family through.

As the voyage proceeds, James's hero continues to insist on his being-unto-self. Together with a fellow passenger, the appropriately named Mrs. Dangerfield, he enters into a kind of community of snobbery against the heroine. On her side, meanwhile, the chaperon heroine contrives a social debut for her parents; under the hero's eye, she introduces them to the ship's captain. Finally, however, when the voyage is almost over, Count Vogelstein momentarily overcomes his doubt and shame and makes an approach to the American heroine. In her turn Pandora Day guardedly suggests that the hero help her put her family through customs: "Well, I have written to a friend to come down, and perhaps he can help us. He's very well acquainted with the head. Once I'm chalked, I don't care. I feel like a kind of black-board by this time, any way. We found them awful in Germany" (373). Mightn't the hero be both something less and something more than an awful German customs officer inspecting a girl's social credentials?

This unspoken question is posed still more sharply by the ordeal by customs itself, an ordeal of self-consciousness if ever there was one:

> The few that had succeeded in collecting their battered boxes had an air of flushed indifference to the efforts of their neighbours, not even looking at people with whom they had been intimate on the steamer. A detachment of the officers of the customs was in attendance, and energetic passengers were engaged in attempts to draw them towards their luggage or to drag heavy pieces towards them. These functionaries were good-natured and taciturn, except when occasionally they remarked to a passenger whose open trunk stared up at them, imploring, that they were afraid the voyage had had a good deal of sameness (376).

Vogelstein, who has learned that Pandora expects her "lover" (377) at the wharf, sees her presenting "an open letter" (378) to a customs officer. He is then introduced by Pandora to this officer: " 'That gentleman is sick that I wrote to,' she rejoined; 'isn't it too bad? But he sent me down a letter to a friend of his, one of the examiners, and I guess we won't have any trouble. Mr. Lansing, let me make you acquainted with Count Vogelstein . . . ' " (379). Evidently there is a transaction open to this hero: let him give over his inspection to the official customs and, instead, take a defaulting lover's part in putting Pandora through them.

As in the myth empowering this story, the heroine now opens a box. She opens a trunk before an audience that includes a customs officer and a hero in two minds:

"Well, Mr. Bellamy says you'll do anything for *him*," Pandora said, smiling very sweetly at Mr. Lansing . . .

Mr. Lansing scratched his head a little, behind, with a movement which sent his straw hat forward in the direction of his nose. "I don't know as I would do anything for him that I wouldn't do for you," he responded, returning the smile of the girl. "I guess you had better open that one." And he gave a little affectionate kick to one of the trunks.

"Oh, mother, isn't he lovely! It's only your sea-things," Pandora cried, stooping over the coffer instantly, with the key in her hand.

"I don't know as I like showing them," Mrs. Day murmured, modestly.

Vogelstein made his German salutation to the company in general, and to Pandora he offered an audible good-bye, which she returned in a bright, friendly voice, but without looking round, as she fumbled at the lock of her trunk.

"We'll try another, if you like," said Mr. Lansing, laughing.

"Oh no, it has got to be this one! Good-bye, Count Vogelstein. I hope you'll judge us correctly!"

The young man went his way and passed the barrier of the dock (379-380).

It is an exposure scene of a kind that is always latent in James's imagination. Pandora's presumably disappointing lover Bellamy has defaulted, leaving his place open to a rival. But now this potential rival also proves insufficient; his sexually anxious self is only the more open for the opportunity, and he can play only the reluctant Epimetheus to his Pandora. In her turn Pandora, who would have disclosed herself voluntarily, is the more open and imploring for her Epimetheus' reluctance. This is why this generally competent heroine fumbles as she stoops; she has had her to-be-rejected self put before her.

The second half of "Pandora" is set in Washington some eighteen months later, when Count Vogelstein unexpectedly re-encounters Pandora Day—in conversation with the President, "the ruler of fifty millions of people" (389) and actually extracting a promise from him; the heroine who has been so painfully aware of a single person's regard has turned out to be a willing cynosure of all eyes. Now very much the social aesthete, Count Vogelstein is more than ever attracted to the self-made, quintessentially American heroine. Near Washington's home, therefore, he nerves himself for the "only approach to intimate conversation" (405) he is ever to have with a girl whom he would now marry. At this moment the hero glimpses the extent of Pandora's previous susceptibility towards him. As she admits, she had indeed been open to him only to be rejected by him as a social inferior. Evidently, then, her social career — an anomalously rapid one even for the extraordinary phenomenon of the self-made girl — has constituted another go on Pandora's part. Her extraordinary celebrity must be a compensation, even a kind of revenge, matching an equally extraordinary exposure — a hurt inflicted by the defensively snobbish hero in a particular episode. For Vogelstein it is as if he were a character in a story at the cruel instant of becoming aware of his own creator's irony towards him. He is altogether theatrical.

He is to be still further exposed to himself. Almost as anxious as when she had fumbled at the New York wharf, Pandora now appears to evade his approach; she has long been engaged, Vogelstein learns from a friend who corresponds to the Mrs. Dangerfield of the earlier shipboard episode, to a Mr. Bellamy of Utica. And while the latter has defaulted in New York, he now emerges triumphantly; he comes down to meet Pandora at the steamer in Washington as if consciously to complete her second go.

The hero stands in a voyeurist relationship to the lovers:

> She was patient for a minute, and then she asked him if he had any news. He looked at her an instant in silence, smiling, after which he drew from his pocket a large letter with an official seal, and shook it jocosely above his head. This was discreetly, covertly done. No one appeared to observe the little interview but Vogelstein. The boat was now touching the wharf, and the space between the pair was inconsiderable.
> "Department of State?" Pandora asked, dropping her voice.
> "That's what they call it."
> "Well, what country?"
> "What's your opinion of the Dutch?" the gentleman asked, for an answer.
> "Oh, gracious!" cried Pandora (411).

It is another Pandora's box situation, and this time an undeniably reactionary one. This time, with the emergence of a once inferior but now superior Epimetheus, there is no place open to the hero. The situation is now sealed; this second-go Pandora's box functions as a precinct guarding a community of knowledge, a precinct powerfully compelling discretion. Just as the hero who has forfeited his social and sexual being-unto-self comes across a desirable secret, he finds himself precluded from it. He is James's awkwardly placed inside-outsider.

Two days later all is indeed out in the open. The would-be ambassador reads in the newspapers that Mr. Bellamy of Utica has been offered the post of Minister to Holland. In the circumstances, the appointment might be a kind of secret reproach to him. He has not really lived, either socially or sexually. He is both a self-conscious might-have-been in the amphitheater of the public's regard and that conscious public at the same time. His nonentity is perfected when he learns that Pandora's "long engagement had terminated at the nuptial altar" (412).

Regarded as a model, "Pandora" suggests that one way of describing psychosocial exposure in James is to say that it involves the feeling of being unexpectedly naked. It is as if his characters are too suddenly and too long — an instant can be too long — seen by their own and other people's eyes. In this fiction of the eye they are hyperconscious of having a front. And no sooner are they conscious of their front than they become even more anxiously conscious of having a vulnerable back or behind.[1] Once these characters' ordeals of self-consciousness have begun, they are in danger of being exposed all around. As we have already seen in discussing James's social imagination, they might be standing out in an oppressive arena or theater of spectators. Alternatively, with Pandora Day's story in mind, one could say that they are or have been at some point too open.

Moreover, exposure is by definition premature or unexpected even when feared and systematically prepared for. The Jamesian hero can never really prevent his being jostled into self-consciousness. His sense of "I am who I am" is always questioned by another's wanting "to see who I am" and by the announcement that "you are not who you think you are." If he is jostled sharply enough, he will become *all* consciousness. This, I think, amounts to a definition of shock. In the more extreme cases in James of such shock, the hero is rendered irrevocably for-the-other, open, theatrical; never again can he be sufficiently unto himself. The epochs, the peripeties, in the lives of these characters are marked by critical discontinuities of identity that it is scarcely possible to accommodate.

One can regard the sense of being exposed and the experience of shock as being the two extremes of the emotion of shame. And one can therefore regard James the psychological novelist as writing predominantly along a shame axis.[2] James's heroes are invariably surprised into self-consciousness, the consciousness of an unready, naive, deficient, unacceptable, incomplete, disadvantaged, vulnerable, even abject self; and their recognition that they have fallen short of their better selves, that they have been caught out in a false position with respect to their cherished self-conceptions, amounts consequently to a kind of shame-shock. Indeed, James's psychological subject could be said to be the varieties of shame.

Shame in James may also be defined by the reaction to it, the compulsion to conceal the exposed self. The hero of "Pandora," for instance, would cover his front with effrontery, thereby to cover a sexually diffident, Winterbourne back; although he has no real choice once he has been exposed, he will nevertheless try to make a tactical choice of exposures. Generally, of course, we speak of the ashamed person's reaction as being a need "to bury the face," "to sink into the ground," or "to die of shame," but it may well be that this reaction involves a compulsive emotional cycle.[3] Exposure breeds resentment, or rage against the eyes of an audience as well as perhaps one's own eyes for having seen an incompetent self. One would put out these reproachful eyes; and, since one cannot do so, one instead conceals, even takes a revenge upon, the unacceptable self. Hurt in James is thus obscured as well as obscure—to the point, we shall see, of generating *ressentiment*. "Pandora" is again a suggestive model here, for its heroine is first open and then, correspondingly, sealed; she has been socially and sexually shamed in such a way as to cause one the misgiving that it may be revenge-feeling that compels her in her subsequent career. Evidently Pandora's boxes in James are not only Freudian boxes but also symbols of suppressed, reactive feeling that is continually re-experienced without its finding any direct outlet.

A Jamesian heroine is exposed. Much later it becomes apparent that she has been seriously wounded in her pride and has sought a compensation to correspond. Might not this story's symbol of an open (or virtually opened) container be a symbol of seriously wounded personality? Certainly the very early Pandora situation "The Romance of Certain Old Clothes," where the heroine seems to die of humiliation or shame, suggests that this is so: "The lid of the chest stood open, exposing, amid their perfumed napkins, its treasure of stuffs and jewels. Viola had fallen backward from a kneeling posture . . . Her lips were parted in entreaty, in dismay, in agony; and on her bloodless brow and cheeks there glowed the marks of ten hideous wounds from two ghostly hands" (318-319).

Moreover, as Maggie Verver says in her story about obscure hurt and the superstition of not hurting, "For such shames and wounds *are* dreadful." They are sometimes so dreadful in James as to produce a curious and, to all appearances, passive reaction in a whole series of his characters. The latter are James's most extraordinary cases of invalid-ism, where revenge-feeling for shortcoming is directed not against others but "extraordinarily," and perhaps self-sacrificingly, against the self. Many of these blushingly blighted heroes and Perdita heroines occur relatively early — Paul de Grey, Clement Searle, the type hero of "A Most Extraordinary Case," Gertrude in "Poor Richard," both the hero and heroine of the fantasy "Longstaff's Marriage." There is also Roderick Hudson, a most important "morbidly special case":

> My mistake on Roderick's behalf . . . is that, at the rate at which he falls to pieces, he seems to place himself beyond our understanding and our sympathy. These are not our rates, we say; we ourselves certainly, under like pressure, — for what is it after all? — would make more of a fight. We conceive going to pieces — nothing is easier, since we see people do it, one way or another, all round us; but this young man must either have had less of the principle of development to have had so much of the principle of collapse, or less of the principle of collapse to have had so much of the principle of development. "On the basis of so great a weakness," one hears the reader say, "where was your idea of the interest? On the basis of so great an interest, where is the provision for so much weakness?" (xix-xx).

But there are a number of later examples as well — Ralph Touchett (insofar as one can regard his invalidism as a rationalized version of the Jamesian social and sexual impotence), Louise Chantry in "The Visits," Grace Mavis in "The Patagonia" (a heroine who, though not invalid, commits suicide in a most extraordinary manner), the writer heroes of "The Middle Years" and "The Death of the Lion," and (at least to the narrator's mind) *The Sacred Fount's* Guy Brissenden and May Server. What these feeble but forcible cases are doing is dying of shame or self-deprecation, quite literally sinking into the ground after being put to shame and having the extent of their weakness proved against them; in them consciousness has turned punitively — and always secretly — upon surprised and vulnerable consciousness. On occasion in James this progressive or cyclic invalidism can be a social phenomenon as well as a matter of individual psychology. For example, when summarizing his impressions of the post-bellum South in *The American Scene*, James observes that

> I can doubtless not sufficiently tell why, but there was something in my whole sense of the South that projected at moments a vivid and painful image—that of a figure somehow blighted or stricken, discomfortably, impossibly seated in an invalid-chair, and yet fixing one with strange eyes that were half a defiance and half a deprecation of one's noticing, and much more of one's referring to, any abnormal sign. The deprecation, in the Southern eyes, is much greater to-day, I think, than the old lurid challenge; but my haunting similitude was an image of the keeping-up of appearances . . . in an excruciating posture.[4]

Insofar as he is a social historian, he is liable to give us what he calls the " 'psychologic' interest,"[5] or a shame psychology, of history.

When serious enough, the chill of exposure in James may actually result in a mortal or near mortal "fever." Thus the hero of "A Passionate Pilgrim" describes himself when near death as being "worn down to a mere throbbing fever-point" (303). And other examples would be the hero of *Watch and Ward* (Chapters 6-7), "The Visits," "The Author of 'Beltraffio,' " "A London Life," "The Death of the Lion," and "The Turn of the Screw." It is, however, "Daisy Miller" that is the type story here. Having unselfconsciously made herself vulnerable to Rome's American cabal, Daisy Miller is then shocked by it into acute self-consciousness. In Jamesian fashion she shows nothing directly but, on the contrary, defiantly affronts the scandalmongers. Finally, she deliberately provokes a scandal by venturing into the Coliseum at night in the company of a local fortune hunter:

> Then he [Winterbourne] passed in among the cavernous shadows of the great structure, and emerged upon the clear and silent arena. The place had never seemed to him more impressive. One-half of the gigantic circus was in deep shade; the other was sleeping in the luminous dusk . . . Winterbourne walked to the middle of the arena, to take a more general glance, intending thereafter to make a hasty retreat. The great cross in the centre was covered with shadow; it was only as he drew near it that he made it out distinctly. Then he saw that two persons were stationed upon the low steps which formed its base. One of these was a woman, seated; her companion was standing in front of her.

Presently the sound of the woman's voice came to him distinctly in the warm night-air. "Well, he looks at us as one of the old lions or tigers may have looked at the Christian martyrs!" These were the words he heard, in the familiar accent of Miss Daisy Miller (201).

This is one of James's most remarkable theater scenes, and it superbly conveys his exposed heroine's seemingly pathological awareness of being seen all round, of having both a back and a front. Daisy might be a martyr at the mercy of an infinite hierarchy of spectators, almost the eye of Caesarean history itself.

Subsequently, of course, Daisy dies of malarial fever. To put it more accurately, she dies of a most extraordinary case of emotional fever that brings on actual malarial fever. But this is to say that even Daisy may not be an unambiguous victim. While she is a martyr for love, she is one in the unsentimental sense that she has sacrificed any assertive voiding of her natural resentment upon others, particularly the hang-fire Winterbourne, and has instead turned it upon herself as someone to be rejected. If she can neither gain the esteem of Winterbourne (especially when she has already forfeited the opinion of the American expatriate cabal) nor aspire to an authentic status in Europe, she may as well be dead for shame: it is a common enough ethic and hardly peculiar to Henry James. In other words, Daisy Miller's passion is more difficult to distinguish from suicidal self-rejection than at first appears.

Daisy Miller, one sees, is not only a type of Jamesian death by fever, she is also typical in dying as a kind of martyr in an amphitheater. Indeed her ordeal suggests that any dying of shame in James may be a fevered-chilled martyrdom before myriad eyes.

Probably the most important example here would be *The Bostonians,* which can be regarded as a story of how a reactionary daughter of New England puts herself on stage, there to die a martyr's death of shame. In a sense, of course, Olive Chancellor stands from the outset in a public amphitheater — in a Jamesian theater of self-consciousness. Suffering from the most acute sexual shame and doubt, Olive has determined to master her abjection only to feel, when it actually comes to a debut before the hero, all the more exposed:

She had instantly seated herself, and while Mrs. Luna talked she kept her eyes on the ground, glancing even less toward Basil Ransom than toward

[*38*]

that woman of many words. The young man was therefore free to look at her; a contemplation which showed him that she was agitated and trying to conceal it. He wondered why she was agitated, not forseeing that he was destined to discover, later, that her nature was like a skiff in a stormy sea. Even after her sister had passed out of the room she sat there with her eyes turned away, as if there had been a spell upon her which forbade her to raise them (I, 11).

Olive Chancellor, James goes on to explain, "was subject to fits of tragic shyness, during which she was unable to meet even her own eyes in the mirror" (I, 11). An all but pathological sense of having a front and a back has brought on in her a kind of seizure of identity.

In Olive's case the compulsion to conceal self has long entered an ideological phase. So effectively has she suppressed her rage that it has come to pervade her personality to such a degree as to be directed not, on the face of it, towards individuals but against a whole system of social values. Hence her reactionary feminism, an ideology by means of which she would out-theater, as it were, the theater of her own and others' consciousness, thus to be other and more powerful than her abjectly exposed self. Like Christine Light after her, Olive would master by being a martyr in an amphitheater of collective eyes: "She could not defend herself against a rich admiration — a kind of tenderness of envy — of any one who had been so happy as to have that opportunity [for self-sacrifice]. The most secret, the most sacred hope of her nature was that she might some day have such a chance, that she might be a martyr and die for something" (I, 14).

The fact that Olive is originally a sexual reactionary leads one to ask whether she is not, following her fever-chilled debut, in love with the hero, in love in a perverse way that is, tragically, the only way open to one whom "no one could help" (I, 13). (On this supposition, her sister Mrs. Luna's design upon Ransom is the conventionally chivalrous reverse of her own feminist reaction.) That is, while Olive deeply desires to establish herself with the manly hero, she also wants to establish herself negatively, even revengefully, for fear of not being able to do so. She might be anticipating the tormented heroine of "A London Life" who "wanted to marry but . . . wanted also not to want it, and, above all, not to appear to" (97). Thus her surprising feeling for Ransom even as she insists, in her ideological role as female emancipist, that he cannot genuinely care for humanity in general. Olive Chancellor, it turns out, is another Jamesian "type of the reactionary" (II, 82) or heroine of the non sequitur: " 'Why, Miss Olive, it's just got up on purpose for me!' cried the young Mississippian, radiant, and clasping his hands. She thought him very handsome as he said this, but reflected that unfortunately men didn't care for the truth, especially the new kinds, in proportion as they were good-looking. She had, however, a moral resource that she could always fall back upon; it had already been a comfort to her, on occasions of acute feeling, that she hated men, as a class, anyway" (I, 25).

On this view, Olive's subsequently attaching herself to Verena Tarrant, the heroine who *will* eventually marry the hero, amounts to a tragically perverse consummation of her own susceptibility to the hero. Being so extraordinarily susceptible to him, yet at the same time denying her susceptibility and, even more, the appearance of it, Olive reacts to her false position with a kind of vampirist rage for compensation; she would seek to live and love vicariously, through a surrogate sexual self, while at the same time protecting herself from further exposure before the hero by means of this same surrogate. To put this another way, almost pathologically theatrical herself, Olive cultivates in Verena Tarrant another self who can retain her composure in any theater, even the seemingly cruel theater of a Basil Ransom's eyes, by virtue of the "strange spontaneity in her manner, and an air of artless enthusiasm, of personal purity. If she was theatrical, she was naturally theatrical" (I, 62). For Olive, Verena might be the secret of which she can most usefully possess herself:

> It was this glance that was the beginning; it was with this quick survey, omitting nothing, that Olive took possession of her. "You are very remarkable; I wonder if you know how remarkable!" she went on, murmuring the words as if she were losing herself, becoming inadvertent in admiration . . . I know not what may have been the reality of Miss Chancellor's other premonitions, but there is no doubt that in this respect she took Verena's measure on the spot . . . "I could only say three words—I couldn't have spoken more! What a power—what a power, Miss Tarrant!" (I, 94-96).

From this moment on, the irrecoverably shame-shocked Olive would *be* the enviable other self whose "essence was the extraordinary generosity with which she could expose herself, give herself away, turn herself inside out" (II, 193).

Not surprisingly, the next phase of Olive's reaction is an impulse to seal this transaction of identity. Olive would bind Verena to herself with a vow, make a cult of her newfound secret. She herself therefore will "give up — I will give up everything!" (I, 97) if on her side Verena will renounce any idea of marriage, "Will . . . be my friend, my friend of friends, beyond every one, everything, for ever and for ever" (I, 96). By virtue of this compact — "So, hand in hand, for some moments, these two young women sat looking at each other" (I, 96) — Olive becomes at once the self-sacrificial martyr and a revengeful master. In her mouth, the Goethean ethic *"Entsagen sollst du, sollst entsagen!"* ("Thou shalt renounce, refrain, abstain!" 1, 102-103) has become a sinister transvaluation as remarkable as any in James.

The Bostonians' first half ends with Basil Ransom's meeting Verena Tarrant in secret; after being robbed of relationship with Verena by Olive, and after being exposed in the meantime to the aggressive Mrs. Luna, he too requires the redress of a secret. This counterreactionary community of knowledge now forms the basis of a second go on Ransom's part, an attempt to master the theater imposed upon him by Olive's use of Verena:

> Verena Tarrant was erect on her little platform, dressed in white, with flowers in her bosom. The red cloth beneath her feet looked rich in the light of lamps placed on high pedestals on either side of the stage; it gave her figure a setting of colour which made it more pure and salient. She moved freely in her exposed isolation, yet with great sobriety of gesture; there was no table in front of her, and she had no notes in her hand, but stood there like an actress before the footlights, or a singer spinning vocal sounds to a silver thread . . . He had read, of old, of the *improvisatrice* of Italy, and this was a chastened, modern, American version of the type, a New England Corinna, with a mission instead of a lyre (II, 52-53).

Undergoing his ordeal of self-consciousness — an ordeal that is also an initiation into a community of knowledge with Olive, the sexual reactionary — Ransom finds himself suddenly falling in love with Verena. As so often in James, however, the hero's recognition of himself as a sexual claimant is accompanied by fear that he may be only a pretender. Basil Ransom is still theatrical. This sense of weakness Olive of course does her best to aggravate. She promotes the claim of a socialite rival, Henry Burrage; threatened with the total loss of her secret, her chaperon-surrogate, she would cover herself, as usual at the cost of all consistency, with this other, altogether unlikely front. (Her

encouragement of Mrs. Luna's designs on Ransom is another conspiratorial initiative on her part.) And when this cover fails, as fail it
must, Olive resorts to her "fearful power of suffering" (II, 85). She
forces Verena reactively to deny Ransom and his rival.

The story's Cape Cod episode sees Ransom once again forcing Olive
to establish herself negatively with him by means of Verena. In yet
another New England interior, yet another community of knowledge is
formed:

> Olive stopped short, and for a minute the two women remained as they
> were, gazing at each other in the dimness . . . From the way it [Verena's
> hand] lay in her own she guessed her whole feeling—saw it was a kind of
> shame, shame for her weakness, her swift surrender, her insane gyration, in
> the morning . . . Olive understood, or thought she understood, and the
> woefulness of it all only seemed the deeper . . . Verena leaned her head
> back and closed her eyes, and for an hour, as nightfall settled in the room,
> neither of the young women spoke. Distinctly, it was a kind of shame. After
> a while the parlour-maid, very casual, in the manner of the servants at
> Marmion, appeared on the threshold with a lamp; but Olive motioned her
> frantically away. She wished to keep the darkness. It was a kind of shame
> (II, 231-232).

Here, in conspiratorial seclusion, Olive prepares for the moment when
she will "bring out Miss Tarrant before the general public—she has
never appeared that way in Boston—on a great scale" (II, 164). That
is, she prepares for her own masterful debut on stage by systematically
dispossessing Verena of her unself-conscious power: "Inspiration,
moreover, seemed rather to have faded away; in consequence of
Olive's influence she had read and studied so much that it seemed now
as if everything must take form beforehand. Olive was a splendid
critic, whether he liked her or not, and she had made her go over every
word of her lecture twenty times. There wasn't an intonation she
hadn't made her practise; it was very different from the old system,
when her father had worked her up" (II, 208). Only, of course, to be
the more theatrical herself, and the more compelled, in a penultimate
reaction, to go into absolute hiding with her secret, Verena.

The maneuver leaves Ransom with the one counterreactive course of
kidnapping Verena into private life, as it were. In order to accomplish
this, however, he must master once and for all a theater of "thousands
of converging eyes" (II, 250): "The place struck him with a kind of
Roman vastness; the doors which opened out of the upper balconies,

high aloft, and which were constantly swinging to and fro with the passage of spectators and ushers, reminded him of the *vomitoria* that he had read about in descriptions of the Colosseum" (II, 251). Denying the power of these eyes—his own sexual self-consciousness if not the actual amphitheater—he wins the secret heroine over. Meanwhile, bereft of her secret, Olive is delivered over to the exposure she has all along both dreaded and arranged. At last Olive Chancellor can die a martyr, a tragic martyr for love who yet asserts a revengeful power over the consciences of others: "If he had observed her, it might have seemed to him that she hoped to find the fierce expiation she sought for in exposure to the thousands she had disappointed and deceived, in offering herself to be trampled to death and torn to pieces. She might have suggested to him some feminine firebrand of Paris revolutions, erect on a barricade, or even the sacrificial figure of Hypatia, whirled through the furious mob of Alexandria" (II, 274-275).

A theory of James's so-called psychological ghost seems appropriate to this discussion of his characters' dying of shame. This ghost—as Saul Rosenzweig pointed out in his pioneering essay—is the ghost of the James hero's unlived life.[6] It is not, therefore, the guilt-ghost of any bad, trespassing life but a shame-ghost representing the life the deficient hero has fallen short of living. Ultimately James writes his ghost story out of the shameful anxiety of not having lived, of being precluded from vital identity. These ghosts arise, perhaps, from the shame of dying of shame, or from the tormenting persistence of the sense of shame even *after* dying of shame. Thus the main characters of the late fantasy "Fordham Castle," both of whom are proven and acknowledged failures in life, are shown in the last stages of losing their identities, actually going under pseudonyms and passing for life. Finally, when they seem to be living on posthumously, it is as if they may as well never have lived. The story ends as the hero, now exposed to himself as his own ghost, "felt as abandoned as he had known he should—felt left, in his solitude, to the sense of his extinction. He faced it completely now, and to himself at least could express it without fear of protest. 'Why certainly I'm dead' " (149).

Since it haunts a hero who has died of shame, James's shame-ghost must also express revenge-feeling (as well as extreme anxiety). If a character cannot bear with his shame, and enters an intensifying cycle of being ashamed of being ashamed, then the revenge-feeling naturally latent in his experience may well result in a visitation from a punitive revenger-ghost. And if the hero now denies that this shame-ghost is his own (in order further to deny his original injury), then he is likely to displace and inflict a revenge-ghost upon others. James's most famous ghost story, "The Turn of the Screw," is an example of this cycle. As we shall see later, the ghosts in this Pandora situation arise from the governess' acute sense of social and erotic shame and doubt before the master; they arise to show her up unbearably as never having lived. These ghosts are then compulsively denied in an effort to conceal from herself her own abject self and are thus displaced by a kind of crusading effrontery upon the children. Eventually she can feel "morally" obliged to inflict the plight of the children, now the instruments of her vengefulness, upon the master; the governess has fomented a situation by which she can both bring herself to the lofty master's notice and punish him ambiguously for his arbitrary neglect of her. The ghosts of "The Turn of the Screw" manifest the ambiguous and treacherous revolt of the slavish acolyte.

However, the other-directed ghost (as in "The Turn of the Screw" and "The Aspern Papers") is in the minority in James. Generally this ghost embodying the life the hero has fallen short of living visits as a secret or extraordinary form of self-punishment for not having lived. The very important early tale "A Passionate Pilgrim" is an example.[7] Here Clement Searle, a self acknowledged "poor nobody of a Yankee" (232), forfeits his American life in order to lay claim to the Searle family estate in England. Turning his apostate's resentment upon himself even before the story has begun, this hero has become a Jamesian invalid: " 'Before I lost my health,' he answered. 'And my property — the little I had. And my ambition. And my self-esteem . . . They are too far gone, — self-esteem especially' " (241). Once arrived in England, however, he can but acquire the identity of a might-have-been: "Sitting here, in this old park, in this old land, I feel — I feel that I hover on the misty verge of what might have been! I should have been born here and not there; here my vulgar idleness would have been — don't laugh now! — would have been elegant leisure" (245). In England it is as if he were living the tenuous posthumous life of a social ghost. But, now, this nobly morbid nostalgia on his part robs him further of such American identity as he still possesses. The more he strives to be the English might-have-been, the more he is a nobody of a Yankee. Indeed, he does not really exist anywhere, in any way.

The passionate claimant's hopes of social transplantation improve momentarily with the chance of his marrying the heiress to the Searle estate. But these hopes are dashed when his cousin and rival, the current incumbent of the estate, emerges. The apostate-claimant now enters into a most extraordinary Jamesian decline at the same time that he identifies himself with an ancestral Clement Searle who has long ago fled in disgrace to America and who still haunts the living Searles: "Searle blazed up into enthusiasm. 'Of course you know,' — and suddenly he began to blush violently, — 'I should be sorry to claim any identity with my faithless namesake, poor fellow. But I shall be hugely tickled if this poor ghost should be deceived by my resemblance and mistake me for her cruel lover . . . But can a ghost haunt a ghost? I *am* a ghost!' " (272). As he says, he is quite "ghost-encumbered" (289). He even claims to see the ghost of the girl "he" has seduced in a bygone century. Finally, having actually impersonated his ghostly forebear and invoked his unlived life, this appealing pretender to life dies. He dies as much from consummating his social apostasy, that is, from self-punishment both for being and refusing to be American, as from punitive shame at his compensatory lost cause in England, his not being and his claiming to be English.

Since James's shame-and-revenge ghost has to do with the hero's unlived life, it will resemble on occasion his alter ego or double. It can be a secret self that completes the hero, but at the same time fatally humiliates him by showing him up as not having lived completely. Or put another way, if the hero fears that he has but half-lived, or that he has not really lived, then any double embodying his shameful fear is bound to have a kind of posthumous, ghostly status.

It is "The Jolly Corner," a story so unrealistic as to seem intelligible only as imaginative psychology, that is the greatest example of this situation. Here the international hero begins by undergoing a kind of cultural shock. Returning to New York after thirty-three years of undistinguished absence in Europe, Spencer Brydon believes "I know at least what I am" (205). Yet in spite of having braced himself for America, he find himself absolutely unready for it. Indeed, he seems to be shocked in proportion to his having been rigidly braced against shock. He suffers the surprise of surprise, so to speak:

Everything was somehow a surprise . . . It would have taken a century . . . it would have taken a longer absence and a more averted mind than those even of which he had been guilty, to pile up the differences, the newnesses, the queernesses, above all the bignesses, for the better or the worse, that at present assaulted his vision wherever he looked.

The great fact all the while however had been the incalculability; since he *had* supposed himself, from decade to decade, to be allowing, and in the most liberal and intelligent manner, for brilliancy of change (193-194).

Overpowered by the America of the billionaires, James's social aesthete has brought home to him the sense that he too might have been powerful. A middle-aged failure looking across half a lifetime to a point where what might have been and what actually has been have diverged, he begins to imagine a hypothetical self:

"What you feel—and what I feel *for* you—is that you'd have had power."

"You'd have liked me that way?" he asked.

She [Alice Staverton] barely hung fire. "How should I not have liked you?"

"I see. You'd have liked me, have preferred me, a billionaire!"

"How should I not have liked you?" she simply again asked (205).

It is not that Brydon simply wants billions; he explicitly denies this vulgarity. Extraordinary vitality or power, however, he does claim. Since, following his initial shock, he fears that he has never really lived, he craves to know how powerful he might have been.

But Spencer Brydon's search for identity is not to be straight-forward. It is true that, having once been decisively overpowered, he will readily admit his failure in Europe:

"I know at least what I am," he simply went on; "the other side of the medal's clear enough. I've not been edifying—I believe I'm thought in a hundred quarters to have been barely decent. I've followed strange paths and worshipped strange gods; it must have come to you again and again—in fact you've admitted to me as much—that I was leading, at any time these thirty years, a selfish frivolous scandalous life" (205).

But he can and will not do any more than "admit as much" concerning his other self. After all, he may well find, after giving away a failed European self, that the unlived American life has no true validity either. This hero, therefore, would cover himself tactically. "I shall readily admit to failure in Europe," he might be bargaining, "on condition that I do not have to admit another failure, one that would render my failure total." A weak man is claiming the luxury of a powerful collateral life for himself; but since he craves power more than any other self, he would not be overpowered by any powerful self. This explains why Spencer Brydon now denies in advance the ghostly double that has begun steadily to enter into his consciousness. "*He* isn't myself. He's the just so totally other person" (206), he tells Alice Staverton.

James's story goes on to dramatize a kind of symbolic pantomime of the consciousness. In absolute secrecy, Spencer Brydon begins to prowl about the house on the jolly corner, "rejoicing above all, as much as he might, in open vistas, reaches of communication between rooms and by passages; the long straight chance or show, as he would have called it, for the revelation he pretended to invite" (207). He patrols this house — considered as autobiography it might, together with the sky-scraper, be Henry James's own house of fiction[8] — in such a way as both to provoke and to harrow the other self. He resembles John Marcher, that so very unready man who would ready himself for any revelation of his emotional and sexual unreadiness: "but he had tasted of no pleasure so fine as his actual tension, had been introduced to no sport that demanded at once the patience and the nerve of this stalking of a creature more subtle, yet at bay perhaps more formidable, than any beast of the forest" (210). The hero's very insistence that there is another self involves an affront to that self. It is as if he would know its secret before losing, on account of its advent, all being-unto-self. "It made him feel, this acquired faculty, like some monstrous stealthy cat; he wondered if he would have glared at these moments with large shining yellow eyes, and what it mightn't verily be, for the poor hard-pressed *alter ego*, to be confronted with such a type" (211). A certain prurience here indicates that Spencer Brydon may be imbued, to an unexpected degree, with a desire for revenge.

But now, in this intensifying reactionary cycle, the hero grows ashamed of his shamelessness or attempt to shame. At one moment he is all-seeing, the next he senses that he himself is all too visible, "definitely followed, tracked at a distance carefully taken and to the express end that he should the less confidently, less arrogantly, appear to himself merely to pursue . . . He was kept in sight while remaining himself — as regards the essence of his position — sightless" (212). He has his back, one might say. In this faintly grotesque pantomime of consciousness, he is a Pantaloon "buffeted and tricked from behind by ubiquitous Harlequin" (213). Consciousness has hived off from consciousness and turned counterreactively upon surprised and vulnerable consciousness. From the ego's point of view, it is as if the alter ego "has 'turned': that . . . is what has happened—he's the fanged or the antlered animal brought at last to bay" (213).

But should a shamed and self- and other self-rejecting self be admitted, then the hero's erstwhile self will be utterly displaced from itself. Spencer Brydon will die of shame, as he has suspected from the outset that he must. Inevitably, then, enormous anxiety accompanies the rout of his identity. Feeling himself "slipping and slipping on some awful incline" (214), Brydon would lapse altogether from the trans-action of identity.

But this panicky reaction is a dying of shame too. For all his panic, then, the hero must stick. Spencer Brydon must insist upon his self-respect. He *is*. It is a further counterreaction that, in this animated dream-pantomime of consciousness, takes the form of a partition: Brydon is shocked to find that a door which would normally be open is now closed, and that it seems to have been closed by the harrowed other self. There is, so to speak, a formal measure of secrecy between the hero's back and front, a partition that more than ever bespeaks the presence of a notionally powerful self that might have been and that the hero would know, but that at the same time he cannot acknowledge for fear of forfeiting what identity he already has, indeed for fear of being exposed as a mere reflex might-have-been by what might have been. Correspondingly, the ego's counterreaction to the alter ego's compulsion to conceal itself is a newfound discretion. Self would now respect exposed self by averting the eyes, by choosing to allow self its "sacred" zone:

> It had turned altogether to a different admonition; to a supreme hint, for him, of the value of Discretion! . . . Discretion—he jumped at that; and yet not, verily, at such a pitch, because it saved his nerves or his skin, but because, much more valuably, it saved the situation . . . He had thus another station, close to the thin partition by which revelation was denied him; but with his eyes bent and his hands held off in a mere intensity of stillness. He listened as if there had been something to hear, but this atti-tude, while it lasted, was his own communication. "If you won't then— good: I spare you and I give up. You affect me as by the appeal positively for pity: you convince me that for reasons rigid and sublime—what do I know?—we both of us should have suffered. I respect them then, and, though moved and privileged as, I believe, it has never been given to man, I

retire, I renounce—never, on my honour, to try again. So rest for ever—and let *me!*" (218-219).

Here is a characteristic Jamesian renunciation of knowing, of an ultimately self-directed act of resentment for being in all probability precluded from vital selfhood. And as in so many of the later James's crises, the renunciation is made upon oath. Spencer Brydon, one can say, commits his identity or honor by invoking all that is sacred to him, and by activating thereby a potential penalty against himself—he will forfeit all right to esteem should he fail to adhere to his oath. Moreover, he ensures that he can never dishonor the other party to the transaction; the latter will remain untouched by any failure on his part. In short, by offering to leave what would be secret secret, Spencer Brydon actually honors the rival self.

But as the James of all the stories employing a discretionary point of view knew well, renunciatory discretion can be only a prudential, containing measure. Once one has begun to know, one is on the way to acknowledging all; properly speaking, it is only revengeful knowing that is for the renouncing. In other words, discretion after the event of exposure at best grants no more than a moratorium on further exposure, and at worst aggravates it. "He knew—yes, as he had never known anything—that, *should* he see the door open, it would all too abjectly be the end of him. It would mean that the agent of his shame—for his shame was the deep abjection—was once more at large and in general possession" (222). Indeed, the erstwhile Spencer Brydon now finds himself virtually dispossessed by this knowledge, so much so that his acknowledgement is translated in the pantomime into renewed panic. The hero flees. And as he deserts the house of his old consciousness in favor of the other self, the latter is inevitably admitted to take possession of it:

> . . . he the next instant saw, by the fact that the vestibule gaped wide, that the hinged halves of the inner door had been thrown far back. Out of that again the *question* sprang at him, making his eyes, as he felt, half-start from his head, as they had done, at the top of the house, before the sign of the other door. If he had left that one open, hadn't he left this one closed, and wasn't he now in *most* immediate presence of some inconceivable occult activity? . . . It gloomed, it loomed, it was something, it was somebody, the prodigy of a personal presence (223-224).

There can no longer be any question of discretion. The hero can but give recognition to the overpowering invasion of the real and true.

It is a great climax of self-consciousness. Here, after systematic resistance, consciousness divides into two. Spencer Brydon's front has been exposed at the outset of the story, now his back, the ghostly implication of a lifetime, the implication of a ghostly lifetime, emerges. There can no longer be any obscurity, or secrecy or refuge, for the hero's self from himself. He seems wholly open in the light of the "thin admitted dawn" (224). It is the climax of a writer who could imagine a character like Hyacinth Robinson, a sensibility on whom nothing was lost.

Not only is James rendering here the failure of a hitherto reliable ego-identity, he also dramatizes the failure of the alter ego's identity. Thus Spencer Brydon might be some William Wetmore Story who, after passing a life of sensations in Europe only "to figure his career as a sort of beautiful sacrifice to a noble mistake,"[9] finds that he has not really lived. In Europe he has lived posthumously, as if he has been his own ghost — in part because of his compensatory indulgence of his unlived, American other life that might have been. But now, thirty-three years later, it turns out that this other, unlived life too is invalid, no more than spectral. The American other self of so deracinated and unlived a life can only be an invalid life, a ghost with "poor ruined sight" and its "poor right hand" (232). Both selves, therefore, merely impersonate and pass for life. Nobody — neither the expatriate hero himself nor the American other self — really lives or has ever lived.

It is an appalling shock of self-recognition that instantaneously involves the compulsion to conceal the self. Spencer Brydon now sees himself burying his face for shame:

> This only could it be — this only till he recognized, with his advance, that what made the face dim was the pair of raised hands that covered it and in which, so far from being offered in defiance, it was buried as for dark deprecation. So Brydon, before him, took him in; with every fact of him now, in the higher light, hard and acute . . . for he could but gape at his other self in this other anguish, gape as a proof that *he*, standing there for the achieved, the enjoyed, the triumphant life, couldn't be faced in his triumph. Wasn't the proof in the splendid covering hands, strong and completely spread? — so spread and so intentional that, in spite of a special verity that surpassed every other, the fact that one of these hands had lost two fin-

gers, which were reduced to stumps, as if accidentally shot away, the face was effectually guarded and saved (224-225).

On Brydon's own part, the compulsion to conceal unspeakable deficiency or disfigurement involves enormous resentment, a lifetime's rage to deny admission to what has had to be admitted in spite of himself:

> Horror, with the sight, had leaped into Brydon's throat, gasping there in a sound he couldn't utter; for the bared identity was too hideous as *his*, and his glare was the passion of his protest. The face, *that* face, Spencer Brydon's? — he searched it still, but looking away from it in dismay and denial, falling straight from his height of sublimity. It was unknown, inconceivable, awful, disconnected from any possibility—! . . . Such an identity fitted his at *no* point, made its alternative monstrous. A thousand times yes, as it came upon him nearer now — the face was the face of a stranger (225-226).

Having *no* authentic identity, the self-rejecting career apostate would once and for all snub himself:

> It came upon him nearer now, quite as one of those expanding fantastic images projected by the magic lantern of childhood; for the stranger, who-ever he might be, evil, odious, blatant, vulgar, had advanced as for agges-sion, and he knew himself give ground. Then harder pressed still, sick with the force of his shock, and falling back as under the hot breath and the roused passion of a life larger than his own, a rage of personality before which his own collapsed, he felt the whole vision turn to darkness and his very feet give way. His head went round; he was going; he had gone (226).

The whole scuffle amounts to a seemingly absolute confusion of identity. Caught in the reactionary emotional cycle of the apostate, he dies of shame for his inanition.

Spencer Brydon has seen, and thereby laid, the shame-ghost. After this, it remains for him to come at last into his proper identity. This man who has died has lived — does live. Further, once it has been seen and laid, the shame-ghost can be completely repudiated by him: *he* it is who has not really existed, never the prodigal "I." As we shall see more clearly when dealing with the role of the lie in James, Spencer Brydon, who has earned the right to trump the damaging evidence of his ghostly double, does so with a heroic, no longer a false, duplicity.

At the end of "Pandora" the hero not only comes upon a Pandora situation that has once been open to him but is now sealed, he also suffers a peculiarly galling shock. A rival whom he has always been able to consider inferior, the naggingly familiar competitor, un-expectedly emerges as a superior joker-competitor. For the hero it is almost as if his uncertain relationship with Pandora has all along been preparing for this: for his being exposed by and to a simulacrum of himself as he might have been. And no sooner has this joker-com-petitor externalized, as it were, than the whole element of rivalry in the situation is paradoxically internalized in the hero; he is painfully wounded, he seems to himself to have divided into two. What is more, the joker-competitor himself is exposed as having been exposed (together with Pandora) in the memorable past. Although he seems to live in the "dying," already ghostly hero's place, he is the hero's superior only on the understanding that he has been, and cannot ever cease to be, compromised by the latter's co-existence. The double too is double-encumbered. Everybody has something of the imploring pretender about them. As the story's ending suggests, everyone, not only the hero, performs quasi-theatrically.

While this theme of "intimate adversaries" ("The Jolly Corner," 220) recurs in all James's Pandora situations, it is in fact to be found everywhere in him. This stands to reason: insofar as the shamed and self-doubting hero feels himself socially and sexually incomplete, he is almost bound to be defined by the presence of a character who does appear to complete him, even if only in a compensatory way that will eventually prove false. If James's theme is the quixotic search for iden-tity and honor in the foreknowledge of a probable failure, then the advent of the compensatory but treacherous double, who announces as no one else that "You are not who you think you are, you are an impostor," is an inevitable turning point. Reversing these for-mulas, one can say that there are always coexistent compensatory doubles in James because there is never enough identity or honor to go around. The James character's life is always likely to be defined against an unlived life that might-have-been; preclusion from satisfactory self-hood seems to be in the mysterious nature of things. Indeed, the merely exoteric initiation into selfhood is so chronic a plight in James that one looks to his early life as well as to his expatriation for its sources — and of course does not look far to find him saying in *A Small Boy and Others* that one of his first perceptions

was that of my brother's [William's] occupying a place in the world to
which I couldn't at all aspire — to any approach to which in truth I seem
to myself ever conscious of having signally forfeited a title. It glimmers back
to me that I quite definitely and resignedly thought of him as in the most exemplary manner already beforehand with me, already seated at his task
when the attempt to drag me crying and kicking to the first hour of my
education failed on the threshold of the Dutch House in Albany after the
fashion I have glanced at in a collection of other pages than these . . . That
failure of my powers or that indifference to them . . . was to leave him once
for all already there an embodied demonstration of the possible — already
wherever it might be that there was a question of my arriving, when
arriving at all, belatedly and ruefully; as if he had gained such an advance
of me in his sixteen months' experience of the world before mine began that
I never for all the time of childhood and youth in the least caught up with
him or overtook him. He was always round the corner and out of sight,
coming back into view but at his hours of extremest ease. We were never in
the same schoolroom, in the same game, scarce even in step together or in
the same phase at the same time; when our phases overlapped, that is, it
was only for a moment — he was clean out before I had got well in. How far
he had really at any moment dashed forward it is not for me now to attempt
to say; what comes to me is that I at least hung inveterately and woefully
back, and that this relation alike to our interests and to each other seemed
proper and preappointed. I lose myself in wonder at the loose ways, the
strange process of waste, through which nature and fortune may deal on
occasion with those whose faculty for application is all and only in their
imagination and their sensibility.[10]

But whatever the biographical situation, both or all the competing
selves in James's stories are incomplete and fractional, and are proved
to be so simply by their coexisting.

An apparent problem with the Jamesian double meets us here. If it
is always an element in James's situations, and is not merely confined
to a story like "The Jolly Corner," why hasn't this double "come out"
along with other nineteenth century doubles?[11] The answer, I think,
has to do with the ambiguous nature of James's psychosocial subject.
In the first place, the other self may actually be welcomed and claimed
by James's hero as a surrogate offering him "another go" or an "extension" ("The Middle Years"):

"You do keep me up," Verena went on. "You are my conscience."
"I should like to be able to say that you are my form — my envelope. But
you are too beautiful for that!" So Olive returned her friend's compliment

. . . To Olive it appeared that just this partnership of their two minds—each of them, by itself, lacking an important group of facets—made an organic whole which, for the work in hand, could not fail to be brilliantly effective . . . Together, in short, they would be complete, they would have everything, and together they would triumph (I, 187-189).

Again it is the childhood autobiography that reveals the emotional basis of this misled, and misleading, welcome for the other self:

I had rather a positive lack of the passion [jealousy], and thereby, I suppose, a lack of spirit; since if jealousy bears, as I think, on what one sees one's companions able to do—as against one's own falling short—envy, as I knew it at least, was simply of what they *were*, or in other words of a certain sort of richer consciousness supposed, doubtless often too freely supposed, in them. They were so *other*—that was what I felt; and to *be* other, other almost anyhow, seemed as good as the probable taste of the bright compound wistfully watched in the confectioner's window; unattainable, impossible, of course, but as to which just this impossibility and just that privation kept those active proceedings in which jealousy seeks relief quite out of the question.[12]

Moreover, the unready, the incomplete, the ashamed hero must be the last person to draw attention to himself. As if caught out in an oppressive theater, he would bolt underground, "sink into the ground." Even when he does attract attention to himself, we suspect him of putting a front on a back. This hero, therefore, will hardly parade with any intimate adversary who can show him up; as James says of the double characters of "The Private Life," "They had nothing to do, the so dissimilar twins, with each other" (preface to *The Altar of the Dead*, xv). Indeed, intimate adversaries will go so far as formally to deny each other. Just as the joker-competitor steals identity from the hero, so the hero would steal identity from the joker-competitor. Therefore, when the latter turns out to be as exposed as he is exposing, to be a vulnerable back to the nominal hero's vulnerable front, he too must conceal himself, possibly by using the hero as a front. Given the potentially total nature of exposure—the whole "I," both front and back, are at issue—concealing must be a function of revealing in James. Thus it is not that the double appears only intermittently in him but, quite the contrary, that it is tenderly and infinitely there, is so likely as to be correspondingly unlikely. James writes too purely along a shame axis for this to be otherwise.

To say that the double poses the question whether the hero has only pretended to live is really to say it arises from the fear of death and that its advent is an earnest of the hero's probable nonentity. This of course had been the theme of the nineteenth century's classic double story, Dostoevsky's "The Double: A St. Petersburg Poem." Here the hero Golyadkin is a character in a weak or dependent social position, a petty official in a bureaucratic anthill. Tormented by shame and self-doubt, he can imagine himself committing suicide, or that he is not himself but someone else strikingly like himself. Eventually he divides into two during an agony of self-consciousness, and his double in every respect manifests itself. After this, he has a back and a front, since Golyadkin, Jr., crowds him out of both the private and official spheres of his life. He even comes to dream that, while he himself is a mere burlesque pretender to his own existence, the upstart Golyadkin, Jr., is the real Golyadkin. In his dream, moreover, the hero seems to redup-licate indefinitely; wherever he goes, exact images of himself spring up from the pavements to harass him.

This hero dreams he is everywhere because he fears he is nowhere. He has no being-unto-self, no place except possibly the corner behind a cupboard or the shelter of a woodstack in which to hide from his imaginary enemies; like any one of James's own characters, he is utterly known and visible. The fact is that the advent of his double and its subsequent success in disestablishing him has shown that this hero has had no genuine identity to begin with. The other self too is exposed as well as exposing, and is likewise an unworthy pretender; he can occupy all Golyadkin's places, official and private, only through the servile careerism that Golyadkin would have liked to master, but which is incapable of ensuring him an authentic place in life. The only place left to Golyadkin is the asylum where, after disembarrassing himself at last of the watching double, he appropriately ends. He might be locked in a kind of a psychosis of humiliation.

Dmitri Chizhevsky has shown that Golyadkin, together with Dostoevsky's later double-encumbered characters Stavrogin and Ivan Karamazov, ultimately arise from nineteenth century ethical ration-alism's questioning of man's existential reality.[13] The resultant anxiety, while it can become in existential theology a source of religious insight, can also create profound psychological and ontological instability; Stavrogin and Ivan Karamazov both fear and are ashamed of their concreteness insofar as this makes them identical with the "least man." And having lost the sense of the "I," the individual in Dostoevsky also forfeits whatever sphere of identity he has had, his "who," and his "place." Hence, Chizhevsky argues, the irruption of the double. When the individual character in Dostoevsky most fears his imposture or nothingness, this double springs forth. The only "place" that can make him invulnerable to this devil-double is his closeness to God.

In contrast, the immediate sources of James's double lie neither in a philosophic nor a religious problem. As we have seen, the double in him is largely a social and sexual matter. Yet it too arises from the extreme fear of nothingness, for not only does James's hero feel no more than indirectly initiated into the society of his choice, he cannot ultimately be confident of the living and changing nature of that into which he is *not* directly initiated. Who are these false gods to whom he has sacrificed himself? If the James of the archetypal Galerie d'Apollon episode stands in an aesthetic relation to society, the hero of *The Sacred Fount* stands only in a theoretical or epistemological relation to it that gives him no more status than that of the prurient house guest of Max Beerbohm's cartoon. On interstitial ground, James's hero seems to forfeit both "I" and "place" — in part because in the first place, on native ground, he had been deeply unsure of his validity. Further, for this hero there is always the thought that to claim social identity on the basis of a false position is but dishonorably to expropriate it. For him, there can only be a factitious identity: spoils, James would have called it.

It is in this death-haunted crisis of identity that the Jamesian compensatory deputy will manifest itself as an inimical double. Indeed, the hero's position may be so unbearable that the double can be said to arise both from the extreme fear of nonentity and from the desire to put an end to this fear of nonentity. On the one hand, "The thought of death is rendered supportable by assuring oneself of a second life, after this one, as a double."[14] On the other hand, conceivably, this double may be awaited in secret as a just self-punishment, or an instrument of self-directed revenge; to quote Otto Rank again, "Thus we have the strange paradox of the suicide who seeks death in order to free himself of the intolerable thanatophobia."[15] In other words, the deeply ashamed and doubting hero may suicidally inflict his double upon himself. His own apostate, as it were, he turns from and thus upon himself, just as another Jamesian revenger will inflict his shame-woundedness upon an enemy, first by devising for him his perfect insolent double, then by insinuating himself between this enemy and his double as the *tertius gaudens*. In such a case the doubling that is a potentiality in all James's situations has become a psychic strategy for refusing or deferring identity.

Because the issue involved in his transaction with his double is one of life or death, any hero who would survive must finally deny his opportunist competitor. The hero whose life is given the lie, who is proved to have only a false claim to life, must in his turn prove that the double is the true impostor; each would deny the other the identity of which there is only enough, and barely enough, for one. "Never for one minute have I taken you for reality," Ivan Karamazov tells his devil-double, "You are a lie, you are my illness, you are a phantom. It's only that I don't know how to destroy you and I see I must suffer for a time. You are my hallucination. You are the incarnation of myself, but only of one side of me . . . of my thoughts and feelings, but only the nastiest and stupidest of them."[16] Therefore the intolerable consciousness of "twin consciousness," as Patrick White has called it in his double novel *The Solid Mandala*,[17] must end in some compulsive disembarrassment, a disembarrassment taking the form either of a "tussle, dishevelment, pushes, scratches, shrieks" (*The Spoils of Poynton*, 49) or, with greater likelihood, of a "noiseless brush" (*The Ambassadors*, II, 68) or a covert scuffle. An almost too discreet case of the latter alternative is *The Tragic Muse* where the tandem heroes, cousins "united . . . by ease of neighbouring" (I, 72), "were both conscious that it was in their interest to keep certain differences to 'chaff' each other about — so possible was it that they might have quarrelled if they had only agreed . . . This served as well as anything else to keep the peace between them; it was a necessity of their friendly intercourse that they should scuffle a little, and it scarcely mattered what they scuffled about" (I, 77). Whether noisy or discreet, however, such scuffling will lead to the reduction or dying of shame or the actual death of one, and probably of each, of the twin pretenders.

One other point should be made here about James's joker-double. So much is it the implication of the ashamed and doubting hero's consciousness that, as in other double literature, it need have no very corporeal or realistic existence so long as it functions as a goad to the hero of what he might have been: "A vague terror seized Gabriel at this answer, as if, at that hour when he hoped to triumph, some impalpable and vindictive being was coming against him, gathering forces against him in its vague world" (Joyce, "The Dead"). Important examples from the stories are "The Aspern Papers," where the narrator in quest of imaginative and sexual identity finds his double in the Byronic Jeffrey Aspern of a bygone age; and "The Beast in the Jungle," where the passionless John Marcher glimpses a passion-ravaged mourner and recognizes in him what he might and should have been. "The Jolly Corner" gives this incorporeal double a seemingly pathological or ghostly status. In these fantasy situations we notice the Jamesian rivalry being progressively internalized, and in "The Jolly Corner" the double is entirely a matter of a single hero's consciousness dividing and turning upon surprised and vulnerable consciousness.

Since James writes primarily along a shame axis, one can expect to find the completing-competing double everywhere in him, whether in an early nouvelle like *Watch and Ward* or in a late novel like *The Ambassadors*. For our purposes, however, the early *Roderick Hudson* may be regarded as a paradigm case. This story begins with an acknowledgment of insufficient identity on the part of the American hero, who is clearly a doubting aspect of the young James himself. "Do you know," asks the dilettante Rowland Mallet, "I sometimes think that I'm a man of genius half-finished? The genius has been left out, the faculty of expression is wanting; but the need for expression remains, and I spend my days groping for the latch of a closed door" (7). The hero feels no more than exoterically initiated into satisfactory selfhood. Now, at this very moment when he would be other than himself, his other self actually manifests itself in the person of the young genius Roderick Hudson. Seeing his opportunity, Rowland immediately adopts Roderick as a complementary self; together they will make a career in Europe. "I can't do such things myself, but when I see a young man of genius standing helpless and hopeless for want of capital, I feel . . . as if it would give at least a reflected usefulness to my own life to offer him his opportunity" (42). "Roderick will repay me," he says at another point in this transaction, "It's a speculation" (67). For his part Roderick, who labors under the feeling of having "to fill a double place. I have to be my brother as well as myself" (36), sees a subsidizing brother in Mallet. If he too can be more than "light ornamental" (49) in America, he may yet, thanks to Mallet's intervention, be "the typical, original, *a*boriginal American artist" (29).

Clearly, this team's relationship is from the beginning a compensatory one based upon a sense of insufficiency. As we have seen, however, the need for compensation is thoroughly ambiguous in James. Invariably arising from a "basis of so great a weakness," any compensation can only further expose the false position it has been intended to compensate; an exposure that, in turn, can lead to a Jamesian revenge cycle. Thus while these heroes' cooperative quest in Europe should by rights make up for their light ornamentalism in America, in the long run it is liable to prove them both specious in Europe and, since they have already forfeited an American life for a European one, nonentities in America. (Rowland recognizes this liability to falling between two stools when he describes himself at the start as "an idle useless creature and . . . he should probably be even more so in Europe than at home" (5); not surprisingly, he experiences "a strange feeling of prospective regret" (28) for America just as he is on the point of proposing the European venture.) One might say, then, that the heroes not only promise to complete each other, they also threaten mischievously to deplete each other. Even at this early moment "there stirred in his [Rowland's] mind an odd feeling of annoyance with Roderick for having so peremptorily taken possession of his nature" (58). Moreover, it transpires unexpectedly that Roderick is Rowland's sexual competitor. No sooner has Rowland fallen secretly in love with the New England heroine — it is an early case of a social aesthete's need for a secret — then he learns that Roderick has already taken precedence over him. A surrogate in every respect, the man who is to live for him professionally also lives for him sexually, and therefore seems to rob him of sexual identity: "Rowland listened to all this with a feeling that fortune had played him an elaborately devised trick. It had lured him out into mid-ocean and . . . given him a singularly sympathetic comrade, and then it had turned and delivered him a thumping blow in mid-chest" (72). Not that Roderick meanwhile lives unencumbered, for his attitude toward Mary Garland is shown up as being entirely self-seeking in comparison with his watcher's and warder's sacrificial devotion. Already, in an unacknowledged fashion, these heroes deplete each other's identity. They are dying suicidally on account of one another even as they live sacrificially for one another.

It is, I think, this unacknowledged ambiguity of the heroes' quest that accounts for the quite extraordinary rate of Roderick's and, necessarily, Rowland's decline in Europe. If their forming a compensatory tandem in America in itself indicates profound self-rejection, then their joint quest for further compensation in Europe can only aggravate their self-rejection, indeed must make it appear almost voluntary. As always in James, the measure of the heroes' unacceptability to themselves is their need for a secret, which they now go about expropriating from each other. While the negligent Roderick is the executive hero in relation to the American heroine Mary Garland, the devoted and self-concealing Rowland also lays claim to her, if only unofficially. Thus Rowland lives for Roderick in an important way, but at the same time reactively steals Roderick's role. In other words, Rowland comes gradually to impersonate Roderick. But this in turn is to render Roderick himself an impersonator. Both heroes, therefore, soon become impostors in terms of American identity. Neither really lives, socially or sexually. Perhaps neither really wants to live.

But this truth of their falsity as Americans is forced upon them by the new, though always half-expected, truth of their falsity in Europe. In the Europe of a Prince Casamassima who can trace his lineage back to the fifth century, Roderick is for all his talent that least man, a barbarian aesthete. Thus even as Rowland reacts secretly towards Mary Garland, Roderick would compensate himself with Christina Light's vengeful ambiguity or secret. Moreover, even in this relationship with Christina Light, Roderick must consciously compete with Rowland. Worse, while he once again plays the nominal hero, the latter unconsciously displaces him. In fact, as Roderick's as yet unavowed double in all respects—as well as the reticent lover he is a secret artist without hope of an authentic artist's career—Rowland arrives at a psychological and moral understanding of Christina that surpasses Roderick's own: "He was not in love with her; he disapproved of her; he distrusted her; and yet he felt it a rare and expensive privilege to watch her, and he found her presence in every way important and momentous" (243). Later, it turns out to be Rowland, not Roderick at all, who guesses the secret of Christina's illegitimacy. Once again, Rowland in effect both displaces Roderick and renders him a mere impersonator (and vice-versa).

That everyone, and not Christina alone, is theatrical is brought out in the Coliseum scene we have already mentioned. Here, in the awkward fashion of doubles, Rowland happens upon a community of knowledge, Roderick and Christina seated together upon a ledge:

"They had apparently an eye to extreme privacy" (226). Undecided whether to withdraw and thus risk giving himself away or to stay on as an involuntary voyeur, Rowland now watches his executive alter ego's performance. Stationed in the wings, as it were, he is as much a "theater" as Christina herself:

> "No, I'm not weak," Roderick returned with vehemence; "I maintain I'm not weak! I'm incomplete perhaps; but I can't help that. Incompleteness is a matter of the outfit. Weakness is a matter of the will."
>
> "Incomplete then be it, since you hold to the word. It's the same thing," Christina went on, "so long as it keeps you from splendid achievement. Is it written then that I shall really never know what I've so often dreamed of?"
>
> "What then have you dreamed of?"
>
> "A man whom I can have the luxury of respecting!" cried the girl with a sudden flame . . . "When I first knew you I gave no sign, but you had struck me. I observed you as women observe, and I fancied you had the sacred fire."
>
> "Before heaven I believe I have!" Roderick broke out.
>
> "Ah, but so very little of it!" (227-228).

Roderick-Rowland (for Christina in effect addresses Rowland as well) is exposed as an impostor. Further, if Roderick-Rowland do not together constitute a genuine "I," it is because they are apostate-aesthetes who will not own to any "place":

> "You've never chosen, I say; you've been afraid to choose. You've never really looked in the face the fact that you're false, that you've broken your faith. You've never looked at it and seen that it was hideous and yet said 'No matter, I'll brave the penalty, I'll bear the shame.' You've closed your eyes; you've tried to stifle remembrance . . . You've faltered and dodged and drifted, you've gone on from accident to accident, and I'm sure that at this present moment you can't tell what it is you really wish" (229).

Christina's unbearable conclusion—"I'm afraid you *are* scant" (230)—now goads Roderick into an act of compensatory defiance. He would master the theater by attempting to fetch a flower for Christina from the ruins above them. Since, however, he is but half a man on his own, the gesture seems foredoomed, even trivial. At the same time, Roderick has always had his chance of sufficiency insofar as he combines with his sponsor half. Rowland as his hidden alter ego, Rowland as Roderick—Rowland himself senses this at this moment: "If the thing were possible he felt a sudden high bold relish of his friend's attempting it. It would be finely done, it would be gallant, it

would have a sort of ardent authority as an answer to Christina's sinister persiflage" (232). Indeed, it looks here as though the incomplete
Roderick were half invoking his supplementary self stationed nearby
(even as Rowland is secretly impelled to urge on *his* incomplete alter
ego).

Of course, such an invocation can at this stage only aggravate what
has been from the first a false position. And when Rowland must "out"
into the arena in order to save his alter ego from fatal embarrassment,
he is both exposing and exposed, a kind of embarrassing back to a
grotesque situation. The advantages of the tandem's cooperation have
turned into the corresponding disadvantages; Roderick and Rowland
henceforward oppress each other as each other's gall and goad. Alike
too conscious of their twin consciousness, they now turn upon each
other in an open rupture. What has previously been a need for
compensation now turns into revenge-feeling, in fact into a revenge
cycle. Roderick defies his watcher and warder and pursues his reactive
relationship with Christina Light, while Rowland asks himself why
Roderick should make off with *all* the sexual identity, a Mary Garland
as well as a Christina Light. Both the mutually exposing heroes seek to
expropriate a secret, Roderick the secret of Christina's esteem (he
knows privately that she esteems Rowland above himself), Rowland
the secret of Mary Garland's devotion to Roderick. One might say that
the selves of the composite apostate hero are painfully snubbing each
other: "He [Rowland] felt himself, in a word, a man cruelly defrauded
and naturally bent on revenge. Life owed him, he thought, a
compensation and he should be restless and resentful till he should
find it. He knew — or seemed to know — where he should find it . . . In
his melancholy meditation the idea of something better than all this
. . . the idea, in fine, of compensation in concrete form found itself
remarkably resembling a certain young woman in America, shaped
itself sooner or later into the image of Mary Garland" (274). While
Rowland's claim upon Mary Garland has always been vicarious, it now
depends upon the death, no longer the life of the other self: "His
uncanny idea persisted; it clung to him like a sturdy beggar. The sense
of the matter, roughly expressed, was that if Roderick were really
going, as he himself had phrased it, to fizzle out, one might help him
on the way — one might smooth the *descensus Averni*" (275).

As an early work *Roderick Hudson* cannot exactly be said to have
the binary form of *The Portrait of a Lady* or *The Bostonians* or *The*

Princess Casamassima, much less the hourglass structure of the last novels. Being a failure-haunted search for identity, however, it too has another go and something of a second half. In the name of the joint quest, Rowland abruptly renounces both his rights of resentment against Roderick and any claim upon Mary Garland, whom he now summons to Europe strictly for Roderick's benefit. But Rowland's redetermining sacrificially to "die for" Roderick at this stage means that he continues in important ways to "live for" him. And this in turn means that he deprives Roderick of his potential selfhood; Roderick must both live and die for Rowland so that Rowland may live and die for Roderick, and so forth. In spite of Rowland's renunciation, the cycle of these intimate adversaries' mutual impersonation has not in fact ceased. Given the basis of their social and sexual weakness, another go just means another compensatory and foredoomed go.

Another of James's theater scenes, a startling nonidentical twin of the earlier scene in the Coliseum, reveals that all is as before in the story's first half. Towards the end, when Roderick is literally dying of shame, the secretly competitive Rowland steps into the stead he has all but vacated.

> One of these [wild flowers] indeed had appeared an easier prize than it was likely to prove, and he had paused a moment at the base of the little peak on which it grew, measuring the risk of further pursuit. Suddenly, as he stood there, he remembered Roderick's defiance of danger and of Christina Light during that sharp moment at the Coliseum, and he was seized with a strong desire to test the quality of his own companion. She had just scrambled up a grassy slope near him and had seen that the flower was out of reach. As he prepared to approach it she called to him eagerly to stop and yield to the impossibility . . . She looked at him in return and then at the flower; he wondered whether she would shriek and swoon as Christina had done . . . Rowland was not a trained acrobat, and his enterprise was difficult; but he kept his wits about him, made the most of narrow footholds and coigns of vantage and at last secured his prize . . . He was red in the face when he offered Mary the flower, and she was visibly pale. She had kept her eyes on him without moving . . . Mary's eyes did not perhaps quite display the ardent admiration anciently offered to the victor by the queen of beauty at a tournament; but they told him that his existence had for the time mattered to her (411-413).

As he shows by his invocation of his other executive self, Rowland is actually living out his fantasy in the Coliseum that "if the thing were

possible he felt a sudden high bold relish of his friend's attempting it."
In a real way, then, Rowland *is* Roderick. And not only in relation to
Mary Garland, but also to Christina Light. Indeed, in the heroes' final
scuffle shortly after this second theater scene, Roderick assures
Rowland that he, Rowland, has as good as ousted himself from
Christina's esteem. He tells the man who has now fully emerged as his
mutinous joker-double that, "on her own word for it . . . you had
pleased her, interested her. I don't say she was dying of love for you,
but she liked you so much that she would have been glad if you could
have become a little aware of it" (444). Since this is exactly the same
reproach that Rowland has made to Roderick concerning his neglect
of Mary Garland, the heroes are now proved incontrovertibly to be
doubles in every respect. Neither, after such mutual exposure, possesses genuine being-unto-self.

If each hero lives only conditionally, or in compensatory terms of
what he himself is not, then neither has fully lived. Both heroes are
might- or should-have-beens—pretenders to life, far less honor,
whether in America or in Europe. The quest has at last proved that,
take them singly or in conjunction, their story has been about too scant
a life-feeling. This is the truth that has been feared from the outset.
But since this is the truth then, after so much strategic and finally
unbearable falsity, it must as truth be welcome. In fact Roderick,
whose living death of shame has been so protracted, has defied and as
good as invited Rowland to punish him by putting his "grotesque" and
"hideous" (450) self before himself. The false claimant thus puts
himself out of the pain of seeking identity without hope. Once he has
been shown that he may as well not have lived, he can disappear to die
of the fiasco of his not really having lived. For Rowland likewise there
is satisfaction as well as pain in the full emergence of his truth-bearing
double. For him, there will even be a certain identity—"repose" (332)
Christina has called it, "serenity" Olive Chancellor will call it—in his
at last bearing with his nonentity. Back in America, at least, Rowland
stoically survives the Jamesian pyrrhic victory.

Writing very purely along a shame axis—exposure, woundedness,
and injury; dying of shame; the shame-ghost; the shame-double; scandal—inevitably the other pole of psychosocial evaluation in James is
identity or, in its public aspect, honor. Identity of course is very much
a contemporary psychoanalytic concern; but I doubt whether an Erik-

sonian sense of it — a conservative pre-Freudian as much as post-Freudian understanding — greatly differs from a late nineteenth-century understanding such as James's. One can therefore speak of identity in James in the confidence that one is not falsely imposing upon him. Honor, however, is a rather different matter. Where we commonly understand the term only in special senses, honor is with James a constant preoccupation. This is not only due to his viewing it as the public aspect, the front, of identity. In all likelihood one will find that identity itself, the sense of a person's being-unto-self, has been subsumed by him under an appeal to honor. James's psychosocial evaluation may very well be described as follows: "Honour is the value of a person in his own eyes, but also in the eyes of his society. It is his estimation of his own worth, his *claim* to pride, but it is also the acknowledgement of that claim, his excellence recognized by society, his *right* to pride. Students of the minutiae of personal relations have observed that they are much concerned with the ways in which people extort from others the validation of the image which they cherish of themselves and the two aspects of honour may be reconciled in those terms."[18] Indeed, a whole cluster of familiar Jamesian positives may be grouped under the notion of honor, identity, self-esteem, success or "decent pride" (as the Ververs put it after their pyrrhic triumph), and even freedom (which in psychological terms is a resolution of the compulsive cycle of shame-shamelessness).

Whether one wants to speak of identity and honor in James or of honor in its dual aspects of claim and right, any Jamesian transaction is likely to involve what may be called the question of the claimant. How can a character, who does not yet possess a solid sense of his identity or who may even have forfeited this sense acquire identity? If we can invent here another loose and baggy formula, we might say that at first James's hero thinks, if he thinks about himself at all, "I am who I am." Now, however, he suffers anything between a jostle and serious shock — an affront, it may be, an insolence or insult. It is as if he has been told, perhaps by the advent of the shame-ghost or double, "You are not who you think you are." Unexpectedly, the hero is subject to a kind of comprehensive awkwardness. He finds himself in a false position of the kind James himself noted in the fiction of Turgenev, whose heroes "are never heroes in the literal sense of the word, rather quite the reverse; their function is to be conspicuous as failures, interesting but impotent persons who are losers at the game of life . . .

Their interest, in his hands, comes in a great measure from the fact that they are exquisitely conscious of their shortcomings, thanks to the fine and subtle intelligence, that 'subjective' tendency, with which he represents all Russians who are not positive fools and grotesques as being endowed. His central figure is usually a person in a false position, generally not of his own making, which, according to the peculiar perversity of fate, is only aggravated by his effort to right himself."[19] Thus open, embarrassed, humiliated, discomfited, he dies of shame. Formally speaking, his crisis of identity is one of admission, a reluctant taking in of an overpowering, overpowered other self. (One can distinguish "admission" here from "confession," in which one acknowledges *with* the self some transgression.) Can he bear with the shockingly abject self he has had to admit, or does he deny it as unreal, as having no power to displace him from himself? Can he win, or win back, his sense of identity?

In theory, meantime, the hero acquires honor insofar as his claim is being evaluated socially. Disencumbering himself of his shame-ghost, disembarrassing himself of his shame-double, he may, in the questioning arena of society, earn the right to valuable selfhood. As Edwin Honig puts it, "No man is honorable alone and by himself; he becomes honorable by means of another person. Having a sense of one's merit, or being virtuous, is not the same as being honorable; honor is achieved."[20] But it is of the essence of honor that it should both seek and find its own level, and in James one may expect the honorable settlement to be an ironized or pyrrhic one. Identity may be won in him, but usually at the expense of honor in the sense of right to that identity; conversely, no sooner is honor accorded than the claim to identity will seem a pretense. Just as there is never enough identity to go round, so there never seems to be enough honor of the right kind at the right time, only too much of a false or unmerited kind. It is as if identity in James, and honor likewise, are irrevocably tainted with a lie, with fraud and imposture.

Another of James's double stories, the superb fable "The Lesson of the Master," will illustrate very clearly the dual aspects of Jamesian honor, as well as the kind of honorable settlement regularly negotiated between them. Here, the acolyte hero Paul Overt is in search of his artist selfhood. He learns, however, that his claim to be a writer raises the question of his social identity. If his authorship of *Ginistrella* (one notes the diminutive) "constituted a degree of identity" (217), Paul

Overt is yet "but slenderly supplied with a certain social boldness (it was really a weakness in him)" (215). The fact is that he is another Jamesian social aesthete who has "spent many years out of England, in different places abroad" (240), and who, when it comes to his craft, inevitably writes "a story that goes on too much abroad" (271). This being so, one might well expect him to be in search of a compensatory, "gentleman" other self:

> Overt, who had spent a considerable part of his short life in foreign lands, made now, but not for the first time, the reflection that whereas in those countries he had almost always recognized the artist and the man of letters by his personal "type" . . . in England this identification was as little as possible a matter of course, thanks . . . to the general diffusion of the air of the gentleman — the gentleman committed to no particular set of ideas. More than once, on returning to his own country, he had said to himself in regard to the people whom he met in society: "One sees them about and one even talks with them; but to find out what they *do* one would really have to be a detective." In respect to several individuals whose work he was unable to like (perhaps he was wrong) he found himself adding, "No wonder they conceal it — it's so bad!" He observed that oftener than in France and in Germany his artist looked like a gentleman (that is, like an English one), while he perceived that outside of a few exceptions his gentleman didn't look like an artist (221-222).

This surrogate self he finds in the distinguished master of *Shadowmere,* Henry St. George, "a patriot" (264) and "an honourable image of success, of the material rewards [Ennismore Gardens and Harrow and Oxford and Sandhurst] and the social credit of literature" (245).

James's vademecum fables regularly mislead, I think, by drawing attention to their tenors rather than their vehicles; they would, perhaps, covertly put a front on a back. So here in "The Lesson of the Master." There is the relatively admissible false position dramatized by the competition of completing-depleting doubles: the acolyte who would lay claim to the mastery that commands honor is as yet no more than a social aesthete, while the master who has earned the right to honor has long been an impostor as an artist. But there is also a relatively inadmissible false position; a back to the story: these doubles are committed to a sexual rivalry. After the would-be master betrays a fear of women (he imagines that Mrs. St. George is St. George's inhibiting Dragon), he is told that "he [St. George] says she [his wife] has been the making of him" (231). Is it marriage as well as being a patriot that makes for mastery? The acolyte, it appears, must venture a sexual debut if he too is to be masterful, indeed if he is to *be*. In the young heroine's presence, accordingly, he grows "conscious that he should have liked better to please her in some other way" (226) than by being merely the author—"so poor—so poor!" (227)—of *Ginistrella*. Subsequently, this sexually hesitant hero becomes the sexually confident St. George's unavowed competitor: "The young man watched them get in; he returned, as he stood there, the friendly wave of the hand with which, ensconced in the vehicle beside Miss Fancourt, St. George took leave of him . . . An indefinite envy rose in Paul Overt's heart as he took his way on foot alone, and the singular part of it was that it was directed to each of the occupants of the hansom. How much he should like to rattle about London with such a girl! How much he should like to go and look at 'types' with St. George!" (248-249). It is not so much that the claimant desires the girl for herself, or even that he intends to displace the master outright. Rather, he desires the heroine because, in his self-rejection and envy, he wants to be masterful. It does not seem absurd to suggest in connection with these sexual politics that the heroine's association with Empire, something upon which the story insists, helps this Jamesian social aesthete to feel "more."

Meanwhile Henry St. George clearly recognizes in Paul Overt his own double. While the acolyte nerves himself for a sexual debut, the socially confident master finds himself shown up as a "successful charlatan" (262); like James's earlier hero, the politician-turned-artist Nick Dormer, he is two men, an incumbent who has the right to a seat and another man, an apostate, who occupies it without a genuine claim to it. In admitting his double successor, however, St. George must surely seem too candid by a half, and it may be surmised that he too would cover a back. If the acolyte's advent has already shown him up as an apostate and impostor, his sexual competition now threatens to leave him without any identity. This *père de famille* who has made up to the heroine, in spite of or on account of his invalid wife, must see the sexual prize going to the splendid, young, and above all eligible talent.

Like all James's double fantasies, "The Lesson of the Master" now has all the makings of a covert revenge cycle. Just as the alter ego's advent represents for St. George the ambiguous lesson of a future master, so St. George as Overt's alter ego will ambiguously punish Overt for his pretension. Accordingly, he advises the acolyte to

[*68*]

renounce all prospect of marriage to the heroine and therewith renounce that train of false gods, Ennismore Gardens and Harrow and Oxford and Sandhurst. In other words, he would maneuver the other self into a false position that mirrors his own: " 'What a false position, what a condemnation of the artist, that he's a mere disfranchised monk and can produce his effect only by giving up a personal happiness. What an arraignment of art!' Paul Overt pursued, with a trembling voice" (269). This oracular lesson, delivered out of an indefinite envy matching Overt's own, is also an eye for an eye.

Henceforward Paul Overt deputizes for St. George as an artist. He renounces the girl (even as his double in all respects has himself pretended to do) and, still the social aesthete, goes abroad to write. During his two year probation, however, he learns of the death of St. George's wife, writes him a letter of sympathy, and receives a reply to the effect that his marriage has been the making of him as an artist: this is precisely what St. George has told Marion Fancourt and precisely the opposite of what he has told his sexual competitor. Of course, the inconsistency seriously threatens the hero, who has renounced his claim on the heroine on the basis of the master's advice. Strengthening himself with the thought of his new novel—he has developed "a certain belief in himself," the new work is "far stronger, he believed, than *Ginistrella*" (274)—he returns to London to prove that he has not committed himself to an empty transaction. He finds the sometime master on the point of marrying Marion Fancourt.

In the ensuing scuffle of doubles, the artist claimant is fully exposed unto himself. He is both a social and sexual aesthete; he cannot really claim to live in social and sexual terms. Indeed, confronted by a "mocking fiend" (283) who gives the lie to his sacrifice to art, Overt dies of shame-shock. After having gained a footing into satisfactory selfhood—Marion Fancourt and England and even Empire—this claimant is then gallingly precluded from it. In the meantime the other self, having been despoiled of his identity, dies as a true artist. Instead, he both makes off and makes do with the social and sexual honors, marriage to Marion Fancourt. The upshot, then, of the doubles' double cross is a pyrrhic division of spoils according to which neither identity nor honor are simultaneously negotiable. What is worse, both heroes mutually render each other successful charlatans. Neither identity nor honor are of an unambiguous value, but are contaminated by a lie, for how can Overt's art, which is suicidally as well as

sacrificially estranged from personal passion, be more than reactionary? "St. George's words were still in his ears: 'You're very
strong—wonderfully strong.' Was he really? Certainly, he would have
to be; and it would be a sort of revenge. *Is* he? the reader may ask in
turn . . . The best answer to that perhaps is that he is doing his best but
that it is too soon to say" (284). At best Overt will survive his scuffle
with Henry St. George as a minor, ever to be shame-ghosted master,
while St. George will live only a posthumous, counterreactive laureate
life.

Our loose and baggy paradigm of shame, identity, and honor seems
even more appropriate to James when it is compared with the kind of
paradigm that is most appropriate to "guilt-axis" imaginations of the
backward look such as Wordsworth's or Hawthorne's or Dickens':
innocence; transgression or crime; guilt or guilt-feeling; confession;
punishment; expiation or atonement. Simply to sketch out the latter
paradigm is to see how little guilt-feeling there is in James, or to see
what guilt there is as a by-product of the shame-shamelessness cycle in
him. Indeed, one would like to see criticism imagining, as much as any
"Hawthorne aspect," a "Stendhal aspect" to James. In many ways
James's first affinities lie with the writers in whom identity and esteem
are the central issues.[21]

Some distinctions, arguable though they will inevitably be, need
developing here between the frequently confused emotions of shame
and guilt.[22] Shame, we have seen, begins with exposure, with the feeling "I am weak." It can arise not only in situations in which criticism
is expressed by an audience of others; it can exist in the theater of the
self. On such a view it might be argued that the emotion of shame is
pre-social and more deeply situated in the personality than guilt-feeling, which results from social adjustment. It is at this point morally
neutral, not yet morally evaluated (as when someone is shameless to
the point of acting shamefully). Guilt, on the other hand, is more
likely to be experienced when a border is touched or exceeded so as to
produce the feeling "I am no good." Guilt arises from what we have
done rather than from what we have omitted to do, or from what we
fear we may have done or may yet do; from the transgression of more
or less specific, even codified, prohibitions.

As we have also seen, shame, being the consequence of exposure or shock, is always unexpected, is an emotion by which one is suddenly overtaken (whether or not one feels prolonged shame after the event). By contrast, guilt-feeling is likely to involve some duration of time, as well as what such a period permits, moral awareness and choice. Furthermore, shame-woundedness can both result from a ridiculously trivial incident and at the same time be pervasive, a matter of back as well as front; on the other hand, any wound associated with guilt arising from a specific transgression is likely to be a specific, penal one. Guilt implies order and relationship (at-one-ment), and may actually be incurred as being preferable to shame as a means either of concealing or of initiating an experience that, because it involves back as well as front, may imply an intolerable abandonment. Again, the compulsion associated with shame is to seal, or to conceal, the wound, while the guilty person may be compelled to confess the thing he has done.[23] The guilty person may address himself more or less directly to a confessor; but the profoundly ashamed person may be able to do no more than equivocally "admit as much" (as "The Jolly Corner" puts it) because what has to be admitted may be a total failure of identity, and because there can be no direct communication when what is at issue is all of the self.

Arguable though such distinctions are, they nevertheless clarify one's sense of James's imagination. Keeping them in mind one can say, for instance, that James writes primarily along a shame axis and a novelist like Dickens primarily along a guilt axis. James imagines stories of the exposure of debutantes (*What Maisie Knew* and *The Awkward Age*) and Dickens, stories of the exposure of potential delinquents (*Oliver Twist* and *Great Expectations*). Since James typically writes an "audience" story about "an odious ordeal, some glare of embarrassment and exposure in a circle of hard unhelpful attention, of converging, derisive, unsuggestive eyes" ("Crapy Cornelia," 355), something of the compulsion to conceal will be present in it to the last; James's story can and will do no more than admit as much. By comparison Dickens, writing according to a crime and punishment pattern of experience, reveals all, it seems almost compulsively; the Dickens plot's charge of secrecy is in the end discharged or confessed, it may be so violently and elaborately as to yield up (as in *Bleak House* or *Great Expectations*) a sentimentally expurgated conclusion. (This is not to say that the guilt-feeling in Dickens is simple. On the contrary, as critics like Julian Moynahan and Taylor Stoehr have shown, one is likely to meet in him the anomaly of the punishment's not fitting the official crime, a misfit that may mean that there is another, recessed crime that is not readily approached or confessed.²⁴ Nor is this to say that there is no concern with exposure in Dickens, whose little boy/girl lost situations made Victorians wait and weep; it is just that exposure in him is exposure to the illegitimate and criminal.)

Again, James creates the hawked-about Christina Light, whose behavior is intelligible only in terms of social and sexual shame and the inability to bear with it; and Dickens creates Edith Dombey, who is also hawked about to her indelible shame but who ends as the guiltiest of magdalens. Dickens gives scant attention to Philadelphian society in *American Notes* (Chapter 7), and a long, ventriloquist, almost too human account of the life of condemned men in Pennsylvania's Eastern penitentiary. In *The American Scene*, by contrast, James praises Philadelphian society as being almost the only one in the United States worthy of the name; and then, since he is interested so much more in what *The Ambassadors* calls "the blush of guilt" (II, 53) than in criminality per se, James offers a brief, somewhat obligatory (Dickens has preceded him), faintly inhuman account of his visit to the same penitentiary, which he regards as a "mean" club prompting speculation "on the implied requisites for membership."²⁵ What the hero is to remember of the surprisingly powerful prison scene at the beginning of *The Princess Casamassima* is his mother's cry, *"Il a honte de moi—il a honte de moi!"* Correspondingly, Pip is turned upside down and shaken by the heels — and it is a perfect image of confusion and shock; but what he remembers are Magwitch's fetters and the "click" at the back of his throat, details that are to be symbols of guilt and atonement. What concerns James in *The Spoils of Poynton* is not so much Mrs. Gereth's virtual theft of the "old things," but the scandal of their despoliation: "It was farcical not to speak; and yet to exclaim, to participate, would give one a bad sense of being mixed up with a theft. This ugly word sounded, for herself, in Fleda's silence, and the very violence of it jarred her into a scared glance, as of a creature detected, to right and left. But what again the full picture most showed her was the faraway empty sockets, a scandal of nakedness between high bleak walls" (63).

And although the Victorian in James will (like Dickens) portray extradomestic sexuality as illicit, it is the dishonor of it that he sees. If

Strether comes to recognize, in the wonderful cynosure scene in Book 11 of *The Ambassadors,* that Mme de Vionnet is engaged in an adulterous liaison, his "sharpest perception yet" (Book 12) is of human weakness exposed:

> . . . it was like a chill in the air to him, it was almost appalling, that a creature so fine could be, by mysterious forces, a creature so exploited . . . She was older for him to-night, visibly less exempt from the touch of time; but she was as much as ever the finest and subtlest creature, the happiest apparition, it had been given him, in all his years, to meet; and yet he could see her there as vulgarly troubled, in very truth, as a maidservant crying for her young man. The only thing was that she judged herself as the maidservant wouldn't; the weakness of which wisdom too, the dishonour of which judgement, seemed but to sink her lower (II, 255-256).

Again, if Prince Amerigo is an adulterer, the Jamesian punishment is the ridiculousness of being in a false position:

> "Sure," Maggie developed, "of your having, and of your having for a long time had, *two* relations with Charlotte."
> He stared, a little at sea, as he took it up. " 'Two' — ?"
> Something in the tone of it gave a sense, or an ambiguity, almost foolish — leaving Maggie to feel as in a flash how such a consequence, a foredoomed infelicity, partaking of the ridiculous even in one of the cleverest, might be of the very essence of the penalty of wrong-doing (II, 168).

The foregoing distinctions between shame and guilt force on us here the question of James's ethic. If the emotion of shame is morally neutral in comparison with guilt-feeling, and if there is also relatively little guilt in James, then where is the beginning of the moral in him? On the face of things a James of the "Stendhal aspect" might be, in his pursuit of identity and honor, an immoralist. After all, there have always been serious conflicts between individualist codes of honor on the one hand and, on the other, what societies regard as moral or licit.

We have seen that James's preoccupation with psychosocial exposure involves a corresponding preoccupation with concealment. Dying of shame, the James hero is compelled to "sink into the ground" or to "bury the face"; if exposure means or has meant weakness, deficiency, abjection, or failure, concealment and even the use of secrecy becomes the unready hero's readiness for life. In theory, this compulsion to conceal is, while fraught with resentment, no less morally neutral than the emotion of shame itself. And although I have so far stressed its negative consequences, it may of course result in morally defensible, not to say positive, uses of secrecy. When caught out in a false position, a James character may equivocate or temporize in order to strengthen himself or others. This is especially true of the later work, for instance of Maggie Verver who "knows" — that is, uses secrecy — in the interests of "general rectification." In *The Awkward Age,* James himself seems to be strengthening his vulnerable heroine by means of a use of secrecy; he negotiates Nanda Brookenham past the perils of the awkward age by withholding her point of view until the end, when she can in a measure trump the other characters' knowingness with what she herself knows. Indeed as we shall see later in discussing the role of the lie in James, it may very well be immoral *not* to conceal.

On the other hand, the compulsion to conceal the exposed self may be the first phase in a Jamesian revenge or *ressentiment* cycle. According to Max Scheler,[26] the feeling of weakness before the superior, whether the conventionally valuable or an "imitation of Christ," is necessarily accompanied by an impulse for revenge. Being based upon weakness, however, such revenge-feeling recognizes that the act of revenge must be postponed. Therefore this revenge-feeling may be repressed, and repressed through successive phases: rancor; an "existential envy" directed at the adversary's very existence, and forgiving everything but what he *is*; the impulse to detract, which is no longer satisfied with being directed against specific aspects of men and affairs but which seeks out targets indiscriminately; and malice and spite, which actively contrive to bring about opportunities for releasing resentment. For Scheler, the final phase of *ressentiment* — so called because the same reactive emotion has been experienced over and over — is entered when revenge is taken not only by falsifying life, but by a systematic devaluation-by-transvaluation of values themselves. *Ressentiment* criticism, it can be said, eventually yields a kind of ideological doubling that is much more comprehensive than any defamation of individuals. This doubling comes about because *ressentiment,* based on the feeling of being without value, cannot lead to any autonomous alternative set of values. The person imbued by it secretly craves the value that he denounces.

The relevance to James of this phenomenology of the emotions associated with weakness will be clear. When shamed, the James hero is compelled to be shameless; he would conceal his front in the ambiguous affront. But such a reaction may in time come to imbue and poison his personality (whereupon his emotional state may be aptly figured by a Pandora situation, by a box symbolizing an obsessive re-experiencing of an original impulse for revenge). The consequence is an essentially revengeful, though ever ambiguous assertion of identity, an assertion culminating in "secret revenge for secret injury" (Calderón). At no point can this revenge take direct form for fear of acknowledging the exposure or injury that has had to be concealed in the first place.[27] Hence one may speak both of the ambiguity of revenge in James, and of the revenge of ambiguity.

Given, then, the moral neutrality of the emotion of shame and the compulsion to conceal, it must be that James's situations become morally critical if and when injury is not admitted or borne. If on the one hand the truth of being caught out in a false position, of being shame-ghosted or double-encumbered, is at least "admitted as much," then no revenge cycle will develop. Furthermore, if as in *The Golden Bowl* there has been a renunciation of the "rights of resentment" in the name of "the superstition of not hurting" or even of love, then a developing revenge cycle may be converted into a "general rectification." But if on the other hand there is either a partial, imperfect renunciation or a false renunciation, then a revenge cycle will certainly develop and James's hero will at least turn his punitive revenge upon himself, at worst inflict it upon others. His shame is now morally evaluable. One would stress once again here that the Jamesian renunciation is not so much a renunciation of life's goods, social and erotic, as common misunderstanding has it;[28] strictly speaking, these life goods cannot be for the renouncing if the hero feels precluded from vital selfhood in the first place. Although it may come to the same thing, what *is* renounced in James is the act of resentment at being precluded from them, and perhaps from vitality itself. Another way of putting the situation would be to say that the false claim, the pretension, the imposture are what are renounced in James. Honorable nonentity is held to be preferable to theatricality — one sees here why those regular pejoratives of James's moral vocabulary, "hideous," "ugly," "deformed," "disfigured," "vulgar," "grotesque," are socio-aesthetic in character and why they have so much to do with "moral appearance" (*The Bostonians*, II, 188).

I want to take three examples of this "secret revenge for secret injury" complex in James: "The Romance of Certain Old Clothes," on which we have already touched, "The Turn of the Screw," another Pandora situation susceptible of a Schelerian (as well as a Freudian) reading, and *The Spoils of Poynton,* which is a case of the most secret of Jamesian revenges, the author's own.

The early Jacob and Esau fantasy of sexual rivalry between two sisters is constructed about a handful of notable scenes. As soon as the elder sister Viola has guessed the secret of the younger Perdita's engagement to the hero for whom they are competing, she collapses before her mirror, "her handsome features sadly disfigured by jealousy" (303). Next, she asks Perdita to comb her hair for her, makes certain of her rival's triumph, and ambiguously curses the forthcoming marriage. It is a scene of shock and intense, suppressed rage. Viola, seeing her rival in the mirror as she combs her own hair, sees herself not only with her own eyes as her own audience but also as if through the eyes of Perdita, now her mirror-self and double. Viola is not only *not* her erstwhile self, she momentarily sees herself as from the point of vantage of a successful rival. She is totally visible. Inevitably, then, she is compelled to conceal herself; indeed, she would already use against Perdita the secret of her intentions—her intentionality—to the point where Perdita would prefer to be cursed outright. With Viola, evidently, it is to be a secret for a secret.

Ultimately the problem for these siblings who have always had to share "but one chamber and one bed between them" (302) is that there is sufficient identity only for one and that in having to share this prize they must seem to rob each other of sufficiency. The problem, aggravated by the availability of but one suitor, is now presented again in a second go mirror scene. Immediately after the wedding,

> Perdita hastened back to her room, opening the door abruptly. Viola, as usual, was before the glass, but in a position which caused the other to stand still, amazed. She had dressed herself in Perdita's cast-off wedding veil and wreath, and on her neck she had hung the heavy string of pearls which the young girl had received from her husband as a wedding-gift . . . Bedizened in this unnatural garb, Viola stood at the mirror, plunging a long look into its depths, and reading Heaven knows what audacious visions. Perdita was horrified. It was a hideous image of their old rivalry come to life again (307-308).

Whereas Perdita has seemed to displace and even to *be* Viola in the earlier scene, by this secret impersonation Viola attempts to be her successful rival.

[76]

It is hardly surprising that, cursed by her sister, Perdita should shortly afterwards become one of James's most extraordinary cases. (Not that James does not rationalize his romance: ostensibly Perdita dies in childbirth as a result of "some indiscretion in the way of diet or of exposure," 310). Since she feels that she has never lived sufficiently, her dying impulse is to live on defiantly and dynastically through her infant daughter's life; she would have her second go. This, accordingly, she tries to guarantee by swearing her husband to guard her wedding clothes for her daughter's future use, "under a double-lock" in "the great chest in the attic, with the iron bands" (312). With Perdita as with Viola it is to be a secret for a secret. Her precaution, it turns out, is well-founded, for after her death Viola contrives to take care of her child so competently as to induce the widowed husband to marry her.

As usual in James, however, a compensatory second go merely aggravates what has been a false position to start with, and when Viola the secret revenger falls short of her Perdita-self both in failing to bear a child of her own and in having to be, on account of money troubles, "perforce less of a great lady than her sister had been" (315), she is goaded into a further act of resentment. Once and for all she would dispossess Perdita of her being-unto-self:

> Viola's thoughts hovered lovingly about her sister's relics. She went up and looked at the chest in which they lay imprisoned. There was a sullen defiance in its three great padlocks and its iron bands, which only quickened her desires. There was something exasperating in its incorruptible immobility. It was like a grim and grizzled old household servant, who locks his jaws over a family secret. And then there was a look of capacity in its vast extent, and a sound as of dense fulness, when Viola knocked its side with the toe of her little slipper, which caused her to flush with baffled longing (316).

She persuades her unwitting husband to break his oath, open his Pandora's secretary, and remove "the sacred key" from its "secret drawer, wrapped in a little packet which he had sealed with his own honest bit of blazonry. *Teneo,* said the motto — 'I hold' " (317). Finally Viola violates her sister's relics in secret.

On the understanding that Viola's story after Perdita's death is a reactionary second go, one can say that, by now, this Pandora's box *is* Viola. It is surely a continually repressed and re-experienced revenge-feeling in her that this chest of romance bespeaks ("There was a sullen defiance in its three great padlocks and its iron bands . . . "), and that must come out into the open at last for having arisen in the first place from a terrible "openness" ("The lid of the chest stood open, exposing . . . its treasure"), from unbearable personal abjection ("Viola had fallen backward from a kneeling posture"). But to say that this Pandora's box represents a state of being is really to say that it represents the heroine's non-being, for this heroine has not really lived; she has lived only reactively. Inevitably, then, she finds a punitive other self and simulacrum in the ghost of another anxious ghost-in-life. "The Romance of Certain Old Clothes" tells us that two ghosts together do not make one authentic life.

"The Turn of the Screw" is another Schelerian secret revenge for secret injury cycle, a cycle that begins (as it ends) with a Pandora situation. A letter arrives to announce Miles's expulsion from school: "I broke the seal with a great effort — so great a one that I was a long time coming to it" (28). This notice of expulsion, the governess tells Mrs. Grose, gives no particulars: " 'They simply express their regret that it should be impossible to keep him. That can have only one meaning.' Mrs. Grose listened with dumb emotion; she forbore to ask me what this meaning might be; so that, presently, to put the thing with some coherence and with the mere aid of her presence to my own mind, I went on: 'That he's an injury to the others.' At this, with one of the quick turns of simple folk, she suddenly flamed up. 'Master Miles! — *him* an injury?' " (29). An opened container, preclusion, injury — the situation contains so many familiar Jamesian elements as to have almost an air of self-parody. Moreover, this is a double Pandora situation, therefore a moment of the most acute self-consciousness; the letter announcing the little gentleman's preclusion is contained within a letter from the god like gentleman, whom the heroine has pledged to serve but never to contact. If the governess has her shocked front at Bly, has henceforth to bear "the fulness of my own exposure" (87), she also has her back, her obligation to the master. Obviously this obligation is very much brought into question by an injurious Miles: will she really be the angel in the master's house? It is the governess' relation with the master that may be said to be injured or "opened" here.

The governess' position with respect to the master is this. Qualified only by her "small, smothered life" (34) and a "scant home" (23), virtually unidentifiable until her employment at Bly, she has been put suddenly "in supreme authority" (21), in fact stands in the master's stead, is a nineteenth century angel in his house.[29] As usual with James's characters, however, the governess' participation in her ideal and vital selfhood turns out to be no more than exoteric. Her inclusion in the master's world is conditional upon her ultimate, and extraordinarily arbitrary, preclusion from it: "she should never trouble him — but never, never: neither appeal nor complain nor write about anything . . . take the whole thing over and let him alone" (22). If she has been nothing before her pledge to the master, she may, worse still, be as nothing while actually in his service. In other words, this acolyte's service has from the outset all the makings of a peculiarly galling false position, a false position that Miles's arbitary preclusion can but aggravate by raising the specter of her own.

Given her sense of front and back, what will be the governess' reaction? One would imagine that, in proportion as she doubts herself, she will need to deny any failure of identity; and that, as a final denial, she will even look for a negative identity as being better than none. On this theory, her natural resentment towards the children for making her aware of her front and back will be suppressed, but suppressed only to re-emerge as an ambiguous revenge for her inadmissible preclusion. It will be a martyr to the "moral" who affronts her destiny at Bly. The governess will use the children as instruments by which she can at once bring herself to the attention of the adored idol and ambiguously punish him for his godlike arbitrariness or negligence.

In the context of this reaction, Quint and Jessel can be viewed as Jamesian shame- and revenge-ghosts. Having once been exposed by the injurious Miles as a nonentity falsely placed in supreme authority, she needs a secret with which to cover or justify herself. She "knows" the children compulsively, therefore. But because her problem is that she may be an unappeasable ghost-in-life, socially and sexually, what she knows, Quint and Jessel, must necessarily be ghostly. It takes a ghost to see ghosts. Of course, arising as they do from the compulsion to conceal an abject selfhood, these shame- and revenge-ghosts cannot easily be acknowledged for what they are, her own psychological ghosts. On the contrary, such is her sense of her own falsity that she must deny that her ghosts have anything but an objective status. And since, finally, her ghostliness is relative to her idol-ideal's mastery, it is to the master that she would deny their merely psychological status. Indeed, she would at once deny before him her own nonentity and ambiguously punish him for his part in it. It is the master who must suffer her turning "infallibly to the vindictive" for her acolyte's abjection before "differences, such superiorities of quality" (40). The governess' ghosts are a subjective, *ressentiment* protest against her conditional station in life, her all and/or nothingness.

Consider the governess' first encounter with Quint soon after her "injury" at Miles's hands. Fantasizing about receiving her master's esteem, she feels she suffices at Bly. She does not lay a false, an unjustified claim to her supreme position:

> It was a pleasure at these moments to feel myself tranquil and justified; doubtless, perhaps, also to reflect that by my discretion, my quiet good sense and general high propriety, I was giving pleasure — if he ever thought of it! — to the person to whose pressure I had responded. What I was doing was what he had earnestly hoped and directly asked of me, and that I *could,* after all, do it proved even a greater joy than I had expected. I dare say I fancied myself, in short, a remarkable young woman and took comfort in the faith that this would more publicly appear. Well, I needed to be remarkable to offer a front to the remarkable things that presently gave their first sign . . . One of the thoughts that . . . used to be with me in these wanderings was that it would be as charming as a charming story suddenly to meet someone. Someone would appear there at the turn of a path and would stand before me and smile and approve. I didn't ask more than that — I only asked that he should *know*; and the only way to be sure he knew would be to see it, and the kind light of it, in his handsome face. That was exactly present to me — by which I mean the face was — when, on the first of these occasions . . . I stopped short on emerging from one of the plantations and coming into view of the house. What arrested me on the spot . . . was the sense that my imagination had, in a flash, turned real. He did stand there!" (35).

Here the repressed coyly returns, the Schelerian, not only the Freudian repressed. So preoccupied is the governess with the master, with compensatory mastery, that "he did stand there!" In the phrase she uses much later, she has "brought on a proof" (114). Is she not justified in occupying her supreme position?

But it is precisely at such a moment that the governess' intense self-doubt and sense of inferiority turn into revenge-feeling. After all, a fantasy of the master can be only a fantasy. May she not have brought on a proof that she is not justified at all? Indeed her fantasy of mastery must, just by being a compensation based on weakness, prove that she does not really exist, either socially or sexually: he is a shame-ghost.

It is an inadmissible recognition. Consequently, the compulsion that has produced the fantasy instantly turns to the vindictive, and the smothered heroine "knows" a revenge-ghost, a ghost both closely associated with her ego-ideal and at the same time a point by point debasement, even insolent mockery, of that ideal. Usurping the stead of the godlike master of her fantasy is someone who is "very much" a "stranger" (44), a "horror" (45), who is not, "never—no, never!—a gentleman" (47), and who, while being "remarkably" handsome (47)—he is even dressed in the master's clothes—nevertheless gives her "a sort of sense of looking like an actor" (47). Exactly in the godlike master's stead stands his debased and debasing joker-double, the ghost of the dead servant Peter Quint. Without allowing herself to know it, indeed without being able to acknowledge it for fear of destroying all she craves, the acolyte defames in fantasy the idol she slavishly adores; it is a servant for a slave.

James's revenge cycle now enters a further, "ideological" phase. Not only is it inadmissible that he should be a reproachful (rather than honoring) shame-ghost, it is equally inadmissible that he should be a revenge-ghost. To acknowledge her obscure but rising revenge-feeling would be to acknowledge that she has something to avenge: her probable preclusion from vitality and value and mastery. And it is just this preclusion—preclusion when she had seemed to be initiate—that is inadmissible in the first place. Therefore, she must further deny her resentment. What better way, now, than to suppress it in the service she has pledged, especially when the force of the pledge has been to do away with all ambiguity with respect to this service? Further, if she asserts herself as angel in *his* house, then she can arrogate to herself a saving or covering moral right. She will be absolutely justified in laying claim to honor at Bly:

> I now saw that I had been asked for a service admirable and difficult; and there would be a greatness in letting it be seen—oh, in the right quarter!—that I could succeed where many another girl might have failed. It was an immense help to me—I confess I rather applaud myself as I look back!—that I saw my service so strongly and so simply. I was there to protect and defend the little creatures in the world the most bereaved and the most loveable . . . They had nothing but me, and I—well, I had *them*. It was in short a magnificent chance . . . I was a screen—I was to stand before them. The more I saw, the less they would. I began to watch them in a sti-

fled suspense, a disguised excitement that might well, had it continued too long, have turned to something like madness. What saved me, as I now see, was that it turned to something else altogether. It didn't last as suspense — it was superseded by horrible proofs. Proofs, I say, yes — from the moment I really took hold (53).

After this, of course, she must bring on further proofs of evil in the children in order to justify her self-justification. More and more committed, not to say dedicated, to a false position rather than to a genuine identity, she actively "knows" the children. She thus begins to maneuver herself to the point when, as the indispensable angel in his house, she will be morally bound to cry scandal. At this foreseeable point she will be able both to appear before him for his approval, that seal upon her honor, and at the same time secretly punish him for his godlike neglect of her. The governess' high morality, therefore, is now also a false or poisoned morality, the beginning of the immoral.

Ghost-encumbered, the governess inevitably brings on another proof of her nonentity, her own personal ghostly double Miss Jessel. Where she herself is an angel in the house, Miss Jessel is "a woman in black, pale and dreadful" (57), an avenger with "awful eyes" revealing "a kind of fury of intention" (58). Where the governess "dies" of "so much respectability" (21), Miss Jessel is "my predecessor — the one who died" (57). And where the governess has only the most dependent social position, Miss Jessel is "a lady," a point Mrs. Grose confirms when she says that Peter Quint had been "so dreadfully below" (59). Evidently the Miss Jessel of the "extraordinary beauty," "Oh, handsome — very, very . . . wonderfully handsome," (59) both compensates this smothered and scant heroine and, as a compensation based upon unappeasable self-rejection, punishes her for her scantness.

But it is the governess' penultimate encounter with Miss Jessel in which their ghostly doubling is most unmistakable. When Miles finally and resentfully strikes for freedom — he will get his uncle to intervene — the governess breaks down in hysteria. It is the one occasion on which she freely acknowledges her shame and self-doubt. She even considers fleeing Bly altogether, thereby to renounce her vengeful self-assertion. Immediately after she returns to Bly from church, however, she dies of shame: "Tormented, in the hall, with difficulties and obstacles, I remember sinking down at the foot of the staircase — suddenly collapsing there on the lowest step and then, with a revulsion, recalling that it was exactly where, more than a month before, in the darkness of night and just so bowed with evil things, I had seen the spectre of the most horrible of women" (96). She will not renounce. Indeed, in her rage of self-rejection, the governess has done nothing less than occupy the stead of her secret sharer. Not surprisingly, then, she once again knows the ghostly double, who in her turn usurps her stead as shining angel in his house. The heroine has no place—no "here" because she can own to no authentic "I." She is an impostor at Bly:

> Seated at my own table in the clear noonday light I saw a person whom, without my previous experience, I should have taken at the first blush for some housemaid who might have stayed at home to look after the place and who, availing herself of rare relief from observation and of the schoolroom table and my pens, ink and paper, had applied herself to the considerable effort of a letter to her sweetheart. There was an effort in the way that, while her arms rested on the table, her hands, with evident weariness, supported her head; but at the moment I took this in I had already become aware that, in spite of my entrance, her attitude strangely persisted. Then it was—with the very act of its announcing itself—that her identity flared up in a change of posture. She rose, not as if she had heard me, but with an indescribable grand melancholy of indifference and detachment, and, within a dozen feet of me, stood there as my vile predecessor. Dishonoured and tragic, she was all before me; but even as I fixed and, for memory, secured it, the awful image passed away. Dark as midnight in her black dress, her haggard beauty and her unutterable woe, she had looked at me long enough to appear to say that her right to sit at my table was as good as mine to sit at hers. While these instants lasted indeed I had the extraordinary chill of a feeling that it was I who was the intruder. It was as a wild protest against it that, actually addressing her—"You terrible, miserable, woman!"—I heard myself break into a sound (96-97).

This is a classic case of a Jamesian character's reluctant acknowledgment of, scuffle with, and compulsive denial of her double. After this, it only remains for the heroine's denial to take its typical, reactive "moral" turn: "There was nothing in the room the next minute but the sunshine and a sense that I must stay" (97). Once more she is the master-martyr.

We saw that the debased and debasing Quint springs from the governess' self-reproach, a self-reproach that she cannot bear and so ambiguously turns outwards upon the children in order ultimately to turn it upon the master. Miss Jessel likewise springs from resentment seeking an outlet. When the governess' alter ego emerges here in full, we notice that, quite apart from unseating the ego-rival, she appears to be writing, evidently under strain, a letter to her sweetheart, and that "her attitude strangely persisted" in spite of the governess' entrance. But one also notices a coincidence here: by now, the affair at Bly has reached a stage when there actually is a letter in the air. The children, trying to bypass their angel in the house and communicate directly with their uncle, are forcing the governess herself to write the master whom she has pledged never, never to bother. This communication is something she dreads; should she write a letter she may forfeit all the approval she craves. But it is also something she secretly craves to bring about — both in order to extort the master's approval, bring on proof that she exists, and ambiguously to punish him for his arbitrary negligence. No wonder, then, that her terrible alter ego turns out to be writing, under very great strain and with her own materials at her own seat, a letter to her sweetheart. No wonder too that this revenge-ghost's "attitude strangely persisted" in spite of the governess' presence. This alter ego reveals that the governess' communication with the master must be an ambiguous eye for an eye — if one likes, a letter for the original, "injurious" letter-within-a-letter. "What is there left for a servant of the lord who has discovered that the idol's hands never move towards the slowly spoiling offerings unless it be to stroke its own stone thighs?"[30]

The acolyte craves mastery, but always on condition that she does not alienate the master without whose approval she herself does not exist. Politically speaking, then, the governess' problem is to contrive to be *morally* bound by proofs of evil to write the master. The evening after having seen that conclusive proof Miss Jessel, she begins the dreaded letter she has always wanted to write. Like "Miss Jessel," however, she writes under such strain that she cannot complete it. She must, accordingly, go in search of Miles, half wanting to be let off from exposing herself to the eyes of the master, but secretly wanting to bring on a further, a supreme proof of the children's evil. (It is in this scene that the first signs of the Jamesian exposure "fever" appear in Miles. "His clear, listening face, framed in its smooth whiteness, made him for the minute as appealing as some wistful patient in a children's hospital," 102. "He gave . . . like a convalescent slightly fatigued, a languid shake of his head," 103.) The following morning this angel in his house cum secret scandal monger tells Mrs. Grose: " 'Yes — I've written.' But I didn't add — for the hour — that my letter, sealed and directed, was still in my pocket" (106). Now, with this letter in her pocket, she anxiously yet desirously awaits still another proof. She interviews Miles:

> This child, to my memory, really lives in a setting of beauty and misery that no words can translate; there was a distinction all his own in every impulse he revealed; never was a small natural creature, to the uninitiated eye all frankness and freedom, a more ingenious, a more extraordinary little gentleman. I had perpetually to guard against the wonder of contemplation into which my initiated view betrayed me; to check the irrelevant gaze and discouraged sigh in which I constantly both attacked and renounced the enigma of what such a little gentleman could have done that deserved a penalty. Say that, by the dark prodigy I knew, the imagination of all evil *had* been opened up to him: all the justice within me ached for the proof that it could ever have flowered into an act.
>
> He had never, at any rate, been such a little gentleman (106).

"Distinction . . . uninitiated . . . extraordinary little gentleman . . . initiated . . . such a little gentleman . . ." —before such superiorities of quality this *ressentiment* ridden exoteric initiate will turn infallibly to the vindictive. Consequently, the moment she senses that Flora is in the grounds, she rushes out to monger evil—leaving Miles, as Mrs. Grose points out, alone in the house with Quint:

> "So long with Quint? Yes—I don't mind that now" . . . But after gasping an instant at my sudden resignation, "Because of your letter?" she eagerly brought out.
>
> I quickly, by way of answer, felt for my letter, drew it forth, held it up, and then, freeing myself, went and laid it on the great hall-table. "Luke will take it," I said as I came back. I reached the house-door and opened it; I was already on the steps (109). .

This raging Blakean angel has, like her equivalent in "A Poison Tree" ("Christian Forbearance"), not once told her wrath but, on the contrary, has devised an ambiguous apple bright. Knowing full well the child's concern with any communication with his uncle, the governess can be morally, so very morally, certain that she is now going to obtain a "thrill of joy at having brought on a proof" (114). Her letter is a *casus belli*. Of course, she shows nothing either to Mrs. Grose or to the readers of her manuscript. But then this paranoic revenger has never been able to tell even her own wrath. Painfully open from the outset unto the splendid but extraordinarily uncaring Epimetheus, she can only extort identity by the most indirect means.

Her inconscient revenge-feeling has at last flowered into apple bright act. Of course the child will open her letter. Of course he will then be open to her for having rendered her open in the first place. In other words, this "knower" can, as she tells Mrs. Grose with vindictive passion, "get it out of him. He'll meet me—he'll confess" (124). Insufficient in her own being-unto-self, she would despoil Miles of his being-unto-self, in order ambiguously to use her knowledge against the master in *his* arbitrary being-unto-self. Next, she "knows" her shame- and revenge-ghost Quint. Lastly, in another reactive "moral" turn, she denies this ghost, and reasserts herself as angel in his house. Thus one smothered life comes to smother another life—with extraordinary, never yet told, rage.

Although our Schelerian account of "The Turn of the Screw" shows its consistency with James's other ghost stories of false claims, for instance "A Passionate Pilgrim," "Owen Wingrave" and "The Jolly Corner," it may appear inconsistent with the story itself in one important respect: it answers only indirectly the problem that has always snagged criticism, namely the ghosts' point by point likeness to the real life Quint and Jessel. How, if the ghosts are purely psychological ones, can they have a status such that Mrs. Grose can recognize them from the governess' descriptions? Why is it that the heroine sees the ghosts when she has not known their real life counterparts, while those who have known their counterparts in real life do not see them? In other words, why does James so stylize the story as to subvert and thereby devalue its status to that of a *jeu d'esprit*?

An answer to this problem should, I believe, eschew any legalist quibbling and try to view the story in the general context of James's development. My own conclusion, then, is that if the story neither unequivocally affirms nor denies the subjective nature of the ghosts, it is ultimately because James himself would disavow his own participation in the situation. This ambiguity covers some content of revenge-feeling—and, therefore, an all but inadmissible sense of injury—in James himself. One may reasonably conjecture that James had despaired of his own claim to a genuine "I" or "here" in England at the time of writing "The Turn of the Screw."[31] One may even go so far as to say that, during this period between the fiasco of *Guy Domville* and the bitter elegy that is *The Spoils of Poynton*, James, the pilgrim of good faith, felt he knew only controversial transformations of the social reality to which he had committed himself: who is this headmaster? who is the master? how to participate in a structure of social power that has taken on the arbitrary, rigid and, above all, withheld character of a secret society? To the James of this period—he is Clement Searle all over again—all that was knowable with confidence was the posthumous life of what might have been. All that was knowable and, therefore, for the denying. Formally speaking, "The Turn of the Screw" is like his own self-sabotaging heroes, a most extraordinary case.

At the end of *The Spoils of Poynton* the passionate pilgrim heroine revisits that latter-day Jamesian picturesque, Poynton, as a last act of worship. Her story has culminated in her renouncing as false all claim upon Poynton and in her espousing instead the role of Poynton's acolyte. Meanwhile, the consequences for the other characters of her cleaving to this role of acolyte have been the destruction of the dowager mistress' hopes in life and the hero's sterile marriage. Now at the end Fleda, a passionate pilgrim become martyr to honor, goes down to Poynton to invest herself with the symbol of her renunciatory passion, a Maltese cross offered to her by the incumbent and master she serves. "She would act with secret rapture. To have as her own something splendid that he had given her, of which the gift had been his signed desire, would be a greater joy than the greatest she had believed to be left her, and she felt that till the sense of this came home *she had even herself not known what burned in* her successful stillness" (my italics, 229).

Evidently Fleda Vetch has not, for all her burning with a martyr's ardor, sacrificed all. In fact, her private investiture represents on her acolyte's standards a kind of triumph: "It was an hour to dream of and watch for; to be patient was to draw out the sweetness. She was capable of feeling it as an hour of triumph, the triumph of everything in her recent life that had not held up its head. She moved there in thought— in the great rooms she knew; she should be able to say to herself that, for once at least, her possession was as complete as that of either of the others whom it had filled only with bitterness. And a thousand times yes—her choice should know no scruple" (229). One may even ask whether this investiture does not amount to a kind of despoliation, in moral quality if not in the letter to something of a feverishly sweet revenge—the self-abasing acolyte's unacknowledged revenge. After all, Fleda would expropriate the essence of Poynton, in effect depriving the rightful incumbents of it. "It should be one of the smallest things because it should be one she could have close to her; and it should be one of the finest because it was in the finest he [Owen Gereth] saw his symbol. She said to herself that of what it would symbolize she was content to know nothing more than just what her having it would tell her" (230). Like Dorothea Brooke selecting the jewelled crucifix at the beginning of her story, Fleda would aggrandize herself without acknowledging the true springs of her feeling. Or, like James's own Charlotte Stant, she "saves up" for a golden bowl. "The whole place was in her eyes, and she spent for weeks her private hours in a luxury of comparison and debate . . . At bottom she inclined to the Maltese cross—with the added reason that he had named it" (230): this expropriation is surely the climax of a vengeful martyr's second go. Not that it is Fleda exactly who is not telling her wrath: if anything, the truth is that James does not tell his.

This speculation helps to explain *The Spoils of Poynton's* anomalous ending, the pyre that despoils the old things. During her journey down, Fleda has been made peculiarly anxious by "the menace of the weather," and by the day's "spoiling for a storm" (230), a spoiling that produces a corresponding fantasy in her: "Something, in a dire degree at this last hour, had begun to press on her heart: it was the sudden imagination of a disaster, or at least of a check, before her errand was achieved. When *she said to herself that something might happen* she wanted to go faster than the train" (my italics, 231). Dismissing this fantasy, she returns to fantasizing about her triumph. She alone seems truly to possess Poynton, while the actual and rightful incumbents are "beyond lands and seas and alienated for ever" (231). In the event, of course, her fantasy of triumph proves false. The heroine who "had even herself not known what burned in her successful stillness" learns that Poynton is "burning still" (233). She must forego not only her acolyte's investiture but also her original foregoing of any claim to Poynton: "Mixed with the horror . . . was the raw bitterness of a hope that she might never again in life have to give up so much at such short notice" (234). On the other hand, the fantasy that "something might happen," a fantasy associated with her impulse to have the Maltese cross, does come true. Is this Jamesian martyr a kind of vengeful arsonist as well? If so, there may be a peculiar ambiguity in the heroine's last attitude: "She came out on the platform: everywhere she met the smoke. *She covered her face with her hands*" (my italics, 234). Fleda may be covering her face with her hands not only as a suppliant but also for shame that the something that might happen has happened.

The point is that this giving up so much perforce is in an important sense inconsistent with the kind of giving up so much that has occupied James so far. While such an "act of God" may cruelly and even tragically ironize the heroine's renunciations, morally speaking it is neutral. On the other hand, it does have a remarkable dramatic consistency with the story, for Fleda's martyrdom to sacred honor has already involved not only a self-rejection but also the destruction of the lives of the incumbents (a destruction that has nowhere been thoroughly acknowledged either by her or by James). And now this wholesale rejection comes spectacularly if ambiguously true: it is almost as if the martyred heroine has lighted the pyre herself, or, to put it more accurately, James has lighted these flames on his self- and other-rejecting martyr's behalf—James, who has not known himself what has burned in his own stillness. Indeed, this final spoliation of Poynton looks very like a most extraordinary case of author's arson.[32]

The *ressentiment* that emerges in *The Spoils of Poynton* is of course unintelligible without an understanding of its ethical crux, Fleda's renunciation of all claim upon Poynton, and, thereby, of all claim to a social place. But a further difficulty is that, on the face of it, this renunciation itself is unintelligible. The sanction Fleda consistently invokes is honor, "honour and . . . good name" (102), "any sort of honour" (211), above all honor committed in a vow: "Nobody had a right to get off easily from pledges so deep and sacred. How could Fleda doubt they had been tremendous when she knew so well what any pledge of her own would be?" (94). Again: " 'The great thing is to keep faith. Where's a man if he doesn't? If he doesn't he may be so cruel. So cruel, so cruel, so cruel!' Fleda repeated. 'I couldn't have a hand in that, you know: that's my position—that's mine' " (172). For this vow, a suprapersonal form, Fleda would sacrifice not only her own place in life but also the happiness of the other characters. Any serious objections to her formalism—for instance, Mrs. Gereth's "No such obligation exists for an hour between any man and any woman who have hatred on one side" (211-212)—appear to represent for her and her creator no more than the damnable terms of this sacrifice.

Unintelligibly destructive as the heroine's appeal to honor may appear, it becomes comprehensible (if not less destructive) when one sees Fleda Vetch as another Jamesian acolyte, "a priestess of the altar"

(33). Fleda, the story insists over and over, has only the most dependent social place. For instance, when she first meets Owen Gereth at Poynton, she feels "Her meagre past" falling "away from her like a garment of the wrong fashion" (10); she "hadn't a penny in the world nor anything nice at home . . . hadn't so much even as a home" (12). Later, Owen Gereth recognizes her situation with clumsy tact: "You don't — a — live anywhere in particular, do you?" (86). Again, "She had neither a home nor an outlook . . . It was, morally speaking, like figuring in society with a wardrobe of one garment"(128). Indeed the weakness of her social basis is such that, in James's evaluation, she may legitimately lay claim to Poynton only in fantasy: "she gave herself . . . up to a mere fairy-tale, up to the very taste of the beautiful peace she would have scattered on the air if only something might have been that could never have been" (39). As mistress of Poynton in Mrs. Gereth's stead, Fleda Vetch would be a barbarian impostor immorally committed to a Jamesian compensation cycle.

It is, in other words, on the basis of her relative nonentity that Fleda protests the honor of Poynton. Being herself so unplaced, so free a spirit, she insists by way of reaction upon a suprapersonal formalism. She cannot, even when disqualifying her own claim on Poynton, be strictly free of reactionary impulse. Only consistent with this externe's conservatism of hers is her protesting Poynton's incumbent master's honor, for the sake of which she is "ready to give an instance" of a "different manner of loving" (94), the acolyte's manner ("You mustn't think I don't adore him when I've told him so to his face. I love him so that I'd die for him — I love him so that it's horrible . . . Darling Mrs. Gereth, I could kiss the ground he walks on," 191). If the godly master's honor has been committed by a vow, a vow which on an acolyte's standards is identical with his existence, then that vow must be observed as an absolute. Likewise consistent with her reactionary formalism is her need not only *not* to "cut in" (124) competitively on Mona Brigstock's claim on Poynton and its master, but also actively to further the latter's claim. If to act in any way as a sexual and social rival is to be an impostor, then let Mona Brigstock be her executive surrogate — so runs this acolyte-aesthete's logic: "There was something in her that would make it a shame to her forever to have owed her happiness to an interference. It would seem intolerably vulgar to her to have 'ousted' the daughter of the Brigstocks: and merely to have abstained even wouldn't sufficiently assure her that she had been straight. Nothing was really straight but to justify her little pensioned presence by her use; and now, won over as she was to heroism, she could see her use only as some high and delicate deed" (94). Whatever her personal charmlessness, Mona Brigstock has a prior, inalienable claim, the birthright of a local or English Esau.

The real problem of *The Spoils,* then, does not lie in the heroine's perfectly consistent inconsistencies. For all her non sequiturs, she is simply a Jamesian social aesthete cleaving to her true identity (or nonentity) rather than laying a false claim to honor. The real problem is the emotional one of her bearing her own noble self-sacrifice, for this heroine is so close to, is so exquisitely fitted for, an expanded selfhood that yet cannot be. And the more the pressure upon her to claim this expanded selfhood, the more she recognizes that it cannot be, indeed that she would not truly *be* should she persist with her claim. Fleda recognizes that she must choose against a life that would be, in her situation, a kind of living death; and choose, after such knowledge of the vital self that might have been, in favor of the protracted half-life of the acolyte-aesthete. In effect, whichever way she turns, this heroine must choose not to live, at least not to live except vicariously. It is as if she were fated always to watch the living from the point of view of a ghost (" 'Somehow there were no ghosts at Poynton,' Fleda went on. 'That was the only fault . . . Yes, henceforth there'll be a ghost or two,' " 220).

Ultimately it is this truth of her twice proven nonentity that Fleda — or, more accurately, a James obviously approving Fleda — must bear. But how to bear a life that so gallingly disinherits one of one's life? To put it another way, where does a professional exoteric initiate's natural resentment go when her nonentity is doubly proved against her? If it has issued in a reactive renunciation during the first half of the story, what becomes of it when this reactive renunciation turns out to yield no genuine alternative life? The novel's distressing ending indicates that this inevitable resentment has never been thoroughly renounced; it has only been reactively renounced, which is to say it has not been renounced at all. Unlike Strether, another servant who bravely and forgivingly recognizes that his only course is "Not, out of the whole affair, to have got anything for myself," Fleda Vetch goes down to Poynton to despoil it, albeit in a high-minded way, of its essence. Because neither she nor James appear able consciously to acknowledge the false or pretentious quality of this act, an inevitably reactionary feeling must out—of course, indirectly. Thus the anomalous destruction of Poynton is really an unacknowledged emotional correlative of the precluded heroine's rage for social essence. *The Spoils of Poynton* is another story, I believe a distressingly flawed one, of a Jamesian acolyte's revenge.

Stendhal, who seems to have cultivated the sixteenth century because its codes of honor allowed him to pose as a laconic dandy, has a story ("Vittoria Accoramboni") in which a certain Cardinal is outraged by the atrocious murder of a nephew. Betraying nothing, however, to the questioning eyes of others, and above all to the Pope, Stendhal's hero retains his dignity intact and thereby paves his way to the papacy. It is a feat of political nonchalance which might be described by a Jamesian term, "consistency." In suffering injury the hero's whole identity is called into question. He is henceforth two persons, the powerful person whom he has conceived himself to be, and another, unacceptably vulnerable person. In dealing with this critical discontinuity of identity he now gives the appearance of being *like* himself, at least his erstwhile self. He instantly seals his wound. He altogether denies the sudden ghostliness of his forfeited self. He repudiates any double who may be enjoying his dividedness. Insofar as his identity and honor have been impugned, he will henceforth live wholly unto himself. Stendhal does not say so in as many words, but his "gran frate's" subsequent career, a jesuitical second go, depends upon his use of what he consummately knows.

James has his own fable in which consistency appears as a way of maintaining or, more accurately, regaining identity. In the relatively early "Crawford's Consistency," a patrician hero is rejected, right on the eve of his marriage, by his beautiful fiancée. (Although there is a reason—her parents fear his financial failure—none is given out at the time.) So severely injured is this hero that, reacting quite extraordinarily, he commits himself to a vulgar woman, thus proving to himself, the ex-fiancée, and his social circle that he has never been fractured into an erstwhile self and an intolerable, to-be-rejected self. Right up to the inevitable unhappy ending there is never the least flaw discernible in his consistency. When forced to recognize that he has dishonorably used his wife as the instrument of his vindication, he still continues to be impeccably like his former honorable self. He compensates his wife for her wrong by consistently enduring her punishment of

him. ("Maud Evelyn," a grotesque late variant of "Crawford's Consistency," is worth noting here. In this fantasy, a rejected lover appears to
take himself at his fiancée's and his own lowest estimate and to determine to be consistent with it. If he is in truth but half a man, then he
will be thoroughly, more than adequately, just that: he engages
himself to, marries, and finally buries a "ghost," a young girl who has
long been dead.)

As a repudiation of a vulnerable self, the principle of consistency is
likely to be implicit in any of James's situations in which there is anomalous or extraordinary or, indeed, inconsistent behavior. Consistency,
however, is something met everywhere in James, not only in his most
extraordinary cases. Being a denial of the loss of all-important identity
or honor it can, as in the type fable "Crawford's Consistency," compel
James's admiration even when a character is committing himself
further to a false position. It is, at least, the peculiar appeal of consistency that makes it so difficult for Isabel Archer in her relationship
with Osmond, who virtually parodies the duty of being like oneself:

> She felt almost sorry for him; he was condemned to the sharp pain of loss
> without the relief of cursing . . . His present appearance, however, was not
> a confession of disappointment; it was simply a part of Osmond's habitual
> system, which was to be inexpressive exactly in proportion as he was really
> intent. He had been intent on this prize from the first; but he had never
> allowed his eagerness to irradiate his refined face . . . He would give no sign
> now of an inward rage which was the result of a vanished prospect of gain—
> not the faintest nor subtlest. Isabel could be sure of that, if it was any satis-
> faction to her. Strangely, very strangely, it was a satisfaction; she wished
> Lord Warburton to triumph before her husband, and at the same time she
> wished her husband to be very superior before Lord Warburton. Osmond,
> in his way, was admirable; he had, like their visitor, the advantage of an
> acquired habit. It was not that of succeeding, but it was something almost
> as good—that of not attempting. As he leaned back in his place . . . he had
> at least (since so little else was left him) the comfort of thinking how well he
> personally had kept out of it, and how the air of indifference, which he was
> now able to wear, had the added beauty of consistency (II, 235-236).

A comparable, late example occurs in *The Wings of the Dove,* when
Lord Mark has his proposal rejected by Milly Theale:

> . . . the perception of that fairly showed in his face after a moment like the
> smart of a blow. It had marked the one minute during which he could
> again be touching to her . . . He quite grasped for the quarter of an hour

the perch she held out to him . . . he was by no means either so sore or so stupid, to do him all justice, as not to be able to behave more or less as if nothing had happened. It was one of his merits, to which she did justice too, that both his native and his acquired notion of behaviour rested on the general assumption that nothing — nothing to make a deadly difference for him — ever *could* happen. It was, socially, a working view like another, and it saw them easily enough through the greater part of the rest of their adventure (II, 143).

In a late essay on Gabriele D'Annunzio, consistency appears not just as a working view but as something virtually identical with identity itself, with the decent and unencumbered sense of "I am who I am": "He [the critic] recognizes as well how the state of being fullblown comes above all from the achievement of consistency, of that last consistency which springs from the unrestricted enjoyment of freedom."[33] Again, James finds a living case of the principle in George Sand:

Of the extent and variety of danger to which the enjoyment of a moral tone could be exposed and yet superbly survive Madam Karénine's pages [James is reviewing a biography] give us the measure; they offer us in action the very ideal of an exemplary triumph of character and mind over one of the very highest tides of private embarrassment that it is well possible to conceive. And it is no case of that *passive* acceptance of deplorable matters which has abounded in the history of women, even distinguished ones, whether to the pathetic or to the merely scandalous effect; the acceptance is active, constructive, almost exhilarated by the resources of affirmation and argument that it has at its command.[34]

Consistency understood as a repudiation of critical discomfiture raises the matter of the lie in James, particularly in the later work. After all, for the shocked hero to act consistently is merely to imitate himself, is therefore in some degree to live what may be called a vital or honorable lie. To put the situation more positively: the triumph of the double — whose advent it is that proves the damaging inconsistency — may in turn be trumped by the hero's calculated duplicity. James finds here a noble use of secrecy, what he himself calls a "virtuous, heroic lie."[35]

As I indicated when dealing with the psychological ghost in James, "The Jolly Corner" provides an important example of the honorable lie. Thus while Spencer Brydon can comfortably enough admit his European failure, he has subsequently to admit the failure of a whole lifetime. If he has never really lived in Europe, neither has he really lived in America: on the evidence of his ghostly American double he has never lived. As we saw, too, Spencer Brydon "dies of shame" as a result of his shock of recognition. Therefore it is not surprising to find that, when he returns to consciousness, he returns "to knowledge, to knowledge" (227). Yet another Jamesian character responding to an access of self-consciousness by concealing himself, he returns to the daylight world with a secret. Never for a moment deflecting into the truth, he lies honorably to Alice Staverton about his experience. "But this brute," he tells her, "with his awful face — this brute's a black stranger. He's none of *me,* even as I *might* have been" (231). Of course Brydon is enormously helped by Alice in this honorable lie, for not only does she not give him back his lie, she actively bears with it and honors it. Indeed, it is possible to put the situation still more positively. Spencer Brydon has at last earned identity, even if a minor one. So Alice is only telling the truth when she both complies and lies: " 'And he isn't — no, he isn't — *you!*' she murmured as he drew her to his breast" (232). Alice's is a forbearing, lovingkindly fraud that ensures that one secret will be guarded by another.

This amounts to saying that the newfound hero's honorable lie is not so much a compulsive self-concealment as an open secret. While he himself is not exactly admitting the truth, he is nevertheless letting Alice "admit as much" on his behalf. In fact, if we are really to believe in this newfound hero, it must be that he tacitly contrives to do just this. At any rate, he accepts Alice's offer to mediate between the intimate adversaries. He gives her mute permission to convene them, and then to arbitrate their transaction of identity. Finally, he allows her to negotiate an honorable solution and to issue what is in essence a communiqué to the world — "And he isn't — no, he isn't — *you!*" The formula satisfies the hero's need for consistency, and also instructs the bystander-reader in a discreet response. The latter, too, should respect this hedging of the sacred.

The matter of the vital or honorable lie necessarily raises the question of the giving of the lie. While in James it may well be honorable (although immoral in a narrow sense) to deceive, to be called a liar in public is to be made to suffer a grave affront. The explanation of this paradoxical point of honor in James goes beyond his feeling on an exposed person's behalf. It depends on whether the honor of the liar has been committed in the first place, that is, on whether the liar

makes a moral commitment to the person he deceives; while withholding the truth, he may nevertheless be withholding it from someone
whom he recognizes as having a right to it and as being worthy of
esteem. Since, then, the right to withhold the truth may be as much
attached to James's honor ethic as the right to know it, to contest this
right is seriously to jeopardize identity and honor.[36] If it can be honorable though "immoral" to deceive, it may well be both dishonorable
and immoral to undeceive by giving the lie.

While the immoral giving of the lie is a possibility in any of James's
situations involving the honorable lie, the classic case of it in him is the
particularly savage story, "The Liar." Here Oliver Lyon, a society
painter, re-encounters a woman he has once loved only to find her
happily married to a certain Colonel Capadose, an extravagant raconteur who "handled the brush . . . with such freedom" (405) as to be a
kind of artist himself. The latter, in fact, turns out to be Lyon's
double, at once his successful sexual rival and a "liar platonic" (411)
who "doesn't operate with a hope of gain or with a desire to injure. It is
art for art and he is prompted by the love of beauty . . . He paints, as it
were, and so do I!" (411-412).

The advent of the gallingly superior-inferior double proves unbearable to Lyon. Having once been rejected by a woman "perfectly incapable of a deviation" (408) from truth—her punning name is Ever-
ina—he now finds that "an adventurer imitating a gentleman" (386)
has succeeded him. Consequently, he enters a crisis of self-doubt and
resentment. If so dubious a rival has succeeded him, has he himself
seemed still more worthless? Is he perhaps a sexual and social
impostor, indeed the real, the career liar of the piece? The presence of
his rival, Lyon at any rate feels, makes "one feel one's self a bit of a
liar, even (or especially) if one contradicted him" (413).

Shaken in his self-confidence, Lyon looks for redress. Above all, he
requires an acknowledgment from the heroine that "her life would
have been finer" (417) with him, that he is a superior would-have-been
rather than an inferior might-have-been. In order to elicit some such
acknowledgment, he determines to put her husband before her, not
as a raconteur of good faith, but as the impostor that he at bottom
feels himself to be. In his essentially revengeful obsession he paints the
Capadoses' child at such length as to seem to expropriate her. Soon
after, he begins "a masterpiece . . . of legitimate treachery" (415), a

portrait of his rival that, when hung publicly, will forever give his rival the lie.

It is a situation that, like any transaction between doubles, must end in a rupture or a wound. In one of James's characteristic voyeurist scenes, Lyon comes upon Colonel Capadose and his wife just as they discover "The Liar." So grave an insult is this picture that its victim reacts by mutilating it "exactly as if he were stabbing a human victim: it had the oddest effect — that of a sort of figurative suicide" (431). The effect of this paroxysm of self-rejection (as well as rejection of Lyon) is that Lyon seems wholly to displace his rival from his identity and to insinuate himself as a superior would-have-been. Indeed, when questioned by a servant about the vandalism, he becomes "The Liar" in the letter as well as the spirit: "Lyon imitated the Colonel. 'Yes, I cut it up — in a fit of disgust' " (432). By telling this lie he consummates his own figurative suicide. He has only painted his own dishonor.

In the story's final twist, Colonel and Mrs. Capadose refuse to be given the lie by their intimate adversary. On the contrary, the man who has been deprived of his name becomes more the painterly raconteur than ever, thus honorably to trump the true liar who, in his consuming mendacity, has intended dishonorably to give him the lie. In their united consistency, the Capadose couple affirm not only the Colonel's original good faith but also the fact that theirs is a "real marriage" (as the precluded hero of "The Real Thing" would put it). The only sign that they might be taking a revenge on the impostor who torments them is the heroine's final use of ambiguity: "For you, I am very sorry. But you must remember that I possess the original!" (440). Even this, however, may not be a parthian shot so much as a final affirmation of the Colonel's moral commitment to the society he entertains.

While, generally speaking, it is immoral and dishonorable to give the lie in James, it may, given a character's rights of resentment, actually be morally heroic to refrain from giving it. For example, Christopher Newman renounces exposing the Europeans' lie in favor of honor, his European adversaries' as well as his own. A comic instance would be the kindly Strether's passing up a chance of vindictively giving the lie to Waymarsh, who has betrayed him to Sarah Pocock. "You don't know," asks Strether while knowing the answer full well, "whether Sarah has been directed from home to try me on the matter of my also going to Switzerland?"

"I know," said Waymarsh as manfully as possible, "nothing whatever about her private affairs; though I believe her to be acting in conformity with things that have my highest respect." It was as manful as possible, but it was still the false note — as it had to be to convey so sorry a statement. He knew everything, Strether more and more felt, that he thus disclaimed, and his little punishment was just in this doom to a second fib. What falser position — given the man — could the most vindictive mind impose? He ended by squeezing through a passage in which three months before he would certainly have stuck fast (II, 171).

As we shall see, too, the moral drama of *The Golden Bowl* depends upon refraining to give the lie.

One can of course dedicate oneself, in a relatively simple ideological sense, to a value or an ideal or an orthodoxy; Isabel Archer would dedicate herself to an Emersonian ideal of an expanding self, and the priestly Fleda Vetch to the aesthetic conservation of "the old things." In James, however, the sacred vow is likely to be an ambiguous thing. It may be less an ideological and more a subjective matter, even a matter of reactive self-assertion. As in the cases of Olive Chancellor and Hyacinth Robinson, the reactionary vow may seem the only way of knowing the real thing. The subjective here has become a way of provoking value, as it were.

Assuming the ideological aspect of the Jamesian vow, we can look here more closely at this subjective side. Thus in the moment of self-consciousness James's hero's sense of "I am who I am" will be overpowered by the announcement that "You are not who you think you are." Beginning to be ruptured into pretender selves, this hero may no longer know who he is, knows only that he must know, that this knowledge alone and the use of it will henceforth constitute his value: the newly self-conscious hero needs intention or intentionality, a secret. Depending upon how seriously he has been exposed, he may now need reactively to fix or formalize his intentionality in a vow by all that is "sacred." This vow represents a kind of identity *fiat*. The hero will stand by the vow or he will be nothing; he *is* his vow.[37] James's self-doubting hero's formalism is, I think, still further reinforced by his no longer knowing sufficiently how others can stand towards him. If he does not know himself, how can he know his society's intention towards him? He not only vows himself, therefore, he proceeds to convert his private vow into an avowal to another or others (just as he seeks to have his claim to identity recognized by society as his right to honor). The force of such avowal is that the hero both knows himself and is henceforth known to and by his society.

Very closely associated with this formalism is the word of honor or oath, something one finds everywhere in James. This oath takes the vow/avowal to a higher power, so to speak, by constituting a ceremonial seal upon it, for the Jamesian oath implies that honor has been formally staked and that all ambiguity as to intention or moral commitment has been eliminated. Moreover, this oath guarantees an implicit penalty against the hero in the event that he should lapse from his vow. By it the hero ensures both that he will be judged as dishonored and that the person or group to whom he has bound himself in understanding will go untouched by his failure. This of course holds true even when he tells an honorable lie on oath, that is, perjures himself. Since he is morally committed here to the character whom he deceives, he cannot be judged as dishonorable if and when it is understood that he is lying.[38]

It is probably *The Portrait of a Lady* that provides the greatest example of the ambiguous vow in James. Suppose here that we take up Richard Poirier's suggestion that "to James's imagination Olive Chancellor is the 'portrait' of Isabel seen from the 'back' "[39]: how far is James's beautiful volunteer for the "multiplied life" (II, 166) a type of the reactionary? One has some right to this question; after all, Isabel's problem is that to follow the ideal as quixotically as she does can but leave her open to falling between two social stools.

Early on, we know, Isabel might have had Caspar Goodwood for the asking. She might have Lord Warburton too—English society illustrated by an eminent case: social quintessence that is all the more readily defined for her by Warburton's own apologetic dis-establishmentarianism. Yet she responds to the latter's approach with "a certain fear"; she even suffers "appreciable shock" (I, 100). Evidently Isabel's social personality is very much at issue. Is she unexpectedly to forfeit her potential American self, a self that might still and always have Caspar Goodwood for the asking?

Undoubtedly it is to emphasize this questioning of her social identity that James introduces Henrietta Stackpole. Henrietta, who has enlisted in Goodwood's cause, functions as a comic cue to Isabel *not* to be "faithless to my country" (I, 119) and, no less obviously, as a kind of programmatic chauvinist upon which she is *not* to model herself. It is exactly at this point—when she has had brought home to her the danger of social faithlessness and when she is reading an appeal from Goodwood himself—that Isabel re-encounters her eminent English "personage . . . a collection of attributes and powers . . . What she felt was that a territorial, a political, a social magnate had conceived the design of drawing her into the system in which he rather invidiously lived and moved" (I, 126-127). Again she betrays anxiety, leaving the disappointed Warburton "really frightened at herself" (I, 138). And again it is because she feels her social identity exposed—the heroine who might so easily claim a Caspar Goodwood in the wings.

At the time Isabel feels that committing herself to Warburton would involve forfeiting what he conceives of as her American "character" (I, 126). Later, in her more considered though not obviously more intelligible rejection, she claims that such a commitment would mean giving up her fate:

> "I can't escape unhappiness," said Isabel. "In marrying you I shall be trying to . . . I mustn't—I can't!" cried the girl.
> "Well, if you're bent on being miserable I don't see why you should make *me* so. Whatever charms a life of misery may have for you, it has none for me."
> "I'm not bent on a life of misery," said Isabel. "I've always been intensely determined to be happy, and I've often believed I should be . . . But it comes over me every now and then that I can never be happy in any extra-ordinary way; not by turning away, by separating myself."
> "By separating yourself from what?"
> "From life. From the usual chances and dangers, from what most people know and suffer" (I, 164-165).

Viewing this classic *Portrait* from the "back," one realizes that one has come upon the original of James's heroines of the non sequitur. It is Emersonian Isabel who is the parent of Fleda Vetch, for instance, and her dilemma in the face of the temptation of "place"; for Isabel (as for Fleda) to claim "place" through marriage would imply, on the one hand, a kind of apostasy and, on the other, laying a false, barbarian's claim to an "other" social system ("It's getting—getting—getting a great deal," I, 164). Such apostasy and such a possession or disposses-sion would together involve her in a separation from true identity, a kind of dishonor, a not-being.

In the midst of this fluctuating transaction of identity, Isabel reminds herself of her responsibility to Goodwood who, "more than any man she had ever known . . . expressed for her an energy — and she had already felt it as a power — that was of his very nature" (I, 142-143). But this is also the "character" whom she has already rejected in America and whom she would now, just after declining Lord Warburton, reject yet again. If Lord Warburton cannot be the real right thing — in part on account of Caspar Goodwood's claim — Goodwood himself seems less than ever this real thing for claiming her after Warburton has done so. It may be then that Isabel has not altogether adhered to her American "character" by renouncing an English marriage. If anything, the opposite may be the case, so that her break with Goodwood is quite epochal for her ("She was not praying; she was trembling — trembling all over . . . humming like a smitten harp," I, 205). With this breaking off Isabel has effectively separated herself from the kind of executive social vitality embodied in the American Goodwood as well as in Lord Warburton — in the name of *not* separating herself from life. Isabel stands forth as the type of James's social aesthetes.

This is a moment of extraordinary virtuality. Soon Isabel will be expanded, elect, "other." The heiress stands to come into a consciousness of multiplied ages:

"You want to see life — you'll be hanged if you don't, as the young men say."
"I don't think I want to see it as the young men want to see it. But I do want to look about me."
"You want to drain the cup of experience."
"No, I don't wish to touch the cup of experience. It's a poisoned drink! I only want to see for myself."
"You want to see, but not to feel," Ralph remarked.
"I don't think that if one's a sentient being one can make the distinction. I'm a good deal like Henrietta. The other day when I asked her if she wished to marry she said: 'Not till I've seen Europe!' I too don't wish to marry till I've seen Europe."
"You evidently expect a crowned head will be struck with you."
"No, that would be worse than marrying Lord Warburton" (I, 187-188).

Yet for all the apocalypticism of her claim, one may believe that Isabel's very need to see already bespeaks a sense of false position. Isabel has too much social freedom and, somehow, too little; and she will come to need both less freedom and, perhaps, more. It is, tragically, as if the still unseen cost of the ideal might be a reactivity in terms of the same ideal.

It can only be this ambiguity in Isabel that leads her subsequently into the startling non sequitur of a relationship with Mme Merle. If Isabel has begun dangerously to separate herself from life in order to be "more," Mme Merle might be the welcome "other" who will vicariously complete, if only gradually to deplete, her. She has long practiced life in the Jamesian interstice, practiced slavishly while yet seeming a mistress of its forms. "If we're not good Americans we're certainly poor Europeans," she acknowledges in her always latently revengeful way:

> "We've no natural place here. We're mere parasites, crawling over the surface; we haven't our feet in the soil . . . A woman perhaps can get on; a woman, it seems to me, has no natural place anywhere; wherever she finds herself she has to remain on the surface and, more or less, to crawl. You protest, my dear? you're horrified? you declare you'll never crawl? It's very true that I don't see you crawling; you stand more upright than a good many poor creatures. Very good; on the whole, I don't think you'll crawl" (I, 246).

If Isabel would *see* Europe's multiplied life, Mme Merle must have its multitudinous "things!" (I, 253). If Isabel admirably, yet also presumptuously, abhors any idea of a crowned head, Mme Merle, a veteran houseguest who has so far failed "to marry Caesar" (II, 324), still schemes to be Caesar's wife: "Her great idea," the Countess Gemini says, "has been to be tremendously irreproachable — a kind of full-blown lily — the incarnation of propriety" (II, 323-324). Above all, just as the debutante commences her coming out, Mme Merle will pretend to a certain esotericism. As in her parable of the iron pot, this "other" is characteristically other-speaking:"I try to remain in the cupboard — the quiet, dusty cupboard where there's an odour of stale spices — as much as I can. But when I've to come out and into a strong light — then, my dear, I'm a horror!" (I, 242).

Of course *The Portrait of a Lady* no sooner perceives the collapse of its idealism into these deep identities and even immanences than it must honorably deny that Isabel is any of a Mme Merle, even as she might yet be. Yet how else does it account for Isabel's susceptibility — not just to Mme Merle, but also to Gilbert Osmond? While Isabel would cleave to her renunciatory aestheticism, the expatriate of the hilltop seclusion and the doctrine of "my studied, my wilful renunciation" (I, 336) professes to live after the style of a work of art. If Isabel determines to civilize her Emersonianism in Europe, Osmond's dream of civilization has long turned into a rage for "convention itself" (II, 19), and for the traditions that are Caesar's:

> His ideal was a conception of high prosperity and propriety, of the aristocratic life . . . He had never lapsed from it for an hour; he would never have recovered from the shame of doing so . . . But for Osmond it was altogether a thing of forms, a conscious, calculated attitude . . . He had an immense esteem for tradition; he had told her once that the best thing in the world was to have it, but that if one was so unfortunate as not to have it one must immediately proceed to make it. She knew that he meant by this that she hadn't it, but that he was better off; though from what source he had derived his traditions she never learned. He had a very large collection of them, however; that was very certain (II, 173-174).

And exactly when an extraordinarily exposed Isabel might be said to need a secret, Osmond comes to hand as a man of taste, a taste of which he alone can be the absolute consultant and arbiter and which he uses as a means of mystifying society into paying him the recognition it would otherwise refuse him. "It was the mask, not the face of the house. It had heavy lids, but no eyes; the house in reality looked another way . . . The windows of the ground-floor . . . were, in their noble proportions, extremely architectural; but their function seemed less to offer communication with the world than to defy the world to look in" (I, 286-287).

One could formulate *The Portrait*'s developing cycle in this way: inasmuch as it is intrinsic to Isabel's idealism that she should obscurely compensate for it just in order to live it, then she must at least be susceptible to the cabalists, who have long lived only in order to revenge themselves for the snub life has dealt them. While Isabel's cleaving to the ideal would in itself require a formal dedication, her social exposure and her further exposure to her as yet unbeknown other in Mme Merle—to a mere pretender self—make some "fixing" of her identity all the more necessary. Meanwhile, the cabalists (whom she in a sense provokes) must correspondingly formulate and fix their identities. Mme Merle, who would "have" (II, 286) Lord Warburton as a Caesarean "tradition" that will complete her social apostasy, has the supreme motive of a second go: "She has failed so dreadfully that she's determined her daughter shall make it up" (II, 324). Therefore she would also have Isabel Archer, at least an Isabel endowed with Touchett money, in order that Pansy should eventually have, if not Warburton himself, then the likes of such spoil. Hence her renunciation, to *her* gallingly youthful and vital "other," of her rights with Osmond and Pansy—a renunciation that is so much a secret, advance transaction in the social marketplace that even Osmond cannot understand how her "ambitions are for me" (I, 305). For his part, Osmond can at last take his secret revenge for the injury personages like Warburton inflict on him simply by existing. Gilbert Osmond will have the woman Lord Warburton all but abjectly wants. The Napoleonist who can say of the quite ludicrous parade of personages he envies—the Pope, the Emperor of Russia, the Sultan of Turkey, an Italian patriot, an English duke—that his "envy's not dangerous . . . I don't want to destroy the people—I only want to *be* them" (II, 5) can now in a manner *be* an English Lord.

Having so involuntarily volunteered for a compensation cycle, it seems inevitable that Isabel should eventually commit herself to it. She would dedicate herself formally to civilizing her ideal; and she must reactively give herself to a form, to tremendous vows, "the most serious act—the single sacred act—of her life" (II, 216). The idealist *is* by virtue of her self-dedication; but she is also absolutely *all* by virtue of her vows and avowal, and *nothing* otherwise. Of course this also holds for the conspirators, who are likewise absolutists.

Nor does this elaborate cycle seem any the less inevitable for James's repetitions of the sequence of Isabel's choices. Isabel has declined Warburton at Gardencourt and subsequently rejected Goodwood; and then, even as Osmond carefully courts her in Rome, she once again rejects both Warburton and Goodwood (just before her marriage). Indeed if there is any apocalypticism in *The Portrait* it would seem to be of an ironized, reverse kind, for James's second half, which sees Isabel wondering whether she might lapse from her vows and then almost convulsively re-affirming them, also recapitulates these "second goes." After Isabel's marriage Lord Warburton duly reappears and proceeds to pay equivocal attention to Pansy, while Goodwood likewise arrives, only to be disappointed. Involved once again in a familiar sequence, Isabel remains ostensibly committed to Osmond—to Osmond, and to a critical false position: she finds she has had no value beyond being "an applied handled hung-up tool" (II, 332) in the

hands of base revengers. Again, after returning full circle to Gardencourt, Isabel re-encounters both Warburton and Goodwood. The
former can make yet another of his equivocal appeals, while
Goodwood yet again shocks as well as energizes her ("His kiss was like
white lightning, a flash that spread, and spread again, and stayed . . .
But when darkness returned she was free," II, 381). And again these
transactions are epochal for her; she seems both to turn and to react
compulsively towards Osmond. "She had not known where to turn; but
she knew now. There was a very straight path" (II, 381).

James's elaborate cycle has run its full course, and the heroine
appears to be as consistent with herself as ever. But if one side of
Isabel's story has been that she has married for love of an ideal and the
other side that she has married out of reaction against the demands of
this same ideal, in what spirit can she be said to copy herself during
this second go? If Isabel knows (and she does know something) she does
not say what she knows. James himself, even after writing his story
twice over, as it were, will not say what he knows. As if he were finding
a discreet form to honor Isabel's new and presumably terrible autonomy, as well perhaps as express a new politics of secrecy in her, he
leaves his story *"en l'air."*[40] A novel about conspiracy makes a formal
use of ambiguity, and turns into its own open secret.

James's characterization throughout the second half can only be
described as consistently equivocal. Isabel the beautiful quester will
now seem infamously brought down within sight of her dream:

> When she saw this rigid system close about her, draped though it was in
> pictured tapestries, that sense of darkness and suffocation of which I have
> spoken took possession of her; she seemed shut up with an odour of mould
> and decay. She had resisted of course; at first very humorously, ironically,
> tenderly; then, as the situation grew more serious, eagerly, passionately,
> pleadingly (II, 174-175).

But now she will draw herself up as a Columbia of moral right, dis-
mayingly determined that her unhappiness should never come to her
through her own fault: "She had spoken of his insulting her, but it
suddenly seemed to her that this ceased to be a pain. He was going
down — down; the vision of such a fall made her almost giddy: that was
the only pain . . . Isabel slowly got up; standing there in her white
cloak, which covered her to her feet, she might have represented the
angel of disdain, first cousin to that of pity. 'Oh, Gilbert, for a man
who was so fine —!' she exclaimed in a long murmur" (II, 241-242).

Now in the Coliseum, just after Mme Merle has taken her revenge of ambiguity as the consummation of *her* second go—Mme Merle has had "Everything" (II, 286) to do with her fate—Isabel might be another Jamesian martyr to Caesarism. She has not really lived; she has had no authentic place because Mme Merle, a party in Europe only to liaison, and now the insolently infiltrating double, has all along occupied this place. Nor does she seem even to be alive to her own present situation: "Isabel started at the words 'her daughter,' which her guest threw off so familiarly. 'It seems very wonderful,' she murmured; and in this bewildering impression she had almost lost her sense of being personally touched by the story" (II, 324). Now, however, Isabel will seem to defy the amphitheater. She will be single-minded in the face of the double. She will never renounce her renunciatory-reactionary vows—when renunciation in James invariably means a giving up of commitment to a compensation cycle:

> Deep in her soul—deeper than any appetite for renunciation—was the sense that life would be her business for a long time to come. And at moments there was something inspiring, almost enlivening, in the conviction . . . It couldn't be she was to live only to suffer . . . To live only to suffer—only to feel the injury of life repeated and enlarged—it seemed to her she was too valuable, too capable, for that. Then she wondered if it were . . . more probable that if one were fine one would suffer? It involved then perhaps an admission that one had a certain grossness; but Isabel recognized, as it passed before her eyes, the quick vague shadow of a long future. She should never escape; she should last to the end (II, 343).

James is never more equivocal and unresolved than in the complex scene in which Isabel tends the dying Ralph (who has by now emerged as Osmond's good double). Here again she is a martyr pitifully ground in the mill of the cabalists' formalism. More important, Isabel is a tragic martyr for love, Ralph's for herself ("But love remains . . . " II, 364) as well as her own for him and for liberty: James comes here as close as he ever comes before *The Princess Casamassima* and the late novels to transcending the ultimately sterile ambiguities of the quest for identity and honor. For all this, and for all her feeling that "nothing mattered now but the only knowledge that was not pure anguish—the knowledge that they were looking at the truth together" (II, 362), Isabel in no real way acknowledges that she might have affronted her fate. "Truth" and "everything" seem here largely to mean that "He married me for the money . . . But he wouldn't have

married me if I had been poor" (II, 362). By no means taking everything on herself for love, as Fleda Vetch tries to do and as Milly Theale
does, Isabel remains at least a potential reactionary.

Ambiguous or unresolved to the end, Isabel can in the end only
resolve upon a life of ambiguity. Having earlier been a baffled acolyte
in the face of Osmond's supreme imposture, his call to her to uphold
her marriage vows, "the honour of a thing . . . something transcendent
and absolute, like the sign of the cross or the flag of one's country . . .
something sacred and precious . . . a magnificent form" (II, 311-312),
she re-dedicates herself in the spirit of a nobly sacrificial mistress of
forms. Henceforth on oath, Isabel Archer will know herself and will be
known as the magnificent formalist.

I am not directly concerned here either with James's sense of the
past, a sense that is inevitably part of his feeling for "the old things" of
Europe, or with his sense of the future, which he usually associates with
his Henrietta Stackpoles and Caspar Goodwoods. This kind of time in
James might be regarded for our purposes as historical or social time. I
am, however, concerned with the psychological time that is of the
essence of James's situations. Thus when James's American hero sets
out to cultivate the old things, and at worst to expropriate traditions,
he must also, as a preliminary, negotiate for time in order finally to
gain this "old" time. In other words, one wants here to define the very
strong time sense of the hero exposed to the Jamesian interstice, or
indeed of this hero caught out in any false position whatever.

At the beginning of the rather maudlin fantasy "The Middle Years,"
James's novelist hero Dencombe sits on his seaside bench of desolation
meditating upon his career. He is middle-aged, he has been seriously
ill (the illness is unspecified), he is filled with a sense of failure: "The
infinite of life had gone, and what was left of the dose was a small glass
engraved like a thermometer by the apothecary. He sat and stared at
the sea, which appeared all surface and twinkle, far shallower than the
spirit of man. It was the abyss of human illusion that was the real, the
tideless deep" (53). Dencombe has with him a copy of his latest novel
"The Middle Years," but this only serves to aggravate his sense of
failure, "as violent as a rough hand at his throat" (56). Indeed, such
are his feelings of failure that he has become strangely alienated from
this book: he has forgotten what it is about. Has there really been a
novel called "The Middle Years," indeed a career, a selfhood, suffi-

cient to be memorable? Has he really lived? is the terrible question he asks himself. "The art had come, but it had come after everything else. At such a rate a first existence was too short—long enough only to collect material; so that to fructify, to use the material, one must have a second age, an extension. This extension was what poor Dencombe sighed for. As he turned the last leaves of his volume he murmured: 'Ah for another go!—ah for a better chance!' " (57).

Exactly at this moment of yearning for another go or extension, Dencombe's revery is interrupted by an encounter with a young man, a certain Dr. Hugh, who is in Bournemouth to attend a patient. There follows an occult recognition scene, for it turns out that the ailing hero does have a kind of extension in the young apostle of health, who happens at this moment to be reading his own copy of "The Middle Years": "The stranger was startled, possibly even a little ruffled, to find that he was not the only person who had been favoured with an early copy. The eyes of the two proprietors met for a moment, and Dencombe borrowed amusement from the expression of those of his competitor, those, it might even be inferred, of his admirer. They confessed to some resentment—they seemed to say: 'Hang it, has he got it *already?*—Of course he's a brute of a reviewer!' Dencombe shuffled his copy out of sight" (57-58). It is another case, however mild, of the scuffle between Jamesian doubles for the prize of identity. The mortally insufficient master would complete himself vicariously through the youthful healthy acolyte were it not that this second go or extension must also bring home to him his basic insufficiency, in fact must seem to rob him of identity just by embodying it. After this initial contact, therefore, it only needs the acolyte properly to identify and honor the master for the latter to "die" of embarrassment. Since he is in very poor health anyway—he might well be dying of some tertiary stage of progressive shame, he is one of James's most extraordinary cases—he loses consciousness altogether: "He . . . then, through a blur of ebbing consciousness, saw Dr. Hugh's mystified eyes. He had only time to feel he was about to be ill again . . . before . . . he lost his senses altogether" (63-64). Although completed by the "extension," he has been all but fatally depleted by him.

James's story now repeats this cyclic transaction of identity. No sooner has the master temporarily recovered than he wonders whether he may well have secured another go through the offices of the acolyte, who has in the meantime pledged himself to his cause. Dencombe learns, however, that any claim he may make upon Dr. Hugh will lead to the latter's being disinherited by the worldly Countess who employs him, and he accordingly renounces any such claim. Meanwhile, the acolyte has as a double in all respects renounced *his* claim upon the Countess in favor of dedicating himself to the master. He returns from attending the Countess (now likewise in a fatal decline) "flourishing the great review of 'The Middle Years' . . . an acclamation, a reparation, a critical attempt to place the author in the niche he had fairly won" (73). But this time the combination of an ardent acolyte's homage and belated public honors can only amount to a fatal embarrassment, and Dencombe now literally dies of his shameful and grotesque inanition. The mortally pretentious impostor sinks into the ground with the words, "A second chance — *that's* the delusion. There never was to be but one" (75). The extension has turned out to be a compensation that has merely aggravated the false position it had seemed to compensate. And the hero dies of having the truth of his imposture proved — in the person of the unwittingly mischievous double — against him.

Used as a model, Dencombe's story suggests that any Jamesian failure-haunted quest for identity or authenticity or honor will imply the appeal: "Grant me an extension; grant me more time so that I can be *more,* so that I can *be.*" Feeling that he has a claim, as yet unsubstantiated, to identity, James's hero submits that society recognize and so substantiate his right to this claim. In this transaction he both puts himself on probation, undertakes to prove himself socially sufficient, and negotiates with society to concede him a moratorium, to suspend its standards until he has in fact proved his sufficiency. His appealing for an extension is, one might say, both to ask for an "accumulation" and a "lapse" of time.[41] (It does not greatly matter whether the term of this extension is specified or unspecified.)

What happens, however, when the probation and/or moratorium the hero has negotiated is up? If time is of the essence of the Jamesian crisis of identity, what happens when there is no more time, when the hero can no longer temporize, and when the situation forecloses upon him? If the second go or extension has proved, as it does in "The Middle Years," just another false position, what then? What kind of time is it when the characters are "time-less"?

Slight though it may be in itself, our model goes some way towards providing an answer. If the hero feels insufficient to start with, and cannot say to himself with conviction "I am who I am," then he is very much for the shocking. He is made for the enviable double who compensates him but whose inevitable advent also shocks him by saying in effect: "You are not who you think you are." This is why that most extraordinary case Dencombe appears to ebb away as if exsanguinated; his scuffle with the acolyte has constituted a fatal jarring of his already invalid being. The experience of shock announces to him that there will be no next time, indeed no more time.

To understand James more fully, then, we need a notion of displacement- or exposure- or shock-time. In order to develop this notion, I want now to examine one of James's "Kindertotenlieder" or "little boy lost" situations, "The Pupil." At the beginning of this story, the hero Pemberton is engaged by the Moreens, an itinerant family of expatriate Americans, as tutor to their youngest child Morgan. The latter, Pemberton learns from Mrs. Moreen, is "all overclouded by *this,* you know—all at the mercy of a weakness—!"; Pemberton "gathered that the weakness was in the region of the heart. He had known the poor child was not robust: this was the basis on which he had been invited to treat" (409-410). The tutor, could he but know it from Mrs. Moreen's equivocation, is already being maneuvered into a false position, for the Bohemian Moreens give only an appearance of offering genuine employment, and are, in reality, "looking out" for a foster parent for their child in the all too possible event of their own default. In a false social position themselves—they are deracinated outsiders trying to qualify for European society—they look on a tutor as a form of insurance.

Inevitably, "the subject of terms" (409) arises at the outset of the situation. When the needy and inexperienced tutor tries to broach it, however, the Moreens negotiate for indefinite terms, partly because they would want the tutor to provide for their child should they ever have to "chuck" the latter. In other words, they want neither "terms" nor a term, far less a termination. Instead, they would temporize, negotiate for an extended moratorium on the exposure of a child they know could prove fatally insufficient. In their shabby-noble insurance scheme, the tutor *is* time.

Insofar as the tutor fails to clarify his position, then, he permits himself to be maneuvered into a most awkward position. Eventually the truth of this is brought home sharply to him by his pupil, who has himself been put in a false position on account of his tutor's false position, and who has been made prematurely to feel himself on probation:

> "How do I know you will stay? I'm almost sure you won't, very long."
>
> "I hope you don't mean to dismiss me," said Pemberton.
>
> Morgan considered a moment, looking at the sunset. "I think if I did right I ought to."
>
> "Well, I know I'm supposed to instruct you in virtue; but in that case don't do right."
>
> "You're very young—fortunately," Morgan went on, turning to him again.
>
> "Oh yes, compared with you!"
>
> "Therefore, it won't matter so much if you do lose a lot of time."
>
> "That's the way to look at it," said Pemberton accommodatingly.
>
> They were silent a minute; after which the boy asked: "Do you like my father and mother very much?"
>
> "Dear me, yes. They're charming people."
>
> Morgan received this with another silence; then, unexpectedly, familiarly, but at the same time affectionately, he remarked: "You're a jolly old humbug!"
>
> For a particular reason the words made Pemberton change colour. The boy noticed in an instant that he had turned red, whereupon he turned red himself and the pupil and the master exchanged a longish glance in which there was a consciousness of many more things than are usually touched upon, even tacitly, in such a relation (419-420).

This tutor is for the shocking. He has never been the employee he would like to think he is but, rather, time for a helpless charge. Correspondingly, Morgan himself is so much the more a chuckable probationer on borrowed time.

This disquieting scene at Nice is more or less repeated a year later. Since by this time the situation has grown unbearably fraudulent, it needs only a further discretionary or honorable lie on the tutor's part to cause the probationer pupil to break down. The upshot is Pemberton's ultimatum to the Moreens: either they come to terms or he will leave immediately and expose them as frauds. However, committed as he is to a weak position, indeed to Morgan's weakness in the region of the heart, he is once again out-maneuvered. And once again his kindly temporizing aggravates his pupil's false position. If a tutor is time, then how much time can a defenseless pupil have? If a tutor is time, it must be because the pupil is regarded as being insufficient against some future day of crisis—because he may yet be exposed, chucked for a "fifth-rate social ideal, the fixed idea of making smart social acquaintances and getting into the *monde chic,* expecially when it was foredoomed to failure and exposure" (442), and therefore denied the right to his life.

The situation at length forecloses in a way entirely characteristic of James. At the very moment when the Moreen family seems doomed to bankruptcy, Pemberton receives a telegram offering him alternative employment: "Found jolly job for you—engagement to coach opulent youth on own terms. Come immediately" (447). What has all along been implicit in the tutor's situation, the desire for his "own terms," at last comes out before the pupil. And what has all along been implicit in the pupil's situation also comes out, a rival or double who is all that the deracinated Morgan might secretly crave to be, a youth who is to be prepared for Balliol, a "little gentleman" (436) who *can* offer genuine terms:

> "I'll make a tremendous charge; I'll earn a lot of money in a short time, and we'll live on it."
> "Well, I hope the opulent youth will be stupid—he probably will—" Morgan parenthesized, "and keep you a long time."
> "Of course, the longer he keeps me the more we shall have for our old age."
> "But suppose *they* don't pay you!" Morgan awfully suggested.
> "Oh, there are not two such—!" Pemberton paused, he was on the point of using an invidious term. Instead of this he said "two such chances."
> Morgan flushed—the tears came to his eyes. "*Dites toujours,* two such rascally crews!" Then, in a different tone, he added: "Happy opulent youth!" (447-448).

The emergence of this hitherto internal competitor virtually means the end of the pupil's privilege or extension. He is proved to be in no position worth speaking of in relation to the man whom by this time he regards as a foster parent. In fact, the opening of the telegram signals an extraordinary access of self-consciousness in him. When the double comes out, Morgan Moreen too must come out; like all of James's child characters, this pupil is something of a premature debutante. Morgan, one might say, comes so far out as to be almost extrinsic to himself, to be his own theater infinitely conscious of himself as an insufficient performer. One might also say then that he suddenly stands outside his own spontaneous or interior or psychological time. Time is as good as up, there is little chance in the theater of consciousness of temporizing; at most he can extemporize in this theater as an unready performer.

The moment—if one can properly attribute temporality to what is timeless or, in a limited and domestic sense, apocalyptic—is one of shock-time. It is the time of psychological implosion and displacement. Socially speaking, it is the non-time of the interstice, the Jamesian non-place. At the same time, of course, James's small pupil shows, and perhaps can show, very little here. It is only with hindsight that his shock at this beginning of the end becomes measureable.

Returning to the Moreens' employment out of kindness to his ex-pupil (whom Mrs. Moreen claims is "dreadfully ill") Pemberton finds himself in a grotesque position. And when it is as good as proposed that he foster Morgan, his impulse, inevitably a resentful one, is to reject any pseudo-parental role—and therefore to reject a child already virtually chucked by his parents: "It was all very well for Morgan to seem to consider that he would make up to him for all inconveniences by settling himself upon him permanently—there was an irritating flaw in such a view. He saw what the boy had in his mind; the conception that as his friend had had the generosity to come back to him he must show his gratitude by giving him his life. But the poor friend didn't desire the gift—what could he do with Morgan's life?" (456). Although in this context it is almost equally cruel to be either kind or unkind, the tutor stays on until the situation forecloses once and for all:

> Confusion reigned in the apartments of the Moreens (very shabby ones this time, but the best in the house), and before the interrupted service of the table (with objects displaced almost as if there had been a scuffle, and a great wine stain from an overturned bottle), Pemberton could not blink the fact that there had been a scene of proprietary mutiny. The storm had come—they were all seeking refuge. The hatches were down—Paula and Amy were invisible (they had never tried the most casual art upon Pemberton, but he felt that they had enough of an eye to him not to wish to meet him as young ladies whose frocks had been confiscated), and Ulick appeared to have jumped overboard. In a word, the host and his staff had ceased to "go on" at the pace of their guests, and the air of embarrassed detention, thanks to a pile of gaping trunks in the passage, was strangely commingled with the air of indignant withdrawal.
>
> When Morgan took in all this—and he took it in very quickly—he blushed to the roots of his hair. He had walked, from his infancy, among difficulties and dangers, but he had never seen a public exposure. Pemberton noticed, in a second glance at him, that the tears had rushed into his eyes and that they were tears of bitter shame (457-458).

All comes out — and quite literally — in this Pandora's box situation; even James's parentheses seem to "open" onto perspectives of collapse. And all must be learned and acknowledged and taken in by the hapless pupil. The tutor does not want him; the scandalous parents, whose "social calendar was blurred — it had turned its face to the wall" (456), would at last chuck him: it is as if his probation or moratorium has all along meant this. It is only *"as if* he had been a little gentleman" (my italics, 436). When, then, Morgan Moreen dies of his weakness in the region of the heart, we know that he has altogether lost heart. He has died of shame-shock. He has accepted an apparently loveless arena's verdict on his pretension to life, and then fatally chucked himself in a paroxysm of self-contempt.

While one kind of formal control over James's stories is their "life-time," another is what may be described on James's own authority as their spatialism.[42] Thus James will "foreshorten" his material when it gives signs of "space-hunger and space-cunning" (*Daisy Miller, Etc.,* xvii); or he will ensure that his story seems powerfully to occupy space, as if in an architectural manner:

> Such is the aspect that to-day *The Portrait* wears for me: a structure reared with an "architectural" competence . . . that makes it, to the author's own sense, the most proportioned of his productions after *The Ambassadors* . . . On one thing I was determined; that, though I should clearly have to pile brick upon brick for the creation of an interest, I would leave no pretext for saying that anything is out of line, scale or perspective. I would build large — in fine embossed vaults and painted arches, as who should say, and yet never let it appear that the chequered pavement, the ground under the reader's feet, fails to stretch at every point to the base of the walls (*The Portrait of a Lady,* I, xviii).

> The dramatist has verily to *build,* is committed to architecture, to construction at any cost; to driving in deep his vertical supports and laying across and firmly fixing his horizontal, his resting pieces — at the risk of no matter what vibration from the tap of his master-hammer. This makes the active value of his basis immense, enabling him, with his flanks protected, to advance undistractedly (*The Awkward Age,* xvii-xviii).

For all this space-scheming, however, James's story is probably still better described as a system. Formally speaking, at least, it is liable to be so predictable (as well as predicable) as to be something of a fearful symmetry: "Each part [of *The Ambassadors*] I rather definitely see in Two Chapters, and each very full, as it were, and charged — like a rounded medallion, in a series of a dozen, hung, with its effect of high relief, on a wall."[43] James, I shall argue, is one of the imaginative system builders.

I have already touched a number of times on the matter of James's binary form and, broadly speaking, it is this that constitutes "system" in him.[44] James indicates as much in the preface to *The Tragic Muse*, where he raises the problem, a spatial one, of his "centre": "The usual difficulties . . . were those bequeathed as a particular vice of the artistic spirit, against which vigilance had been destined from the first to exert itself in vain, and the effect of which was that again and again, perversely, incurably, the centre of my structure would insist on placing itself *not,* so to speak, in the middle (I, xii)." Under this eye for a false position, James's stories almost seem a series of impostures:

> It mattered little that the reader with the idea or the suspicion of a structural centre is the rarest of friends and of critics . . . the terminational terror was none the less certain to break in and my work threaten to masquerade for me as an active figure condemned to the disgrace of legs too short, ever so much too short, for its body. I urge myself to the candid confession that in very few of my productions, to my eye, *has* the organic centre succeeded in getting into proper position.
>
> Time after time, then, has the precious waistband or girdle, studded and buckled and placed for brave outward show, practically worked itself, and in spite of desperate remonstrance, or in other words essential counterplotting, to a point perilously near the knees — perilously I mean for the freedom of these parts. In several of my compositions this displacement has so succeeded, at the crisis, in defying and resisting me, has appeared so fraught with probable dishonour, that I still turn upon them, in spite of the greater or less success of final dissimulation, a rueful and wondering eye. These productions have in fact, if I may be so bold about it, specious and spurious centres altogether, to make up for the failure of the true (I, xii).

It seems that James sets out, over and over again, to build the "hour glass" structure, as E.M. Forster called it, of *The Ambassadors*.[45] His story must be all hourglass or it is nothing.

That James's systematic, binary form should stand here for "freedom" over against "disgrace . . . displacement . . . dishonour" argues that it derives directly from his primary concerns. A subsequent remark in his confession of off-center centers indicates how: "The first half of a fiction," James continues, "insists ever on figuring to me as the stage or theatre for the second half, and I have in general given so much space to making the theatre propitious that my halves have too often proved strangely unequal" (I, xiii). Evidently binary form has directly to do with the James theater, with his social and sexual aesthetes' ordeal of self-consciousness, their autonomy or being-unto-self on the one hand and, on the other, their being-for-the-other and loss of freedom.

Suppose we enumerate again the main possibilities of the Jamesian scenario. According to this the hero will, in his quest for identity and honor, inevitably risk a failure of identity and dishonor; and insofar as he has his failure proved against him he will vow himself to, that is to say predict for himself, another go, a consummate reiteration of his quest that will both annul and complete his first go. To put this situation another way, if and when he does have failure proved against him, he will die of shame-shock; in which event his reaction may well be an extraordinary case of consistency understood as a form of the second go or as a kind of psychological system. Alternatively, the hero's fear of dying of shame or of his having already died of shame will give rise in him to the sense — either premature or posthumous — of his own ghostliness; unappeasable and peregrine, this ghost will haunt and try for life even though it can succeed only in living factitiously. Alternatively, the Jamesian acolyte hero may find that he has been no more than exoterically initiated into masterful selfhood, and he may now dedicate himself in secret to his rage for mastery. Again, James's hero will find that he has either maneuvered himself or been maneuvered into a false position — he is not who he thinks he is, he lives and has lived a lie; subsequently, he either duplicates his unwitting duplicity by "consummately masking the fault and conferring on the false quantity the brave appearance of the true" (*The Tragic Muse,* I, xiii), or he ambiguously gives the lie to the adversary who has impugned him. Yet again, the quester may well find that his first go has been double- as well as ghost-haunted; consequently, any second go at authentic selfhood must both invoke (perhaps as a self-punishment) and defeat this double, must in fact be a thorough redoubling or reduplication as well as a reiteration. Finally, as James himself implies in the preface to *The Tragic Muse,* his social aesthete or debutante heroine will find that they have entered a theater of self-consciousness in which they are liable to be seriously shame-wounded or disfigured, and in which they must therefore "figure" if they are to survive.

Given these possibilities, it is not difficult to see why they should come regularly to be expressed in binary form. If the Jamesian hero's quest for identity and honor implies another or a second go, then his story may very well take a one-two form. Insofar as this hero quests compulsively for being-unto-self, then his story may well turn into a fiction system that is by definition supremely unto itself. Of course I am not saying here that James's fiction itself is necessarily compulsive (although in specific cases like *The American* or *The Spoils of Poynton* it appears to be so). I am saying that the element of compulsion in his characters is generally acknowledged, morally evaluated, and then "admitted as much" in creative form.

Moreover, since the compulsion associated with the Jamesian quest for identity is the compulsion to conceal, the Jamesian halves are liable to stand in an anomalous as well as systematic relation to each other. Formally speaking, the second half of any of James's binary systems will, in appearing by episodes, images or whatever to tell the first half's story over again, also appear correspondingly redundant, as much a static irony as a narrative development. It is conspicuously redundant, not only in its being a reiteration as such but also in its eliciting in the reader — by virtue of its redundancy, its insubordination, its ornamentalism — a sense of its being somehow more than it appears. The self-concealment of the exposed James hero has become the open secret of an ironic, discretionary form.

As a remarkable double Pandora situation, "The Aspern Papers" suggests itself here as a model of James's form. The first "half" of this story reveals yet another Jamesian hero who fears that he has never really lived, and who as a consequence seeks a kind of extension in the vital past. If he can only make his "life continuous, in a fashion, with the illustrious life" (306) of the Byronic Jeffrey Aspern (who sounds very like a successful Roderick Hudson), then he can prove to himself that he really exists. It is a Jamesian acolyte's quest for mastery or, in this case, godhead.

Of course the quest to *be* the past master can but be failure-haunted. Hence, it would seem, the acolyte's extraordinary, post-humous prurience: not only would he commune with his vital god through his relics, he would violate this god for being a goad to him in his own nonentity. It is as if his attempt to exhume the past were, in spirit, a way of humiliating and conclusively mastering it—always towards the end of proving himself comparatively alive. It is this vicious impulse in him that Juliana Bordereau tries to forestall when she gives him her "extraordinary eyes" (362) for his prurient eye during the fiasco of his first go at the Aspern papers. As we are told after his Pandora's death from shock, "She had an idea that when people want to publish they are capable . . . 'Of violating a tomb' " (374-375).

But it needs a second "half" or rehearsal fully to reveal the "back" of this hero's problem. It turns out here that behind his ambivalent cultivation of the past lies an ambivalent attitude towards the present. Not only does he fear he has never really lived, he also fears ever really living. It is precisely because he fears ever to "let go" that he has dedicated himself to knowing the secrets of the Aspern love letters. That he is this professional Epimetheus is proved when Juliana's niece Miss Tita emerges from the past in a timid effort to live in the flesh and blood. Miss Tita, ironic thanks to himself, is a second, a debutante Pandora; she would offer him a portrait of the godly Aspern—exactly as Juliana Bordereau has done in the first half—a portrait, what is more, that suggests to him a sexually masterful other self, a Byronic Roderick Hudson who is "free and general and not at all afraid" (311). And should he accept this offer and in turn offer to take up another role, she would offer him a further right: access to the box of Aspern papers. These papers are no less than her dowry—just as another, now deceased Pandora, has intended.

As if overwhelmed by Maenads on all sides, back as well as front, the hero bolts for shame. The re-vitalizing god has turned out to be a mocking goad: "He seemed to smile at me with friendly mockery, as if he were amused at my case. I had got into a pickle for him—as if he needed it! He was unsatisfactory, for the only moment since I had known him" (372). Eventually, however, cued by "the terrible *condottiere* who sits so sturdily astride of his huge bronze horse" (378), he swings from agonized self-rejection back to the will to mastery that is the other extreme of his chronic emotional cycle. Seized overnight by "a passionate appreciation of Miss Bordereau's papers" (380), he actually nerves himself for a second go at the Aspern papers; with this Epimetheus it is more than ever a matter of the box, and nothing but the box. After all, the problem for this hero who fears ever to let himself go is that he cannot forfeit the box any more than he can bear to be "boxed." Accordingly he ends in a kind of hell of chagrin, a false position only half-relieved by Miss Tita's arson and remarkable forgiveness. Just as he will always be both initiated into and precluded from "esoteric knowledge" (306), so will he be compelled always to "know."

We have already touched on the binary form of *Roderick Hudson, The Bostonians, The Portrait of a Lady,* and *The Princess Casamassima,* and we shall meet it again later when discussing the even more stylized major phase novels. In the meantime I want to take *The Spoils of Poynton* as an example of the most important of the exceptions to the Jamesian rule, the so-called "dramatic" novels of the nineties, and show how even these are only apparent exceptions. James of course wrote *The Spoils* just after his experience in the theater, which seems to have been so much a means of keeping in touch with London life as to make him reluctant to take any artistic risks.[46] In these circumstances, it is natural that criticism should read the novel (which James himself originally conceived in "three chapters, like three little acts"[47]) as a dramatic narrative. Walter J. Isle, for instance, has argued that although it does not hold to James's original conception, it nevertheless has an essentially dramatic, four-phase movement (five, including a kind of epilogue). According to this argument the first of these phases includes the opening six chapters, which set the scenes at Waterbath, London, Poynton, and Ricks and establish the conflict among the characters over the old things. This first phase, which concluded with Fleda's encountering the adored but already committed Owen in London, corresponds to "the exposition in a play."[48]

The second phase of the novel, Isle argues, includes Chapters VII-XII, all of which are set at Ricks. In this phase, the fate of the old things becomes more and more Fleda's moral problem. Having arrived at Ricks (that community of exoteric initiates) to find that Mrs. Gereth has despoiled Poynton, Fleda is torn between her loyalty to Mrs. Gereth and her acolyte's love for the now openly ardent Owen, a conflict that results in her honorable lie to the former about Owen's love for her. This so-called second phase ends with the renunciatory Fleda characteristically waiting for something to happen. When urged by Mrs. Gereth to act positively towards Owen, she can only flee back to London.

The remainder of the novel, Isle argues, "it is tempting to see . . . as a third act, the resolution of the action" were it not that "it would be disproportionately long, as long as the first two acts combined."⁴⁹ In the face of this obstacle to his "dramatic" argument, Isle divides the remainder of the novel into two smaller phases approximately equal in length to each of the first two sections, Chapters XIII-XVI, and Chapters XVII-XX. (The final two chapters form an epilogue outside the main action.) Each of these phases follows a pattern of three chapters set in London followed by a chapter in which Fleda visits her sister Maggie. The whole of the third phase is devoted to developing Fleda's distressed but consistently renunciatory relationship with Owen Gereth; no sooner does she avow her own love for the latter than she binds him to Mona Brigstock. A fourth phase is concerned with Fleda's relationship with Mrs. Gereth, with the latter's daring return of the spoils to Poynton, and with Mona's taking advantage of Fleda's scrupulosity and Owen's weakness; at the end of this section, Fleda and Mrs. Gereth are presented in a state of collapse after hearing the news of Owen's marriage to Mona. The novel's last two chapters—Fleda's return to Ricks and visit to Poynton—may be seen as an epilogue. Isle would argue that the last chapter in particular stands "in a sense outside the movement of the book; the action is complete, and order has been restored in the preceding chapter."⁵⁰ At the same time, he believes, this almost anomalous epilogue fulfills our expectations of the action; witnessing the fire, Fleda "experiences once again her sacrifices and all the pain with them."⁵¹

Isle's analysis quite correctly moves from a consideration of the theater's influence on its form to a sense of its emotional and moral form ("The basic form . . . is essentially a form of sacrifice, a 'tragedy of renunciation'. "⁵²). But this kind of analysis is, I believe, limited by its "dramatic" assumption, however justified this may seem. If James is writing during the nineties with his reactive theatrical system, he still remains the builder of binary, ornamental systems. In other words, *The Spoils of Poynton* can also be seen as falling naturally into two parts, Chapters I-XII (its so-called first and second phases) and Chapters XIII-the end (its third and fourth phases together with the epilogue). These are the customary Jamesian halves (Isle himself notes that his first two phases "comprise only a little over half the novel"⁵³) with their characteristic misplaced center. The first half presents Fleda's first go, her recognition of her chance of possessing both Owen and Poynton and of thereby finding a place in life, and her subsequent renunciation of this chance on seeing that such a place in life (as distinguished from a priesthood) would constitute a false position. This first half concludes on a pyrrhic note, with Fleda's holding herself to her renunciation by holding Owen to his vows to Mona, and with her return to London. The second half sees a corresponding second go, a reiteration of Fleda's struggles that amounts, to James's conscious mind, to an heroic martydom, but that also represents an unacknowledged reaction on his part. In London again, and with another chance of Owen and Poynton as a result of Mona's postponement of the marriage, Fleda experiences exactly the same fantasy that she has had at the outset (Chapter 1: "she stared at . . . a future full of the things she particularly loved"): "Fleda lost herself in the rich fancy of how, if *she* were mistress of Poynton . . . " (129). The remainder of this second half sees Fleda re-experiencing the false temptations of the first half, as well as reaffirming her renunciation of Owen after the latter actually proposes. Finally, this half sees her on the way highmindedly to despoil Poynton, partly at the behest of Owen, but chiefly on account of her inability to bear with her pyrrhic self-sacrifice. Far from being a detached epilogue, the open secret of this conclusion consummates this second half's ambiguous second go.

In order to round out the notion of binary system in James, we need a case of it in the process of coming into being. By far the best example of this would be *The Sacred Fount,* the subject of which might almost be the compulsion to create Jamesian binary systems. The hero here is a familiar one, a tantalized probationer standing on the hither side of "secret society": "These things — the way other people could feel about each other, the power not one's self, in the given instance, that made for passion — were of course at best the mystery of mysteries" (15). "It would have been almost as embarrassing to have to tell them how little experience I had had in fact as to have had to tell them how much I had had in fancy" (80). "It was none of my business; how little was anything, when it came to that, my business!" (87). "I think the imagination, in those halls of art and fortune, was almost inevitably accounted a poor matter; the whole place and its participants abounded so in pleasantness and picture, in all the felicities, for every sense, taken for granted there by the very basis of life, that even the sense most finely poetic, aspiring to extract the moral, could scarce have helped feeling itself treated to something of the snub that affects — when it does affect — the uninvited reporter in whose face a door is closed" (123). And, as such, he rages to know. In spite of his both reminding himself and being advised to renounce his distasteful scandal-mongering, this hero *will* know the *"Intimissima"* (28).

So preposterously does he pretend to initiate knowledge that he can imagine himself as an "effective omniscience" (134) or a "providence" (134, 138). "I alone," crows this would-be esotericist, "was magnificently and absurdly aware—everyone else was benightedly out of it" (139); "I wanted her [Grace Brissenden's] perplexity—the proper sharp dose of it—to result both from her knowing and her not knowing sufficiently what I meant" (197). By the end of the story he *is* by virtue of his secret knowledge or he is *nothing*: "And I could only say to myself that this was the price—the price of the secret success, the lonely liberty and the intellectual joy. There were things that for so private and splendid a revel—that of the exclusive king with his Wagner opera—I could only let go . . . I was there to save my priceless pearl of an inquiry and to harden, to that end, my heart" (230-231). By this stage, indeed, he might be a prototype of that later aesthete and reactionary, Prince Amerigo, who likewise adorns himself with the spoils of identity: "It had all been just in order that his—well, what on earth should he call it but his freedom?—should at present be as perfect and rounded and lustrous as some huge precious pearl . . . the pearl dropped itself, with its exquisite quality and rarity, straight into his hand. Here precisely it was, incarnate" (I, 321).

But what is it that the hero knows? Although he cannot be directly initiated into the social and sexual life of Newmarch, he can nevertheless know its appearances and outward forms. As a might-have-been he can invent a theory of sacred identity:

> "One of the pair," I said, "has to pay for the other. What ensues is a miracle, and miracles are expensive. What's a greater one than to have your youth twice over? It's a second wind, another 'go'—which isn't the sort of thing life mostly treats us to. Mrs. Briss had to get her new blood, her extra allowance of time and bloom, somewhere; and from whom could she so conveniently extract them as from Guy himself? She *has*, by an extraordinary feat of legerdemain, extracted them; and he, on his side, to supply her, has had to tap the sacred fount. But the sacred fount is like the greedy man's description of the turkey as an 'awkward' dinner dish. It may be sometimes too much for a single share, but it's not enough to go round" (24).

The so-called vampirism of this "apologue or . . . parable" (24) might be better described as an economy or, better still, compensation system of identity or honor (the "sacred" in James). According to this, it is of the mysterious nature of things that there is either a surplus or a deficiency of identity. And any surplus is compensatory, "a second wind, another go," a quantity always relative to a first go or depletion or failure; sacred fount cases are, one might say, most extraordinary one-two or binary affairs. Further, such transactions are liable to be ironic or cyclic or merely reversible. Indeed, the sacred fount is at best a figure for the ambiguities of the shame and honor plane of experience, a purely psychosocial plane, and at worst a figure for the Jamesian revenge cycle. No authentic or intrinsically valuable transcendence — namely the superior plane of love that emerges in James's subsequent novels — is implied by the sacredness of this fount. The only freedom involved is the false, "aesthetic" one that has compelled the hero to create his scenario in the first place.[54]

A compensation system, then, is all that the hero knows, for it compensates him to know that others should be involved in compensation cycles. Managing to defame even the ambiguous life of Newmarch, he knows that completion always covers depletion (and vice versa). If Grace Brissenden blooms as "a most extraordinary case — such as one really has never met" (9), it must be as a second go at the expense of the blighted poor Briss, that most extraordinary case in reverse. The hero might even be parodying here James's own feeling for the feeling of having a "back":[55]

> I seemed perpetually, at Newmarch, to be taking his [Brissenden's] measure from behind.
>
> Ford Obert has since told me that when I came back to him there were tears in my eyes, and I didn't know at the moment how much the words with which he met me took for granted my consciousness of them. "He looks a hundred years old!"
>
> "Oh, but you should see his shoulders, always, as he goes off! *Two* centuries — ten! Isn't it amazing?" (178).

And, if Gilbert Long blooms most extraordinarily, then his bloom likewise must constitute another go at the expense of the blighting of May Server. The hero knows the latter's deficiency in the same way that he knows Brissenden's back:

> She was absolutely on my hands with her secret . . . But if, though only nearer to her secret and still not in possession, I felt as justified as I have already described myself, so it equally came to me that I was quite near

enough, at the pass we had reached, for what I should have to take from it all . . . Beautiful, abysmal, involuntary, her exquisite weakness simply opened up the depths it would have closed . . . I saw as I had never seen before what consuming passion can make of the marked mortal on whom, with fixed beak and claws, it has settled as on a prey. She reminded me of a sponge wrung dry and with fine pores agape. Voided and scraped of every- thing, her shell was merely crushable. So it was brought home to me that the victim could be abased, and so it disengaged itself from these things that the abasement could be conscious. That was Mrs. Server's tragedy, that her consciousness survived — survived with a force that made it struggle and dissemble. This consciousness was all her secret — it was at any rate all mine (105-107).

Raging for compensation, the hero has inflicted a binary system upon the Brissenden marriage and then, as a further compensation for this inevitably insufficient compensation, a liaison between Gilbert Long and May Server. He thus rehearses the social structure of the familiar Jamesian international situation, in which a cabal springs up and coexists alongside a marriage that represents manifest society.[56] But now these cycles must in turn match each other, even as a first and a second or reflex go match one another. There must also exist — it is the obsessive compensator's logic — a "dim community" (133), perhaps even a conspiracy, between both the extraordinarily complete Grace Brissenden and Gilbert Long and between the extraordinarily depleted poor Briss and May Server. The result is a binary system built of binary sub-systems: "These opposed couples balanced like bronze groups at the two ends of a chimney-piece, and the most I could say to myself in lucid deprecation of my thought was that I mustn't take them equally for granted merely *because* they balanced. Things in the real had a way of not balancing; it was all an affair, this fine symmetry, of artificial proportion. Yet even while I kept my eyes away from Mrs. Briss and Long it was vivid to me that, 'composing' there beautifully, they could scarce help playing a part in my exhibition" (143).

Possessed of the knowledge of this dim community — it is the James- ian misplaced half-way mark — the hero is convinced that he exists. Certainly he will never be better than this. Since, however, he has all along occupied a false position, it must turn out that, even as he con- summates his system, he invites an awkward exposure, "the peril of . . . public ugliness" (139). In fact, one wonders whether his preposterous "wizardry" (101) is not a half-conscious invocation of the fatal criticism of the real thing, for how else than by means of a perverse and punishable vainglory should so precluded a hero relate to "secret society"? The system he builds against the knowledge of his unreality also amounts to a welcoming acknowledgment of this truth. To put this situation in another way: like other James heroes he lives so systematically as to deny any recessed and shocking double, but he also lives so as effectively to elicit, if not this double exactly, then at least an account of affairs at Newmarch that will rival his own. Like Strether in his tale of Paris, he both dreads and invites a "smash" at the hands of life.

But ultimately this view of *The Sacred Fount's* second half can be only a speculative one, for even though Grace Brissenden's account of things thoroughly ironizes the hero's, it appears to be too defensive or even reactive, too much a matter of "her tone" (249), to be the real thing that will unequivocally give his pretensions the lie. James, presumably, can guarantee nothing in *The Sacred Fount*. Indeed, the second half culminating in Grace Brissenden's counter-statement may only be another, compensatory go at reality, a reflex of the hero's first go. And insofar as this is so, the novel itself has a kind of ornamental sacred fount form: "It may be sometimes too much for a single share, but it's not enough to go round." Formally speaking, *The Sacred Fount* takes after its light ornamental hero, who tells us at the very end that he "*should* certainly never again, on the spot, quite hang together, even though it wasn't really that I hadn't three times her method. What I too fatally lacked was her tone" (249).

III. Child-Cult and Others

I now abandon my specialized feelings because I am trying to find better ones, so I must balance myself for the moment by imagining the feelings of the simple person. He may be in a better state than I am by luck, freshness, or divine grace; value is outside any scheme for the measurement of value because that too must be valued.

William Empson, *Some Versions of Pastoral*

Was it after all a joke that he should be serious about anything?

James, *The Ambassadors*

I have been very much gratified and very much hurt by your Letters in the Oxford Paper: because independent of that unlawful and mortal feeling of pleasure at praise, there is a glory in enthusiasm; and because the world is malignant enough to chuckle at the most honorable Simplicity. Yes on my Soul my dear Bailey you are too simple for the World — and that Idea makes me sick of it — How is it that by extreme opposites we have as it were got discontented nerves — you have all your Life (I think so) believed every Body — I have suspected every Body — and although you have been so deceived you make a simple appeal — the world has something else to do, and I am glad of it — were it in my choice I would reject a petrarchal coronation — on account of my dying day, and because women have Cancers. I should not by rights speak in this tone to you — for it is an incendiary spirit that would do so. Yet I am not old enough or magnanimous enough to annihilate self — and it would perhaps be paying you an ill compliment.

Keats, *Letters*

At the outset of the story of Maisie Farange's exposure, there occurs an epochal, "a great date" (15). Maisie, who is being prepared by her newly divorced mother for a rebound to her father's new establishment, finds herself being instructed to tell the latter "that he lies and he knows he lies" (17). Too innocent yet to be able to evaluate the situation, she asks her governess Miss Overmore whether her father does in fact know he lies, and whether she is really to tell him so. Her innocence, it happens, catches Miss Overmore out in a false position, for the latter has already begun to seduce her charge's papa. Maisie is met, therefore, with an equivocation: "It was then that her companion addressed her in the unmistakable language of a pair of eyes of deep dark grey. 'I can't say No,' they replied as distinctly as possible; 'I can't say No, because I'm afraid of your mama, don't you see? Yet how can I say Yes after your papa has been so kind to me, talking to me so long the other day, smiling and flashing his beautiful teeth at me the time we met him in the Park?' " (17). Thus Maisie is initiated into a secret, the knowledge of a relationship that, evidently, requires concealment.

This initiation, however, is not a simple but a complex one. Since Maisie obviously cannot know the social and erotic substance of the adults' situation, she can know only the form or appearance of it. She can know only indirectly, as a Jamesian exoteric initiate knows. "It gave her often an odd air of being present at her history in as separate a manner as if she could only get at experience by flattening her nose against a pane of glass" (97). "How and when and where, however, were just what Maisie was not to know—an exclusion, moreover, that she never questioned in the light of a participation large enough to make him [Sir Claude] . . . shine in her yearning eye like the single, the sovereign window-square of a great dim disproportioned room" (144). "It was in the nature of things to be none of a small child's business, even when a small child had from the first been deluded into a fear that she might be only too much initiated" (146). Standing in this manner on the hither exposed side of the truth, Maisie is potentially in a false position. At best she stands on the outside-inside of established adult norms, at worst outside and therefore "below" them.

Sensing her exposure, Maisie reacts. Being merely for-the-other, she grows correspondingly aware of her being-unto-self: "on which a new remedy rose . . . the idea of an inner self or, in other words, of concealment" (15). More than this, the episode with Miss Overmore sows in her "the seeds of secrecy" (15). In the face of adult intentionality Maisie even develops her own knowledge or secret—her joke, James might have said: "She puzzled out with imperfect signs, but with a prodigious spirit, that she had been a centre of hatred and a messenger of insult, and that everything was bad because she had been employed to make it so. Her parted lips locked themselves with a determination to be employed no longer. She would forget everything, she would repeat nothing, and when, as a tribute to the successful application of her system, she began to be called a little idiot, she tasted a pleasure new and keen" (15).

So far Maisie is the familiar Jamesian exoteric initiate in a comparatively naive, child form. Yet Maisie turns out to be atypical in an important, perhaps revolutionary way. In her the phases of reaction to exposure are transvalued pari passu by "prodigious spirit," as James calls it here. Maisie's prodigiously spiritual knowing actually constitutes a remarkable renunciation of all part, passive or active, in "knowing," in the "rights of resentment" cycle that might otherwise have been associated with her lowly status. It places her decisively above her situation. If "she saw more and more" (15), it is to be both less and genuinely more.

The point is that with *Maisie* (much more successfully than with *The Spoils of Poynton*) James's exoteric initiate begins to be accorded a spiritual superiority that entirely makes over his or her inferiority. Maisie and her successors Nanda Brookenham, Strether, and Milly Theale still occupy James's international-interstitial ground but, in comparison with Isabel Archer and Fleda Vetch, they are more authentically "true" than the bitter truth of their tasting full selfhood only to be precluded from it. Maisie's identity, at least, is far from being confined to a psychosocial plane of experience, the ironic, sacred fount plane on which the James hero either acquires honor or commits himself to a revenge cycle. Indeed, while psychosocial insufficiency is her complex fate, she shows that the psychosocial plane itself is relatively insufficient, that identity and honor are not available purely on their own terms, are too much the other aspect of shame and dishonor to be so. In other words, Maisie's story discovers a further, higher plane of experience, that of prodigious spirit or love. James, who on the evidence of *The Spoils* might have seemed to be running out of love, discovers more love.

[*130*]

In a sense, then, Maisie is two exoteric initiates at once. She might have been a little nineteenth century girl lost — she is "below"; she is a "poor little monkey" (5); she is prematurely exposed. Equally, she might have been "above" in all the good faith of a nineteenth century angel in the house. She is James's "ironic centre" doomed to a first and then to a second go:

> Whereas each of these persons had at first vindictively decided to keep it from the other, so at present the re-married relative sought now rather to be rid of it — that is, to leave it as much as possible, and beyond the appointed times and seasons, on the hands of the adversary; which mal-practice, resented by the latter as bad faith, would of course be repaid and avenged by an equal treachery. The wretched infant was thus to find itself practically disowned, rebounding from racquet to racquet like a tennis-ball or shuttlecock . . . The child seen as creating by the fact of its forlornness a relation between its step-parents, the more intimate the better, dramatic-ally speaking . . . the child becoming a centre and pretext for a fresh system of misbehaviour, a system, moreover, of a nature to spread and ramify: *there* would be the "full" irony (v-viii).

But, equally, she functions as a kind of pastoral center with but one foot in this world:

> not only the extraordinary "ironic centre" . . . she has the wonderful impor-tance of shedding a light far beyond any reach of her comprehension; of lending to poorer persons and things, by the mere fact of their being involved with her and by the special scale she creates for them, a precious element of dignity. I lose myself, truly, in appreciation of my theme on noting what she does by her "freshness" for appearances in themselves vul-gar and empty enough. They become, as she deals with them, the stuff of poetry and tragedy and art (xiii).

In short Maisie, exoterically initiated twice over, becomes a Jamesian divine fool.

But insofar as Maisie is this, she must also meet the problem that has always obtained with divine foolishness. Even though the divine fool can scarcely be said to live in "normal" terms, he must nevertheless live and claim community with "normal" persons. He would *be* by being "other," if not "other almost anyhow." However, his standing simul-taneously above and below while yet claiming community with the establishmentarian now involves the divine fool in catching the latter in a kind of pincer and making him aware of both front and back. His foolery, awkwardly allied as it is with his being too good to be true, proves to be a source of acute discomfiture; the establishmentarian has no sooner considered himself the natural superior of the fool than he is shown up as being a spiritual inferior. But then his being too good to be true on the basis of his weakness now grotesquely re-embarrasses the establishmentarian; the latter recognizes not only that he himself is inferior but also that he falls below someone who has clearly been his inferior — indeed inferior to the point of being stigmatized. In other words, that twice-over exoteric initiate, the divine fool, twice over excludes the establishmentarian from his cherished self-conception. He might be a kind of reproachful arena or theater in which the normal man is momentarily shown up as an impostor. Not surprisingly, then, his claim to community is met with equivocation and the lie and, as a last disembarrassment, with his expulsion. "People could put up with being bitten by a wolf but what properly riled them was a bite from a sheep" (*Ulysses*).

How to break this tragic "imitation of Christ"/*ressentiment* cycle? How to be free? The later James answers paradoxically: just when it seems most open to his civil alien of the ardent good faith to pursue and claim a place, an esoteric initiation, or what might be called a "pastoral of happiness,"[1] he must sacrifice all chance of doing so. His pastoral vision of community must be renounced for the pastoral vision of prodigious spirit. Rather than asking as a complex man for a simple fate, he should simply accept his complex fate. In so doing James's renunciatory exemplar reaffirms true pastoral vision, which puts "the complex into the simple" (Empson) but which is nevertheless properly adhered to only when it is subsequently determined to put the simple, the prodigiously spiritual, back into the complex.[2] On the other hand, were he not to abstain he would be inconsistent with his being at once below and above and therefore outside. He would be aggravating an apostasy from true selfhood, perhaps suicidally taking revenge upon himself both for his original insufficiency and for the mistaken claim based upon this insufficiency.

Another of the great dates in Maisie's life will bring out both the problem of the divine fool in *Maisie* and something of James's answer to it. This occurs at the end of Maisie's first go (and the novel's first half), when she finally forfeits all claim to her parents and finds herself handed down to stepparents. By this time of course her father's presence (not to speak of his absences) has become an outright fraud. Now, in order to cover his supreme imposture — his desertion of his child in the name of conscientious parenthood — he lies to Maisie; he tells her that he is going to America with his so-called American countess. In the event, however, it proves awkward to lie to a child who can embarrass him as a pitiably poor monkey, and who then re-embarrasses him by virtue of her good faith. Accordingly, the fraud must lie twice over: once to the gullible victim in her, and once again to the "divine" child. Speaking with two voices, a false shepherd insinuating the complex into the simple, he tries to induce the divine fool to enter forgivingly into the spirit of her own exposure at his hands:

> "Do you mean to say you'd really come with me? . . . That's a way, my dear, of saying, 'No, thank you!' You know you don't want to go the least little mite. You can't humbug *me!*" Beale Farange laid down . . . "Your mother will never again have any more to do with you . . . Therefore of course I'm your natural protector and you've a right to get everything out of me you can. Now's your chance, you know — you won't be half-clever if you don't. You can't say I don't put it before you — you can't say I ain't kind to you or that I don't play fair. Mind you never say that, you know — it *would* bring me down on you. I know what's proper. I'll take you again, just as I *have* taken you again and again" (166-167).

But if Beale Farange lies and knows he lies, his daughter knows and knows she knows. In the first place she knows as James's ironic center. Once again she is to be ambiguously tormented as the instrument of her parents' revenge cycle: "Wasn't he trying to turn the tables on her, embarrass her somehow into admitting that what would really suit her little book would be, after doing so much for good manners, to leave her wholly at liberty to arrange for herself?" (167). What she knows therefore is prematurely differentiated selfhood: "it rolled over her that this was their parting, their parting for ever" (167). At the same time, however, the dupe and fool knows divinely, not resentfully — just as her pseudo-pastoral guardian has calculated: "To give something, to give here on the spot, was all her own desire . . . She was ready, in this interest, for an immense surrender" (163). Maisie will go quietly. She will surrender her right, which still appears to be worth something, to give her father the lie. That is, she renounces her claim to the truth and therefore to community. To do otherwise in the circumstances would only further falsify the already false.

Yet Maisie the ironic center knows one other thing. All but chucked, she nevertheless retains one secret as the basis of survival and a second go. She surrenders to her father "everything but Sir Claude . . . everything but Mrs. Beale. The immensity didn't include *them*" (163). Her retention of this knowledge, however, and thus of her poor monkey's sufficiency in the face of her father's fraud, only has the effect of goading Beale to further cruelty. After all, for Maisie to lay claim to Sir Claude means that his hated wife's lover will displace him and so give the lie to his own pretensions. Even more embarrassing, however, is Maisie's loving clemency. Against her father's suggestion, she asserts that no irregularity in Sir Claude's relationship with Mrs. Beale can " 'prevent them from loving me. They love me tremendously.' Maisie turned crimson to hear herself" (169).

Embarrassed and then grotesquely re-embarrassed, Beale Farange responds with feline and comprehensive cruelty that appears less ugly than it is only on account of Maisie's undaunted good faith:

Her companion fumbled; almost any one — let alone a daughter — would have seen how conscientious he wanted to be. "I daresay. But do you know why?" He braved her eyes and added: "You're a jolly good pretext."

"For what?" Maisie asked.

"Why, for their game, I needn't tell you what that is."

The child reflected. "Well, then, that's all the more reason."

"Reason for what, pray?"

"For their being kind to me."

"And for your keeping in with them?" Beale roared again; it was as if his spirits rose and rose. "Do you realize, pray, that in saying that you're a monster?"

She turned it over. "A monster?"

"They've *made* one of you. Upon my honour it's quite awful. It shows the kind of people they are. Don't you understand," Beale pursued, "that when they've made you as horrid as they can — as horrid as themselves — they'll just simply chuck you?"

She had at this a flicker of passion. "They *won't* chuck me!"

"I beg your pardon," her father courteously insisted; "it's my duty to put it before you. I shouldn't forgive myself if I didn't point out to you that they'll cease to require you." He spoke as if with an appeal to her intelligence that she must be ashamed not adequately to meet (169-170).

It is the poor monkey's "divinity" that has proved too much for the fraudulent parent. Totally exposed before it, he retaliates by desecrating her good faith. He revengefully "knows" her stepparents, gives her faith the lie, and thus ensures that he will ghost any second go on her part. Finally he consummates the injury he has dealt out with insult: the highest term of his damnable sacrifice of his daughter is his latest mistress' "no end of money" (171). For these pains he suffers the conclusive embarrassment of the divine fool's absolutely refusing to give him up, far less repudiate him in her turn by giving him the lie.

The problem of the Jamesian divine fool emerges still more clearly in the matching scenes at the end of the novel's second half, when society's moratorium on Maisie's exposure is at last up ("*Et vos billets?—vous n'avez que le temps . . . Ah vous n'avez plus le temps!*" 305-306). As her false father has foretold, Maisie eventually finds herself for the chucking by her stepparents. And, as before, the chucking—the shocking—of the poor monkey commences with a lie; Sir Claude, who has allowed himself to be maneuvered into an awkward position between Mrs. Wix and Mrs. Beale, lies and knows he lies when he implies that he is not living with Mrs. Beale at Boulogne. It is soon after this cue that Maisie realizes the full extent of her exposure:

> "She *is* your mother now, Mrs. Beale, by what has happened, and I, in the same way, I'm your father. No one can contradict that, and we can't get out of it . . . Mrs. Wix is the obstacle; I mean, you know, if she has affected you. She has affected *me,* and yet here I am. I never was in such a tight place: please believe it's only that that makes me put it to you as I do. My dear child, isn't that—to put it so—just the way out of it? That came to me yesterday, in London, after Mrs. Beale had gone: I had the most infernal atrocious day. 'Go straight over and put it to her: let her choose, freely, her own self.' So I do, old girl—I put it to you. *Can* you choose freely?" . . . He smoked a minute, with his head thrown back, looking at the ceiling; then he said: "There's one thing to remember—I've a right to impress it on you: we stand absolutely in the place of your parents. It's their defection, their extraordinary baseness, that has made our responsibility. Never was a young person more directly committed and confided" (296-300).

Although shocked here into the knowledge of her complex fate, Maisie still cannot be shocked into reactive knowing. She has never been more the poor little monkey but, equally, she is never more "divine." "Now in truth she felt the coldness of her terror, and it seemed to her that suddenly she knew, as she knew it about Sir Claude, what she was afraid of. She was afraid of herself" (299). It is not so much that she fears for her chuckable self. What she does fear is her own failure to love and to offer the necessary earnest of this love ("I love Sir Claude — I love *him*," 318), that is, the sacrifice of her by now embarrassing claim to community with Sir Claude and Mrs. Beale. Not for her (any more than for Fleda Vetch) any pastoral of happiness like the one promised with kindness but without conviction by Sir Claude: "My idea would be a nice little place — somewhere in the South — where she and you would be together and as good as any one else. And I should be as good too, don't you see? for I shouldn't live with you, but I should be close to you — just round the corner, and it would be just the same. My idea would be that it would all be perfectly open and frank. *Honi soit qui mal y pense*, don't you know?" (296). To persist in her claim to this happiness would entail her being "other almost anyhow," other at the expense of truth as well as of an expulsion of Mrs. Wix in favor of Mrs. Beale.

Therefore, rather than protract a false position, Maisie renounces her claim upon community. She determines to disembarrass the establishmentarians of herself, even at the cost of momentarily embarrassing them. For her it must be a pastoral of prodigious if unhoused spirit. A case of what Erving Goffman calls "the embarrassment of limits" that characterizes social life, the poor monkey realizes that

> The stigmatized individual is asked to act so as to imply neither that his burden is heavy nor that bearing it has made him different from us; at the same time he must keep himself at that remove from us which ensures our painlessly being able to confirm this belief about him. Put differently, he is advised to reciprocate naturally with an acceptance of himself and us, an acceptance of himself that we have not quite extended him in the first place. A *phantom acceptance* is thus allowed to provide the base for a *phantom normalcy*.[3]

This is what Maisie lovingly and forgivingly knows, indeed divines.

James's biographer Leon Edel has argued very justifiably that, from the mid-nineties on, James was both reliving his career and rewriting his earlier novels; the children, pubescents, and adolescents of this nineties phase represent "an extensive personal allegory of the growing up of Henry James."[4] My own view, however, is that these are even more symbolic juveniles than Edel maintains. Morgan Moreen and Maisie and Nanda and Mamie Pocock have still more to do with the older James's inmost life-feeling, and specifically with a new acceptance of his anomalous social position ("The stranger who was for the most part saved from being inconveniently strange but by being inconveniently familiar," as *The Wings of the Dove* puts it with bitter blandness). It is as if James, faced at this time with the intractable irony of his complex fate, were temporarily retreating under cover of child characters to a state of comparative simplicity, thence to "come out" a second time and so re-encounter this complex fate. His making himself small, as it were, in the "low posture" of a child may even constitute an attitude of humility, a purification of motives, a truer restatement of the passion of the early pilgrimage. In James's life and career the child debutante is, hopefully, the moral father or shepherd-chaperon of a new man.

This is why the child Maisie is, as Edel says, only half "real."[5] Maisie is in large part a pastoral figment; and pastoral, whether shepherd-cult or child-cult, has never been altogether real. With Maisie, James is removing complex reality, all that precedes and then proceeds from shocks of recognition, into the realm of prodigious spirit. "Maisie," therefore, is a temporary state of freedom from cycle and irony. She is an embodiment of what will become in Strether, the divine fool whom she fathers, "the oddity of a double consciousness" whereby James can look both at his own complex fate from the perspective of his original and seemingly simple idealism and, simultaneously, at simplicity itself from the point of view of a man unexpectedly embarrassed by a complex fate. The relative or interim freedom of such a double consciousness provides auspices, as one might say, for another and more hopeful go. Indeed Maisie the child and lamb functions for James, as well as for the adults of her own story, as an extraordinary chaperon or shepherd. It is the sort of thing one says about the revolutionary child figures of "The Songs of Innocence."

But if it is true that "Maisie" is a state of being to which James retreats, it is also true finally that she is a state of being from which he must return. Like Isabel Archer, Maisie cannot escape for long into any pastoral of happiness; and the true value of her pastoralism is revealed only when her time is up and she goes out into the world. The same thing, I believe, may be said of her story as a whole in the context of James's second go. *What Maisie Knew* is the preliminary story, both initiative and initiation, that James had to write even as Blake, for example, wrote "The Songs of Innocence," or Patrick White the remarkable *The Aunt's Story*. The artist himself comes to the pastoral realm only for the time being, in order to clarify his purpose of doing the subsequent "work of my life."[6] Maisie is a stay in a great good place against the time when its author goes out into nearby, international theaters of exposure.

It is Maisie that fathers *The Ambassadors*, another story about a complex sense of differentness, of being at once valuable and discountable. If Maisie is a divine child, Strether is a fully fledged divine fool. Moreover, if Maisie prematurely undergoes the awkward age, Strether experiences his awkward age at an awkward age. Strether too is a valuable yet discountable hero who would claim community, who would be like any other person, who would *be* other, other almost anyhow. After a lifetime of falling short of doing all the usual human things, he might almost be welcoming the spring of his particular beast in the jungle: "*Would* there yet perhaps be time for reparation? — reparation, that is, for the injury done his character; for the affront, he is quite willing to say, so stupidly put upon it and in which he has even himself had so clumsy a hand?" (I, vi). That is to say, Strether stands open to welcome the other self who will promise to complete him — and who of course will compete with him eventually to deplete him. Lambert Strether stands to know what Maisie knows: that he can earn only a phantom normality on the basis of a phantom acceptance.

In Strether's case it requires the jostle of Europe, the force of unexpected criteria for life, to render self susceptible to its other. Thus right at the outset he realizes the extent of his "failure to enjoy" (I, 15) as he might otherwise have enjoyed. Later, as a novice in an overwhelming Paris, he has to acknowledge not only that he scarcely exists by Europe's criteria, but also that he scarcely passes on New England's. He has his claimant's front only to discover his apostate's back. Indeed Strether recognizes that he has lived only a posthumous, ghostly existence in America. He has lapsed from his marriage vows (a failure underscored by Waymarsh's marital situation); and he has never fulfilled a "vow taken in the course of the pilgrimage" to Europe, "a private pledge . . . to treat the occasion as a relation formed with the higher culture" (I, 75). He is, consequently, James's light ornamental man on the outside-inside of identity: "They [the spoils of his earlier pilgrimage] represented now the mere sallow paint on the door of the temple of taste that he had dreamed of raising up — a structure he had practically never carried further" (I, 76). Even on the provincial criteria established by the Newsomes and the Pococks, Strether has never been anything but insufficient on account of being too idealistic to be true. Has Lambert Strether ever really existed?

Unexpectedly falling between two stools, James's hero inevitably reacts. Since he may as well not have lived, he will put at risk his small capital of American identity and try for a better return on his money in Europe. Like his Tweedledee Waymarsh, he develops a "sacred rage" (I, 39) to *be* other. If he stands exposed and all-visible in the interstice, then by way of reparation he "now at all events *sees*" (I, vi). Strether would *see* where a Maisie knows in reaction to the feeling of being known about.

Of course, the more this claimant sees, the more he will be seen. And the more he is seen, the more he will need reactively to see. And so on. In other words, Strether enters a Jamesian compensation cycle according to which reaction reproduces itself in further or counter-reaction. If he sees from "one of the high sides of the old stony groove of the little rampart" (I, 15) at Chester, it is to be seen for a mere nobody of a Yankee. In turn, his forfeiture of American identity leads him to see at the theater with Maria Gostrey, that is to feel himself more visible, more "theatrical," than ever: "the figures and faces in the stalls were interchangeable with those on the stage . . . He had distracted drops in which he couldn't have said if it were actors or auditors who were most true" (I, 46). But if he is indeed an all too visible man, he will in turn prosecute and see the other that might have been. But this, by another turn of his compensation cycle, is to be seen by the potentially humiliating other: "There were 'movements' he was too late for: weren't they, with the fun of them, already spent? . . . If the playhouse wasn't closed his seat had at least fallen to somebody else. He had had an uneasy feeling the night before that if he was at the theater at all . . . he should have been there with, and as might have been said, *for* Chad" (I, 77-78). But if the hero does not live sufficiently, then he must once more renew his claim to *be* other. He rages to see from the point of view of the youth he would have been:

> There was youth in that, there was youth in the surrender to the balcony, there was youth for Strether at this moment in everything but his own business; and Chad's thus pronounced association with youth had given the next instant an extraordinary quick lift to the issue. The balcony, the distinguished front, testified suddenly, for Strether's fancy, to something

that was up and up; they placed the whole case materially, and as by an admirable image, on a level that he found himself at the end of another moment rejoicing to think he might reach. The young man looked at him still, he looked at the young man; and the issue, by a rapid process, was that this knowledge of a perched privacy appeared to him the last of luxuries. To him too the perched privacy was open (I, 86).

But, yet again, he sees from this new station of reaction only to feel overseen, as if caught out in a theater, or in "the most baited, the most gilded of traps" (I, 100).

At length Strether actually entertains his vital other in Chad Newsome. Always on account of the insufficiency that derives from his being too idealist to be true, he sees in the latter a miracle of young manhood, sees realized in him his ideal of a civilized marriage of life-styles: "What could there be in this for Strether but the hint of some self-respect, some sense of power, oddly perverted; something latent and beyond access, ominous and perhaps enviable? The intimation had the next thing, in a flash, taken on a name — a name on which our friend seized as he asked himself if he weren't perhaps really dealing with an irreducible young Pagan . . . Pagan — yes, that was, wasn't it? what Chad *would* logically be. It was what he must be. It was what he was" (I, 137-138). But of course the same turn of his reactionary cycle finds Strether utterly overturned. To have welcomed the other as he does, at the Comédie, is unexpectedly to find himself performing at the center of a theater of consciousness. Lambert Strether, not only Chad Newsome, has made an awkward debut. Indeed, exposed like "kings, queens, comedians and other such people" (I, 120), involuntarily seen, he asks whether "*he* carried himself like a fool. He didn't quite see how he could so feel as one without somehow showing as one" (I, 122).

And so on. At the same time, however, this latest of Jame's reactionaries is, so to speak, ex-Maisie. In Strether too the cycle of reaction to exposure is continually checked by prodigious spirit. Strether after all would see in terms of an imaginative idealism (or of an idealist imagination) that does not by definition allow him to compensate or to "take" (II, 253) in any ordinary sense. When one might have expected only a "rights of resentment" voyeurism of him, one finds as well an "amount of comedy" (II, 248), something like the artist's ethic of disinterested contemplation. Not of course that this imaginative idealism turns out to be any less problematic than his insufficiency. This hero of "rather too much" (II, 218) imagination inclines to see too much when he doesn't see too little; in his case imagination might be another, "good" word for insufficiency, since it is partly on its account that he has so tenuous a footing in the world. However one takes him, Strether remains out of it all, an exoteric initiate twice over who does not really live except in ironic or in pastoral terms. "He had at that time gathered them in, the explanations—he had stored them up; but it was at present as if he had either soared above or sunk below them—he couldn't tell which" (II, 12).

All the more urgent, then, his claim in Europe, where he is more out of it than ever, to community with the real live thing. It is the same with this divine fool as with Milly Theale: "If it established thus that they couldn't or wouldn't mix, why did Milly none the less feel through it a perverse quickening of the relation to which she had been in spite of herself appointed? What queerer consequence of their not mixing than their talking—for it was what they had arrived at—almost intimately?" (I, 144). And all the more awkward his impact upon the status quo. For being both "above" and "below," Strether imposes upon others, and particularly upon *the* other, "the oddity of a double consciousness" (I, 5). At one moment his social and sexual ignorance, embarrassingly allied as it is with his being "too good to be true" (II, 211), will show Chad Newsome up as being monstrous when he is in fact the successful lover of Mme de Vionnet. At another, his being too good to be true on the basis of his comprehensive ignorance has the effect of showing Chad up a second time round. The latter is made out to be a "miracle" (II, 270), the too-good-to-be-true self's too-good-to-be-true other, when he really is, and knows he is, "none the less only Chad" (II, 255), indeed when he has begun to react against his own false position in Europe by chucking his miracle-worker.

All told, Strether might be a kind of disturbing, lately come inquisitor. He brings about a fairly embarrassing, not to say provocative disestablishment of his other, the average sensual man. Not unnaturally, therefore, this other counterreacts. Just as Strether would deny his failure in life by claiming another self that would have been, so Chad now seeks to cover his potentially awkward barbarian's retreat from Europe by means of a deputy in Strether. *His* other, the yeastily reactive idealist Strether, will pass for himself with Mme de Vionnet even as he backslides from his exploit. "My idea—*voyons!*—is simply that you should let Madame de Vionnet know you, simply that you should consent to know her" (I, 206). As Maria Gostrey guesses, "you'll do . . . Why, for *them*—for *ces dames*. He [Chad] has watched you, studied you, liked you—and recognized that *they* must" (I, 165-166). At the very least, Strether as deputy will ease "the damnable terms of my sacrifice" (I, 207) of his mistress. In other words, Strether's awkward connection with his other develops into a version of the too-good-to-be-true/reactionary cycle that appears in *Maisie* (and, in still more tragic form, *The Wings of the Dove*). Strether too can be said to be something of a divine provocateur insofar as he pursues the ideal only to cause a negative, even conspiratorial counterreaction against it. The more he would be a truly civilized man, the more he seems merely to be a party to an embarrassing and embarrassed barbarian's liaison. It is the complex fate.

How to cleave unto the ideal? In James's ethic, we know, the answer is a paradox: a formal renunciation of the pursuit of the ideal. Even as it becomes open to the claimant Strether to compensate himself, to *see* and to *be* the other, he should give up all his chances of doing so. He should heed Waymarsh's advice absolutely to "quit this" (II, 173). The more he is initiated (with the other's complicity) into what might have been, the more determinedly should he remain the exoteric man. For him *not* to abstain will involve him in being increasingly false to his divine fool's nature, thus to visit fiasco upon himself and all concerned.

Yet for Strether to renounce at this point would be to short-circuit his story. The hero is not yet ready for formal renunciation because he has not yet run the course of his reaction. He does not even know yet that he has a choice of false positions. Perhaps one could say that he is not quite an ethical man because he is, necessarily, so much the "free" aesthetic man. On the other hand, this social and sexual aesthete is by no means an unethical man. Insofar as he suspects his falsity, he declines actively to disestablish the other even when offered the latter's establishment. He at least attempts to accommodate his claim to a life to his sense of the truth, namely that he is not fitted to live except as a kind of imaginative ghost.

The hobbled, two-steps-forward, one-step-backwards nature of Strether's progress is brought out clearly towards the end of the story's first half. Here, divinely yet pruriently as usual, he again *sees* the other only to overestimate him:

He had signed to the waiter that he wished to pay, and this transaction took some moments, during which he thoroughly felt . . . that Chad's higher spirit, his youth, his practice, his paganism, his felicity, his assurance, his impudence, whatever it might be, had consciously scored a success . . . "But is this lady against your interests at home?" Strether went on.

"Not directly, no doubt; but she's greatly in favour of them here."

"And what — 'here' — does she consider them to be?"

"Well, good relations!"

"With herself?"

"With herself."

"And what is it that makes them so good?" (I, 208-209).

And overestimates him so embarrassingly as to cause the latter to counterreact by maneuvering *his* other into his own place: "What? Well, that's exactly what you'll make out if you'll only go, as I'm supplicating you, to see her." In the same breath Strether characteristically underestimates Chad:

"Excuse me, but I must really — as I began by telling you — know where I am. Is she bad?"

" 'Bad'?" —Chad echoed it, but without a shock. "Is that what's implied — ?"

"When relations are good?" Strether felt a little silly, and was even conscious of a foolish laugh . . . What indeed was he talking about? His stare had relaxed; he looked now all round him. But something in him brought him back, though he still didn't know quite how to turn it. The two or three ways he thought of, and one of them in particular, were, even with scruples dismissed, too ugly. He none the less at last found something. "Is her life without reproach?" (I, 209).

And underestimates him so embarrassingly as to cause him to redouble his counterreactive persuasion:

"Absolutely without reproach. A beautiful life. *Allez donc voir!*"

These last words were, in the liberality of their confidence, so imperative that Strether went through no form of assent; but before they separated it had been confirmed that he should be picked up at a quarter to five (I, 210).

Strether *sees* the other that much more to *be* the other. From the time of his visiting Mme de Vionnet at Chad's instigation he is not only the passionate acolyte at the shrine of quintessential European things, but he may even be said to have become Mme de Vionnet's true lover.

At the same time, Strether has begun to live perceptibly beyond his divine fool's means. Although he may yearn to live like a pagan, especially from the moment when he encounters Mme de Vionnet in the Faubourg Saint Germain, nothing in his past life seems to have qualified him to do so. He may have his sacred rage; but what gives him "the right to the sacred rage" (II, 169)? No sooner then is Strether initiated into an unexpected consciousness of himself as Mme de Vionnet's true lover than he begins to renounce any claim of his own upon her. "There was something in her [Fleda Vetch] that would make it a shame to her forever to have owed her happiness to an interference." And as the earnest of this renunciatory determination, he undertakes to save Mme de Vionnet with Chad, her rightful lover. He himself is not fit for life, for all that he wants to live. Chad, let it be, then—who will live for him, who will effect on his behalf the ideal relation with a higher culture—"Let them face the future together!" (I, 252).

The first half of *The Ambassadors* has seen its hero foregoing an authentic life of his own in Europe ("he [Waymarsh] thinks that *I've* a life of my own. And I haven't!" I, 236), yet nonetheless claiming an extension, a second go, a vicarious life. As usual in James, however, even such a reduced claim is ghost-encumbered. After all, the other still owns the precious identity that promises to compensate the hero, and can make off with it at any time without notice: "the main truth of . . . everything was none the less that everything represented the substance of his loss" (II, 205). For this reason, Strether's second go in Europe must itself give rise to another go, or a second half to his story. The shame-ghost must be laid by a reiteration; it must be absolutely laid by a systematic reiteration.[7] It is as if two half lives taken together in sequence might be able to produce one whole and sufficient life.

Therefore it is still as "a case of reaction against the mistake" (I, 191) of not living that Strether encounters Mme de Vionnet in Notre Dame Cathedral, carrying herself "in the sacred shade, with a discernible faith in herself, a kind of implied conviction of consistency, security, impunity" (II, 6). The international claimant sees the private honor he has met with in Mme de Vionnet's *intérieur* in its cultural aspect: "It was, to Strether's mind, as if she sat on her own ground, the light honours of which, at an open gate, she thus easily did him, while all the vastness and mystery of the domain stretched off behind. When people were so completely in possession they could be extraordinarily civil; and our friend had indeed at this hour a kind of revelation of her heritage" (II, 8-9). Already converted to the miracle she has worked in Chad, he promptly converts to her as the worker of the miracle.

But once again Strether proves embarrassing as an acolyte. Having previously imagined horrors when the reality has been a genuine erotic passion, he now sees a worker of miracles when the reality is a woman of a certain age on the point of being deserted by her lover. It is hardly surprising, then, that Mme de Vionnet should not undeceive him of his fool's paradise, and hardly surprising that she should see in him a brake on her backsliding barbarian; in default of one true lover, a tandem of halfhearted, complementary lovers will have to do her for the time being. Like Chad himself under the divine fool's peculiar pressure, Mme de Vionnet begins to live a fable and a fiction. If Strether will vow himself "in honour" (II, 20) to her cause she will more than oblige him with "sublimity" (II, 270). As she will confess to her dupe at the end, "At any rate . . . we've thrust on you appearances that you've had to take in and that have therefore made your obligation. Ugly or beautiful — it doesn't matter what we call them — you were getting on without them, and that's where we're detestable" (II, 257-258).

For his part Strether has no sooner converted to the worker of the miracle than he virtually forfeits all his standing with Woollett. For the apostate-claimant time is up, as his awkwardly schismatic Tweedledee duly announces. And as his counterreactionary other also announces: Chad, eager to free himself from his false positon in Europe, now openly suggests that his idealist other take his place with his mistress, "Only for a month or two — time to go and come. Madame de Vionnet . . . would look after you in the interval" (II, 31). Placed thus in the "Grotesque!" (II, 31) position of all but actually deputizing for a repatriated other, Strether has it brought sharply home to him that he has been completed only to be depleted: does he really exist? All the more difficult, then, "to give him [Chad] up"; "I want to see him a little further" (II, 36), he tells Maria Gostrey. Still a case of the sacred rage, Strether would continue to claim his pastoral of happiness: "But nevertheless I'm making up late for what I didn't have early . . . They may say what they like — it's my surrender, it's my tribute, to youth. One puts that in where one can — it has to come in somewhere, if only out of the lives, the conditions, the feelings of other persons. Chad gives me the sense of it . . . and *she* does the same . . . Yes, they're my youth; since somehow at the right time nothing else ever was" (II, 44). The more, consequently, he is the apostate. And, by Woollett's immunized criteria, a sexual scandal. And the more, ironically, he stands to be proven a sexual nonentity:

> Strether took it in; then as if an echo of Miss Barrace were in the air: "She's wonderful."
>
> "You don't begin to know *how* wonderful!"
>
> There was a depth in it, to Strether's ear, of confirmed luxury — almost a kind of unconscious insolence of proprietorship; but the effect of the glimpse was not at this moment to foster speculation: there was something so conclusive in so much graceful and generous assurance (II, 58).

The tyro has all but "come out" into the interstice, so it is appropriate that his whereabouts should be signalled at this point by one of James's "ados" about little girls and debutantes.[8] Having step by step claimed a vicarious life in Europe, Strether has found this claim being met to an extent quite beyond his expectations. "It's only for you — absolutely you alone — that I speak," Marie de Vionnet confides, thus affording him the sense he "so often had . . . of being further and further 'in' " (II, 111-112). He even appears to stand on the same footing as his counterreactionary other, the erotic, executive man — the Chad, what is more, who in his time has stood on the same footing as an absentee husband: "It was the first time she had spoken to him of her husband, and he couldn't have expressed how much more intimate with her it suddenly made him feel" (II, 111). It is open to the "virginal knight" (*The Idiot*) to claim his place with Mme de Vionnet.

However this new degree of "otherness" on Strether's part is gained at the cost of a shock of recognition:

> He stood in the middle, slightly lingering, vaguely directing his glasses, while, leaning against the door-post of the room, she gently pressed her cheek to the side of the recess. "*You* would have been a friend."
>
> "I?" — it startled him a little.
>
> "For the reason you say. You're not stupid." And then abruptly, as if bringing it out were somehow founded on that fact: "We're marrying Jeanne."
>
> . . . He had allowed for depths, but these were greater: and it was as if, oppressively — indeed absurdly — he was responsible for what they had now thrown up to the surface. It was — through something ancient and cold in it — what he would have called the real thing (II, 110-113).

What is shockingly ancient and cold about this arranging for debutantes is not just European *vieille sagesse*. Chad Newsome it has been
who has arranged for Jeanne, the Chad for whom Jeanne would have
come out. Jeanne, it follows, is one of the damnable terms of Chad's
sacrifice. And if Chad has sacrificed Jeanne for the sake of good relations with her mother, the latter has damnably sacrificed an awkward
daughter for the sake of *her* continued good relations with Chad.
"*We're* marrying Jeanne." In other words, what is ancient and cold for
a tyro is evidence of an exposure or expulsion at both Chad's and Mme
de Vionnet's hands. Evidently vulnerable debutantes like Jeanne (like
his own awkwardly aged self?) can make endings that are at least as
tragic as they are happy.

On the other hand, Strether can be said to have a life like Mamie's
as well. He too has fulfilled himself without, somehow, having quite
fulfilled himself: "What Mamie was like was the happy bride, the
bride after the church and just before going away. She wasn't the mere
maiden, and yet was only as much married as that quantity come to.
She was in the brilliant acclaimed festal stage" (II, 66). And if there
is something foolish about Mamie Pocock as an American deb — "she
was bland, she was bridal — with never, that he could make out as yet,
a bridegroom to support it . . . She was dressed . . . less as a young lady
than as an old one; the complexities of her hair missed, moreover, also
the looseness of youth; and she had a mature manner of bending a
little, as to encourage and reward, while she held neatly together in
front of her a pair of strikingly polished hands" (II, 131)—there is
likewise something foolish about Strether's career in Europe. Awkwardly aging at an awkward age, Strether likewise could be both a
tender novice and a dowager past it all.

Having all but "come out" into the international interstice, Strether
has also decisively forfeited his American identity. All the more, consequently, does he *see* from the point of view of his other. On Chad's
balcony once again, he seems to have come into his inheritance of
identity. He is free: "But the freedom was what was most in the place
and the hour; it was the freedom that most brought him round again
to the youth of his own that he had long ago missed" (II, 204-205). In
Chad, by whom he is "exceptionally confronted" (II, 205) and with
whom he feels "deep identities" (II, 217), he entertains almost to the
full another life that might have been. At the same time, of course,
this claimant is more than ever the all too visible man. No sooner has

he forfeited his American life possibilities than he finds himself wholly committed to his other's false position in Europe, for this counter-reactionary other comes out in his turn with the announcement that, while caring very much for his European ties, he also does not want to care: he would even prefer Mamie to a Marie de Vionnet. Under ever more embarrassing pressure from his too-good-to-be-true other, he would decisively forfeit his false European place in favor of his quixotic other. In short, self and its other, whether Strether or Chad, are exceptionally confronted only to become liable exceptionally to embarrass one another. Strether and Chad have arrived at that late awkward pass to which James's tandem enterprises (for instance Roderick-Rowland, Olive-Verena and even Hyacinth-Paul) regularly come.

The point therefore about the claimant on his excursion outside Paris is that he has virtually disestablished his initiator Chad and graduated to being Mme de Vionnet's true lover himself. So much is he this true lover that he is, it would seem, tempted to live still further beyond his divine fool's means. It has been ambiguously offered to him, at least, to be other almost anyhow — just as it has been offered to Fleda and Maisie:

> He had really feared, in his behaviour, a lapse from good faith; if there was a danger of one's liking such a woman too much one's best safety was in waiting at least till one had the right to do so. In the light of the last few days the danger was fairly vivid; so that it was proportionately fortunate that the right was likewise established . . . It hadn't been till later . . . that he remembered how, with their new tone, they hadn't so much as mentioned the name of Chad himself . . . and it was amazing what could still come up without reference to what had been going on between them . . . It had served all the purpose of his appearing to have said to her: "Don't like me, if it's a question of liking me, for anything obvious and clumsy that I've, as they call it, 'done' for you: like me — well, like me, hang it, for anything else you choose. So, by the same propriety, don't be for me simply the person I've come to know through my awkward connexion with Chad" (II, 223-224).

Never has he been "truer." And never more pretentious.

At this moment Strether comes out. The very type of the Jamesian reactionary aesthete, he might be seeing with "special-green vision" (II, 220). "For this had been all day at bottom the spell of the picture — that it was essentially more than anything else a scene and a stage, that the very air of the play was in the rustle of the willows and the tone of the sky" (II, 226). He sees divinely yet foolishly, moreover, from what might be a box in a theater, "a small and primitive pavilion that, at the garden's edge, almost overhung the water . . . the full grey-blue stream" (II, 227-228). He is indeed in a theater — another Jamesian amphitheater of self-consciousness. Not only does he at last exceptionally confront his other, but he is at last exceptionally confronted by this other. More than this: self, whether Lambert Strether or Chad Newsome, sees its other, whether Strether or Chad, as its other sees it. With the possible exception of "The Jolly Corner's" climax, it is the classic shock of recognition in James.

Like the comparable scene of Chad's advent at the Comédie, this crisis records a "sharp rupture of an identity" (I, 121). Instead of completing one another and thereby being sufficient for Europe and for life, the tandem of Strether plus Chad breaks down, bespeaks only insufficiency. Just by coexisting, Strether and Chad now seem to rob each other of all social and sexual identity. They disembody one another, as good as give each other's lives the lie. Strether, by now Marie de Vionnet's true intimate in so many respects, discovers in Chad another, rightful kind of intimate. If he has been on the point of liking Marie de Vionnet too much he is, under his expert erotic double's eye, discredited as an impostor. If he has not really allowed for this real live thing, he himself is a Parson Adams bedding down incongruously with Joseph Andrew's girl, a scandal of impotence, a fiasco. At the same time, if Chad is Mme de Vionnet's rightful lover he is also proved, under the eye of the idealist claimant, conclusively false. If Chad too likes a woman too much for his comfort, he is also, upon Strether's advent, a backsliding impostor, a barbarian like another who would have his liaison and his exploit. Indeed in this great scene of invalidating exposure everyone, not only Strether, is false. For the lovers as well as the novice extra, "intimacy, at such a point, was *like* that" (II, 237-238). Like, and only like.

An awkward age ends here, just as it generally ends in James, pangfully. Strether has looked to a new lease of life in Europe only to find this lease abruptly terminated. He has recognized in Gloriani's garden in the Faubourg Saint Germain that he probably has no authentic place in life; now in this corresponding second go scene he knows that he cannot even claim a vicarious life. It has not only been a mistake for him not to have lived, it is at best a beautiful mistake for him ever to aspire to live: how can a man who is light ornamental at home be anything other than a divine fool abroad? And while he has been encouraged to live like any other person, it has all the time been on the basis of a phantom acceptance. Lambert Strether has turned out to be another of James's cases of the embarrassment of limits.

What of this ex-claimant's sacred rage? Having already forfeited his American life possibilities, he is now precluded from identity and honor in Europe. Yet rather than continuing grotesquely to assert himself in the face of failure, Strether now goes quietly—even as his moral parent Maisie has gone quietly. He may on the basis of his weakness have aspired to *be* other, but he has also consistently renounced being other *anyhow*. If he has appointed Chad to live for him, he himself has nonetheless lived for Chad: "It was in truth essentially by bringing down his personal life to a function all subsidiary to the young man's own that he held together" (II, 206). And if, now, his consistent self-deprecation has been insufficient, he will bring himself to a thorough-going renunciation of his pastoral of happiness. In contrast to Fleda Vetch, who must have her symbolic spoil at least, he has the capacity "not, out of the whole affair, to have got anything for myself" (II, 292). Strether's only morality is to be the acolyte-epiphyte, never the barbarian vampire-parasite. He makes the familiar Jamesian choice of the higher of two false positions.

Therefore, although recognizing that "you've been chucked, old boy," he can also ask "but what has that to do with it?" (II, 264). Although shocked by the truth that intimacy at such a point was like that, Strether can ask himself "what in the world else would one have wished it to be like? It was all very well for him to feel the pity of its being so much like lying; he almost blushed, in the dark, for the way he had dressed the possibility in vagueness, as a little girl might have dressed her doll. He had made them—and by no fault of their own—momentarily pull it for him, the possibility, out of this vagueness; and must he not therefore take it now as they had simply, with whatever thin attenuations, to give it to him?" (II, 238). Indeed, while being so disappointed that Chad's and Marie's relation should be so contaminated with a lie, he can still admit that he likewise has been living a fable and a fiction in Europe, "really been trying all along to suppose nothing" (II, 238), for fear of a conclusive proof that he himself is not properly qualified for life. Therefore there will be no more sacred rage on Strether's part, no more saintly prurience, and no righteousness: "He was mixed up with the typical tale of Paris, and so were they, poor things—how could they altogether help being? They were no worse than he, in short, and he no worse than they—if, queerly enough, no better" (II, 243). There will be no act of resentment at this climax of his compensation cycle—"It would have sickened him to feel vindictive" (II, 264)—for Strether determines in no way to act *"because* of what he had forfeited. That was the refinement of his supreme scruple—he wished so to leave what he had forfeited out of account. He wished not to do anything because he had missed something else, because he was sore or sorry or impoverished, because he was maltreated or desperate; he wished to do everything because he was lucid and quiet, just the same for himself on all essential points as he had ever been" (II, 264).

On account of such renunciatory determination there can be no more moral room, as it were, than for a farewell encounter with Marie de Vionnet. Undeceived at last of his fool's special-green paradise, Strether sees the latter clearly as a creature of the sacred fount, stricken by cycle and irony:

> With this sharpest perception yet, it was like a chill in the air to him, it was almost appalling, that a creature so fine could be, by mysterious forces, a creature so exploited. For at the end of all things they *were* mysterious: she had but made Chad what he was—so why could she think she had made him infinite? . . . The work, however admirable, was nevertheless of the strict human order, and in short it was marvellous that the companion of mere earthly joys . . . should be so transcendently prized. It might have made Strether hot or shy . . . but he was held there by something so hard that it was fairly grim . . . the real coercion was to see a man ineffably adored (II, 255).

To use Stendhal's terms, Strether sees that Marie would try for the black as compensation for the red that she cannot have:

> "And I don't mean now about *him.* Oh for him—!" Positively, strangely, bitterly, as it seemed to Strether, she gave "him," for the moment, away. "You don't care what I think of you; but I happen to care what you think of me. And what you *might,*" she added. "What you perhaps even did . . . What's cheerful for *me,*" she replied, "is that we might, you and I, have been friends. That's it—that's it. You see how, as I say, I want everything. I've wanted you too" (II, 257-259).

It is the divine fool's moment of greatest danger of liking a woman too much. Accordingly, he must renounce once and for all. " 'Ah but you've *had* me!' he declared, at the door, with an emphasis that made an end" (II, 259). Thus Strether at last avows the love that it is not for divine fools to avow, but at the cost of getting nothing at all out of the affair in the way of the real thing. If Marie has tried for the black in lieu of the red, he likewise makes his Stendhalian gesture. He gives the earnest of his special kind of love in his apparently suicidal, but actually sacrificial and life-affirming self-committal to "prison," the non-place of the international interstice ("so very *much* out . . . He was out, in truth, as far as it was possible to be," II, 288).

Necessarily the next but last of the damnable terms of Strether's self-sacrifice is a formal farewell to Chad and to all hope of being "secret" or "other." Having committed himself to this earnest of his divine foolishness, however, Strether becomes free to claim a divine fool's right, not to love like any other person, but as it were to love love. If he expels himself from Europe (not in the spirit of any reactionary "revulsion in favour of the principles of Woollett," II, 265) and if he thereby takes upon himself all responsibility for a still "restless" (II, 285) Chad's barbarism, then Chad in his turn should pay *his* tribute to the ideal by renouncing *his* American life possibilities. Strether even manages to exact from Chad a vow never to forsake his European mistress; should the latter ever do so he will be "a brute . . . guilty of the last infamy" (II, 276), "a criminal of the deepest dye" (II, 279), a barbarian like another and despoiler of civilized quintessence. Thus a Jamesian imagination of love, as one might call it,[9] holds out the only hope of redeeming the Jamesian compensation cycle. And when Strether has arranged his final renunciation—of a life with Maria Gostrey: "It's you who would make me wrong!" (II, 292)—he may be said to have done all that is humanly possible to free this offer from equivocation. In the circumstances, nothing short of the pilgrim's laying down his life will do.

If Milly Theale is not really there,[10] it is not because of any failure of James's genius but because she cannot be expected to be altogether there. It simply is not for her to live like any other person. Milly not only stands below the norms of experience—the plane of the sacred fount and the marketplace—as an invalid and an outsider for the duping, she also stands above these norms in a spiritual sense. Milly Theale is another Jamesian "virginal knight" or "white soul"[11] who never quite exists in the way, for instance, her "other" Kate Croy exists; with the latter she can sense only "a sort of failure of common terms" (I, 169). As James shows in the emblematic Alpine scene in which she makes her debut, she has on the one hand her extraordinary "liability to slip, to slide, to leap, to be precipitated by a single false movement, by a turn of the head—how could one tell?—into whatever was beneath" (I, 111). On the other hand she might be a disinterested, a prodigiously spiritual presence "in a state of uplifted and unlimited possession . . . looking down on the kingdoms of the earth" (I, 111). However she appears, Milly Theale remains out of it all. Like Maisie or Strether, she is two falsely placed exoteric initiates at once, the divine fool who does not really live save in confused (and confusing) ironic and pastoral terms.

Like Maisie and Strether, therefore, she is also an exquisite reactionary bent on claiming community with the living. If strictly speaking she does not "mix" with the realms of the sacred fount and the marketplace, she must nonetheless, indeed all the more, *be* other. This "potential heiress of all the ages" (I, 98) would lay her claim, too, to all the European old things. She goes so far as to invite a possibly fatal exposure to Europe; she might be a divine provocateur. "It would be a question of taking full in the face the whole assault of life, to the general muster of which indeed her face might have been directly presented as she sat there on her rock" (I, 112). It would be a mistake for Milly not to risk living even if it should turn out to be a mistake—and James raises the possibility of her suicide—actually to risk living. It would be a mistake not to make the mistake. As usual in James, the protagonist's choice is one of alternative false positions: "Since I've lived all these years as if I were dead, I shall die," determines Milly, "as if I were alive" (I, 176).

Meanwhile, the "other" whom this true pretender will claim is a mirror-other, a Jamesian revenger on the point of entering a dehumanizing cycle. Kate Croy has "tasted the faint flat emanation of things, the failure of fortune and of honour. If she continued to wait it was really in a manner that she mightn't add the shame of fear, of individual, of personal collapse, to all the other shames" (I, 3-4). In her own way, Kate is as falsely placed in life as Milly: "Why should a set of people have been put in motion, on such a scale and with such an air of being equipped for a profitable journey, only to break down without an accident, to stretch themselves in the wayside dust without a reason?" (I, 4). Worse still, she inherits a damaging sense of dishonor from her father Lionel Croy, who has been a man "like nothing" (I,

18) pretending to be like something. Kate, James suggests, may even have been subtly deracinated on account of the latter's pretentiousness: "He looked . . . the man in the world least connected with anything unpleasant. He was so particularly the English gentleman and the fortunate settled normal person. Seen at a foreign table d'hôte he suggested but one thing: 'In what perfection England produces them!' . . . Those who knew him a little said 'How he does dress!' — those who knew him better said 'How *does* he?' " (I, 7). And she herself has as a girl lived so much abroad that "there stuck to her . . . the religion of foreign things" (I, 83).

Already standing fever-chilled in a recognizably Jamesian interstice, Kate Croy is yet to forfeit even her apology for an inheritance. Offering to give away her chances with her wealthy but arbitrary aunt in favor of caring for her father, she nevertheless finds herself chucked with all of a Beale Farange's mercenary conscientiousness. The upshot is that, on nothing more than the basis of her "fellowship in abjection" (I, 32) with her family, Kate ventures to be *other* at Lancaster Gate: other almost anyhow, since to take her compensation at Lancaster Gate is but to aggravate her basic abjection, to consent to "a surrender, though she couldn't yet have said exactly of what: a general surrender of everything . . . to Aunt Maud's looming 'personality' " (I, 27). It is as Mme Merle might have said, to "crawl" before "material things": "She had a dire accessibility to pleasure from such sources" (I, 26). And inasmuch as she has been deracinated, it is to fall beneath the heavy charm of "Britannia of the Market Place — Britannia unmistakable but with a pen on her ear" (I, 28). Of course eventually it is to make herself ripe for conspiracy. Being so much for-the-other — whether at Chirk Street or at Lancaster Gate, where she is the instrument of her Aunt Maud's second go — Kate must seek out a fellowship in secrecy.

Kate Croy's fellow conspirator Merton Densher likewise occupies a false position in life. Densher, James tells us, falls just short of identity: "He suggested above all, however, that wondrous state of youth in which the elements, the metals more or less precious, are so in fusion and fermentation that the question of the final stamp, the pressure that fixes the value, must wait for comparative coolness" (I, 44). Although precious, he is also subject to question: specifically, he has "strength merely for thought" and "weakness, as he called it, for life" (I, 47). Falsely placed in this way in life, the sexually aesthetic Densher has found a compensatory self-completion in Kate Croy, whose "value would be in her differences" (I, 46) and particularly in her manifest "talent for life" (II, 160, 318). (Kate in her turn has found a compensatory value or difference in Densher, who offers "what her life had never given her and certainly, without some such aid as his, never would give her," I, 46.)

Besides, while Kate has been obscurely displaced, Densher has been deracinated to a still greater degree. He is another of whom it might be said in foreign places, "In what perfection England produces them!" In fact, there are so many "more foreign things" in Densher than in Kate that the latter regards him "as if he were a map of the continent or a handsome present of a delightful new 'Murray' " (I, 83). "Something had happened to him that could never be undone. When Kate Croy said to him as much he besought her not to insist, declaring that this indeed was what was gravely the matter with him, that he had been but too probably spoiled for native, for insular use" (I, 84). In these circumstances it seems only appropriate that Densher should drift into a fellowship in abjection at Lancaster Gate; he is another, uncertain Jamesian social aesthete in quest of Britannia Unmistakable. Not that his taking his compensation here can appease him any more than it does Kate. Densher too compensates only to recognize that "decidedly there was something he hadn't enough of" (I, 70), that he is a "queer creature" and a "social anomaly" and "but half a Briton" (I, 82). To say nothing of that "great ugliness" (I, 56), his want of means, Densher is a stigmatized person who can never pass in contexts that he should otherwise have been able to assume: "the mark on his forehead stood clear; he saw himself remain without whether he married or not" (I, 57).

In due course James's have-nots constitute a community of knowledge. Kate engages herself to Densher forever, pledges every spark of her faith and every drop of her life; the lovers kiss upon the vow, "sealed their rich compact, solemnised . . . their agreement to belong only, and to belong tremendously, to each other" (I, 86). These lovers, however, formalize their relationship in a reactive spirit; they might be said to love too much by virtue of their vows. Consequently, as Kate well knows and as Densher points out, they involve themselves in something so much like lying (*The Ambassadors*): "Of course it will never do—we must remember that—from the moment you allow her to found hopes of you for any one else in particular. So long as her view is content to remain as general as at present appears I don't see that we deceive her. At a given hour, you see, she must be undeceived: the only thing therefore is to be ready for the hour and to face it" (I, 86). Their fellowship in abjection has taken on the character of a dangerous fellowship in secrecy:

"Yes; no doubt, in our particular situation, time's everything. And then there's the joy of it."

She hesitated. "Of our secret?"

"Not so much perhaps of our secret in itself, but of what's represented . . . by it . . . Our being as we are."

It was as if for a moment she let the meaning sink into her. "So gone?"

"So gone. So extremely gone. However," he smiled, "we shall go a good deal further." Her answer to which was only the softness of her silence — a silence that looked out for them both at the far reach of their prospect (I, 87).

The advent of Milly Theale among James's incipient secret revengers now sets in train the most tragic of James's "imitation of Christ"/ *ressentiment* cycles. While the long lost heiress would claim another European life that would have been, she herself is consummately "other" from the point of view of her other. She embodies to an unbearable degree what Kate Croy would have been. For the outsider Milly with "her funny race, her funny losses, her funny gains, her funny freedom, and, no doubt, above all, her funny manners" (I, 223), the Milly to whom an established Kate might have been superior — this Milly can also own to "luck all round" (I, 229), a luck that is too good to be true. For all that she is the discountable exotic, she is socially quintessential to a degree Kate Croy will never be: "It was New York mourning, it was New York hair, it was a New York history . . . it was a New York legend of affecting, of romantic isolation, and, beyond everything, it was by most accounts, in respect to the mass of money so piled on the girl's back, a set of New York possibilities" (I, 95). No sooner, then, can the would-be established Kate take any compensation in the outsider than she has her own outside-insider self brought home to her, her own cheap value or hidden stigma. What is more, no sooner does Milly embarrass her other in this way than she promptly re-embarrasses her. Milly is invalid, extraordinarily liable, ghost-encumbered; her most beaux moments take place as if in a handsome cemetery. However at the same time that she is shown up by Kate's "talent for life," she manifests her own superior talent for spirit, so to speak. On Kate's own ambivalent admission, she is "impossibly without sin" (I, 200). In fact Milly is impossible altogether and should, from the all too possible, latently conspiratorial Kate's point of view, be prevented from being possible. No sooner then can Kate prize her own immunity and talent for life as against Milly's liability than she finds herself shown up for being worse than she might otherwise have been, spiritually of the left hand, poisoning herself and her other. In short, if as Mrs. Lowder says "together they could do anything" (I, 191), Milly and Kate also compete with one another and, in their different ways, deplete one another.

Like Strether, therefore, Milly Theale reacts against her mistake of not living only to become a kind of divine provocateur. Meanwhile, again as in *The Ambassadors,* the already reactive, all too human other counterreacts against her as *her* other. It is a cycle the nature of which is made clear in a scene towards the end of the novel's first half. Here, when the divine fool suggests in her good faith that Britannia of the Marketplace may be something of an idealist, Kate is compelled to undeceive her, as much however from suppressed resentment as from any loyalty to Milly or to the truth. Kate must inflict the "mere mercenary" (I, 248) realm upon the impossibly ideal other; she must bring down Milly's differences into the marketplace.

> "Oh but she has . . . plenty of use for you! You put her in, my dear, more than you put her out. You don't half see it, but she has clutched your petticoat. You can do anything—you can do, I mean, lots that *we* can't. You're an outsider, independent and standing by yourself; you're not hideously relative to tiers and tiers of others." And Kate, facing in that direction, went further and further; wound up, while Milly gaped, with extraordinary words. "We're of no use to you—it's decent to tell you. You'd be of use to us, but that's a different matter. My honest advice to you would be"—she went indeed all lengths—"to drop us while you can. It would be funny if you didn't soon see how awfully better you can do. We've not really done for you the least thing worth speaking of—nothing you mightn't easily have had in some other way. Therefore you're under no obligation. You won't want us next year; we shall only continue to want *you*. But that's no reason for you, and you mustn't pay too dreadfully for poor Mrs. Stringham's having let you in. She has the best conscience in the world; she's enchanted with what she has done; but you shouldn't take your people from *her*. It has been quite awful to see you do it" (I, 247-248).

Kate's advice, given here in the knowledge of her underground ambivalences and all her liability to conspiracy, amounts to a revengeful use of ambiguity. Kate the counterreactionary "knows" Milly. Deprived of her being-unto-self, she would secretly deprive Milly of her otherness.

But now the divine fool turns the screw tragically once again. If Britannia of the Marketplace can seem to her disinterested, then in spite of everything Kate Croy remains and will always remain a friend; like her prototype Maisie, Milly forgivingly includes everyone. In the event, however, it is precisely this general clemency of hers that constitutes a final goad to the self-rejecting, very probably precluded other: "It had been at this point, however, that Kate flickered highest. 'Oh you may very well loathe me yet!' " (I, 248). It is as though the pastoral fool's very failure to reproach were the supreme reproach to the always self-reproachful Kate. Indeed Kate's abject-incendiary spirit is appeased only when she has elicited from Milly "a small solemnity of remonstrance" (I, 248), that is when she has brought down the "differences" that gall her, put Milly before herself as someone who is all too human, perhaps even less than human:

> This unexpectedly had acted, by a sudden turn of Kate's attitude, as a happy speech. She had risen as she spoke, and Kate had stopped before her, shining at her instantly with a softer brightness. Poor Milly hereby enjoyed one of her views of how people, wincing oddly, were often touched by her. "Because you're a dove." With which she felt herself ever so delicately, so considerately, embraced; not with familiarity or as a liberty taken, but almost ceremonially and in the manner of an *accolade . . . That* was what was the matter with her. She was a dove. Oh *wasn't* she? (I, 248-249).

As in *What Maisie Knew* and *The Ambassadors,* the first half of James's story sees its protagonist having to forego the hope of an authentic life, yet sublimely-foolishly claiming an extension or second go. Fatally exposed and stigmatized, Milly would have a secret on the model of Sir Luke Strett's merciful fraud: "Going too far was failing to try at least to remain simple. He would be quite ready to hate her if she did, by heading him off at every point, embarrass his exercise of a kindness that, no doubt, constituted for him a high method . . . It came round to the same thing; him too she would help to help her if that could possibly be; but if it couldn't possibly be she would assist also to make this right" (II, 112). Undertaking to live out a true pretension, to die as if she were alive, she establishes "the thorough make-believe of a settlement" (II, 121) in Venice. Here it is that the exquisite barbarian would reiterate her ghost-encumbered London life.

Meanwhile, the all too human mirror-other counterreacts. In order to free herself from her false position at Lancaster Gate, where she likewise enjoys only the thorough make-believe of a settlement, in order to be other anyhow, Kate Croy arranges to offer Milly a false lease of life. If Milly seeks to live vicariously through herself and Densher, Kate will extend to her a phantom normality on the basis of a phantom acceptance. Kate will vacate her place with Densher in Milly's favor, but vacate it with the object of treating her in a mercenary, defamatory spirit, as if she were dead. Kate too lives a lie, a *ressentiment*-imbued one. She might be taking her cue from Mrs. Lowder's affably specious " 'You must stay on with us; you *can,* you know, in any position you like; any, any, *any,* my dear child' — and her emphasis went deep. 'You must make your home with us; and it's really open to you to make the most beautiful one in the world' " (I, 190); or from Densher's "desire . . . to be like everyone else, simplifyingly 'kind' to her. He had caught on already as to manner — fallen into line with every one else; and if his spirits verily *had* gone up it might well be that he had thus felt himself lighting on the remedy for all awkwardness" (I, 264).

Always like her ideal mirror-other, Kate is committing a kind of suicide — as one might expect given her original, punitive self-rejection. Ultimately she is wreaking a kind of secret, inadmissible vengeance upon what is most precious, yet also most insufficient for her, her "being as we are" with Densher. Working the principle of the sacred fount, Kate exploits the element of the compensatory that has always characterized their intimacy; if Densher with his weakness for life has been drawn to her own talent for life, she will systematically withhold herself from him. Expertly equivocating and temporizing, Kate thus reduces their relationship to a reactionary, feeble-forcible cycle in itself, to an "abjection of love" (II, 68) that must always give rise to a corresponding fellowship in mastery, an ever more dangerous community of knowledge.

> He hadn't come back to hear her talk of his believing in her as if he
> didn't; but he had come back — and it all was upon him now — to seize her
> with a sudden intensity that her manner of pleading with him had made, as
> happily appeared, irresistible. He laid strong hands upon her to say almost

in anger, "Do you love me, love me, love me?" and she closed her eyes as with the sense that he might strike her but that she could gratefully take it. Her surrender was her response, her response her surrender . . . The long embrace in which they held each other . . . was stronger than an uttered vow . . . This settled so much, and settled it so thoroughly, that there was nothing left to ask her to swear to. Oaths and vows apart, now they could talk (II, 17-18).

James's divine provocateur has but aggravated all that is negative in the situation. Not that Milly has ever pressed her claim to a life so very far beyond her divine fool's means; like Maisie and Strether, she recognizes that it is not for her to live and love in the usual human, the "middle" or "other" way, and that she is only fitted charitably to love love:

The choice exhaled its shy fragrance of heroism . . . She would be charming to Kate as well as to Kate's adorer; she would incur whatever pain could dwell for her in the sight—should she continue to be exposed to the sight—of the adorer thrown in with the adored. It wouldn't really have taken much more to make him wonder if he hadn't before him one of those rare cases of exaltation—food for fiction, food for poetry—in which a man's fortune with the woman who doesn't care for him is positively promoted by the women who does (II, 72).

More formal still is her renunciation of a marriage in Europe, of the pastoral of happiness falsely offered by Lord Mark (in the second go scene that corresponds to the "Bronzino" scene of the first half):

She shook her head with her slowness, but this time with all her mildness. "No, I mustn't listen to you— that's just what I mustn't do. The reason is, please, that it simply kills me. I must be as attached to you as you will, since you give that lovely account of yourselves. I give you in return the fullest possible belief of what it would be—" And she pulled up a little. "I give and give and give—there you are; stick to me as close as you like and see if I don't. Only I can't listen or receive or accept—I can't *agree*. I can't make a bargain. I can't really (II, 145).

Characteristically, Milly mixes here only to have to refuse to mix for fear of being false to herself and to others. There is to be no question either of getting or taking, of anything but a "white" barbarism on her part.

But again it is precisely this tragic waver, this innocent teasing out of self-esteem on the pastoral dove's part, that so provokes the other sacred fount or marketplace world. Bad enough to be precluded from her wealth and power when it has seemed so very accessible; intolerable, now, to be precluded from the too good to be true that has seemed so very susceptible of being patronized. "No man, she was quite aware, could enjoy thus having it from her that he wasn't good for what she would have called her reality" (II, 142-143). Although Lord Mark's expert consistency does not permit him openly to complain, "the perception of that fairly showed in his face after a moment like the smart of a blow" (II, 143). Doubly embarrassed by the divine fool — to whom he has actually had to sue as if she were not one — he takes an ambiguous revenge on her: "the sign of his smarting . . . reappeared for her — breaking out moreover, with an effect of strangeness, in another quite possibly sincere allusion to her state of health. He might for that matter have been seeing what he could do in the way of making it a grievance that she should snub him for a charity, on his own part, exquisitely roused" (II, 144). And when the divine fool innocently directs him back to his true reality, to his obligation to Kate Croy, the humiliated Mark retaliates by "knowing" her: "But don't you really *know*?" (II, 147). With Lord Mark — "a fellow who isn't a fool" (I, 194), as he himself would put it — it is to be a fool for a fool, for the fact is that Milly has inflicted on him his superior-inferior joker-double, Merton Densher who, in spite of being a nobody, has won precedence over himself with both Kate and Milly. Milly's innocent ignorance has put no one less than Lord Mark in a "theater" with vulgar impostors and thieves. It has of course always been the way of virginal knights and doves with the way of the world.

The climactic turn of James's "imitation of Christ"/*ressentiment* cycle is Milly's celebration in honor of Sir Luke Strett (a scene corresponding to the first half's "dove" transaction between Milly and Kate). But while Milly makes a supreme bid here for a pastoral of happiness, her reaction against her mistake of not living is no more spiritually disfigured than it has ever been. Transvalued as much as possible by renunciatory spirit, indeed impossibly without sin, her gesture would include everyone. On account of its "amount of comedy" no one need any longer be a mere, exoteric initiate. Above all the saintly Milly loves the Judas-like lovers Kate and Densher, whom on Mark's word are conspiring against her.

But once again it is Milly's spiritual "difference" that most provokes the realm of the sacred fount and the marketplace. That Milly should possess a fortune while being a doomed invalid might be sufficiently provoking for her other self Kate. But that she should also be too good to be true on the basis of her ignorance of others proves as supremely galling to Kate as it has to Lord Mark. Consequently Kate must, out of her incendiary ambivalence, once and for all defame Milly's genius, reduce difference to a matter of spoil:

> . . . he felt her diffuse in wide warm waves the spell of a general, a beatific mildness . . . But Milly, let loose among them in a wonderful white dress, brought them somehow into relation with something that made them more finely genial . . . "But she's *too* nice," Kate returned with appreciation. "Everything suits her so—especially her pearls. They go so with her old lace. I'll trouble you really to look at them." Densher, though aware he had seen them before, had perhaps not "really" looked at them, and had thus not done justice to the embodied poetry—his mind, for Milly's aspects, kept coming back to that—which owed them part of its style. Kate's face, as she considered them, struck him: the long, priceless chain, wound twice round the neck, hung, heavy and pure, down the front of the wearer's breast . . . "She's a dove," Kate went on, "and one somehow doesn't think of doves as bejewelled. Yet they suit her down to the ground."
>
> "Yes—down to the ground is the word" . . . Milly was indeed a dove; this was the figure, though it most applied to her spirit.' Yet he knew in a moment that Kate was just now, for reasons hidden from him, exceptionally under the impression of that element of wealth in her which was a power, which was a great power, and which was dove-like only so far as one remembered that doves have wings and wondrous flights, have them as well as tender tints and soft sounds . . . All this was a brighter blur in the general light, out of which he heard Kate presently going on.
>
> "Pearls have such a magic that they suit everyone."
>
> "They would uncommonly suit you," he frankly returned.
>
> "Oh yes, I see myself!"
>
> As she saw herself, suddenly, he saw her—she would have been splendid; and with it he felt more what she was thinking of. Milly's royal ornament had—under pressure now not wholly occult—taken on the character of a symbol of differences, differences of which the vision was actually in Kate's face. It might have been in her face too that, well as she certainly would look in pearls, pearls were exactly what Merton Densher would never be able to give her. Wasn't *that* the great difference that Milly to-night symbolised? (II, 191-197).

As elsewhere in James, the exoteric initiate's perception of authentically superior differences has led infallibly to the vindictive. So near, yet so far from the "royal" herself, Kate would be different almost anyhow. But since she cannot openly displace her other self for fear of destroying her own self absolutely, she contrives to destroy her secretly: she proposes that Densher should marry Milly as if he were not already pledged to herself, that he should offer the dying Milly the simulacrum of a life in return for her money after her death. With this proposal Kate perfects her vengeful imitation of the divine fool's now perfected career. Kate too would renounce—exactly what Milly has renounced. She arranges a damnable, a black sacrifice of what has been most precious to her, her own being "so gone" with Densher.

Of course, in consummating her secret revenge for the injury of life, Kate has also perfected Densher as her dupe and instrument. Indeed it is a question whether she has not revenged herself upon him for not being a Lord Mark for whom she might have felt so gone. Not surprisingly, then, Densher reacts against her the very moment he becomes her consummate, her abject, dupe. If Kate has withheld herself from him in order to compensate him and thus manipulate him, he in turn demands a kind of justifiable retribution. If Kate has contrived "without a pang, to see him ridiculously—ridiculously so far as just complacently—exposed" (II, 160) to a false position, indeed laid him open to the ultimate Jamesian penalty of appearing the fool, "the ass the whole thing involved . . . Lord Mark had caught him twice in the fact—the fact of his absurd posture" (II, 189), then Densher counterproposes to be "master in the conflict" (II, 207). To this end he has found, like any other Jamesian reactionary, something of his own, a cover against his sense of being theatrical—private rooms occupied during earlier days in Venice. And it is here, in the dangerous spirit of an eye for an eye, that he insists upon sealing his community of knowledge with Kate.

In the final phase of the lovers' "secret society," the masterful Kate operates on a "law of silence": "Letters? Never—*now*. Think of it. Impossible" (II, 240). (In this she yet again imitates her other self who, stricken with disappointment, has turned her face against the wall.) Densher meanwhile endures an agonizing ordeal of self-consciousness, for by the familiar Jamesian paradox he is both an underground and an all-too-visible man. Suddenly and arbitrarily excluded from the palace, he finds himself exposed to a "vulgar view, the view that might have been taken of an inferior man" (II, 231) on the part of Milly's expert mercenary Eugenio. "One had come to a queer pass when a servant's opinion so mattered. Eugenio's would have mattered even if, as founded on a low vision of appearances, it had been quite wrong. It was the more disagreeable accordingly that the vision of appearances was quite right, and yet was scarcely less low" (II, 233). Merton Densher has never been the man of distinction manqué that he likes to think he is; he is, rather, a pretentious version of a common fortune hunter. In fact, Merton Densher is but a specious imitation of that more genuinely (in one respect) pretentious fortune hunter, Lord Mark. Encountering the latter, who turns up in the Piazza di San Marco like the bad double he is, he might be occupying a most terrible amphitheater, "the drawing-room of Europe" (II, 234)—a pretender alone and mastered and divested of identity. Even worse, Densher is confronted in Mark, the double who *is* his own duplicity, not only with what he is not but also with his innermost but unacknowledged motive, "base revenge"; for Mark's denunciation of himself and Kate amounts to nothing else but a revenge taken both against Densher, who has upstaged him with Kate and Milly, and, presumably, Milly herself for having rejected him in favor of Densher. Merton Densher, secret revenger, has had altogether to come out—hence his protesting the double too much. This other is altogether other, none of Densher, "an idiot of idiots," "exactly the inevitable ass," "the ass at his worst" (II, 254-255):

> "Then it *was* mere base revenge. Hasn't he known her, into the bargain." the young man asked—"didn't he, weeks before, see her, judge her, feel her, as having for such a suit as his not more perhaps than a few months to live?"
> Mrs. Stringham at first, for reply, but looked at him in silence; and it gave more force to what she then remarkably added. "He has doubtless been aware of what you speak of, just as you have yourself been aware."
> "He has wanted her, you mean, just *because*—?"
> "Just because," said Susan Shepherd.
> "The hound!" Merton Densher brought out (II, 259).

Milly Theale, divine fool heroine of the beautiful delusion and the wasted charity, fails utterly. It is not only that she is proved a would- or might-have-been, not only that she may as well *not* be; she has also divinely-foolishly provoked and aggravated a situation that might or would have been better without her intervention. For Milly to persist, then, in the compensatory quest for a life for which she is unfit would be to persist in an immorality (as the Ververs will call it)—both to be false to her own prematurely ghostly self and fatally to falsify her exquisite reaction, to act revengefully against the conspirators to whom she has after all offered herself as an opportunity. Therefore she must renounce her barbarian's provocation, even if this should mean in effect that she gives up the effort to live all she can. When she turns her face to the wall in fatal disappointment, she also does so as what Densher recognizes as an "act of renouncement" (II, 301) of an entirely false course. Better to choose a higher false position, and not to try to live while yet not committing spiritual suicide than to choose a base false position, and to assert herself reactively on a false basis and in false hope. More important still, Milly's turning her face to the wall is an act of renouncement in favor of the ultimate Jamesian value, on behalf of what Kate recognizes as "the peace of having loved" and "of having *been* loved" (II, 296)—"for love," as *The Golden Bowl* puts it. Like her moral parents, Maisie and Strether, therefore, Milly Theale goes quietly in the end, not only refusing vindictively to reproach or expose the conspirators but even making over to them, as the earnest of her loving-kindliness, a share in the fortune of which they would have defrauded her. In this way she holds out the possibility that a dehumanizing revenge cycle may be redeemed. The divine fool has failed utterly only to succeed extraordinarily in asserting the hope that everyone is valuable. As Richard Poirier says of Strether, this idealist who cannot but fail shows that "people really ought to try to live up to such an imagination of them."[12]

Not that Milly can mix altogether with the conspiratorial lovers' reality. Milly can instruct Densher in the need for renouncing, for love of her love, the money, and Kate in the need to renounce Lancaster Gate as a recognition of her dove-likeness; but her loving-kindliness cannot actually revoke "the knowledge of each other that they couldn't undo" (II, 347). Indeed, if she herself has had to choose a higher as against a lower false position, Milly can only hold out to the lovers a similar choice. Her intervention frees Kate and Densher from their abjection of love, but only to bring them to the recognition that they will "never be again as we were!" (II, 359). Love is unequivocal, James might be saying, but making a life remains a matter of making a choice of false positions.

IV. For Love

"For love," said the Princess.
The Golden Bowl

Maisie, James's most lowly exemplar and the humble beginning of his own second go, goes quietly for love of Sir Claude. Strether meets the complexity of his fate by going quietly for love of the lovers, Chad and Marie de Vionnet. Milly Theale turns her face to the wall ultimately for love of the lovers Densher and Kate Croy, as well as for Sir Luke Strett. In each of these situations one might say that a higher pastoral plane of experience has separated from the psychosocial plane of the sacred fount and the marketplace, and separated because in a sense it has never been anything but separate. In each case, too, it separates only to "mix" again and affirm and redeem what could not otherwise be sustained. It is in *The Golden Bowl*, however, James's greatest work, that the pastoral plane emerges most clearly. Indeed *The Golden Bowl* comes out unequivocally: the Jamesian renunciation is not only against all vicious revenge cycles, it is "for love" (II, 102). It is all for love.

Like the other late novels, *The Golden Bowl* develops into an "improbably good"/reactionary cycle (I, 352). It likewise is about the ideal's problematic, even false, position in the world. Accordingly Maggie and Adam Verver too are Jamesian divine fools (a fact which accounts for the majority of the ambiguities that worry the more moralistic critics of the novel). Maggie Verver is "divinely blind" (I, 354), "the scapegoat of old . . . charged with the sins of the people . . . gone forth into the desert to sink under his burden and die" (II, 207), while Adam is an "incredible little idealist" (I, 250), "a revelation of simplicity" (I, 289), or a "too inconceivably funny," even "stupid" (II, 119) person. Moreover, and again like Strether and Milly, these divine fools might be provocateurs of a kind. Reacting against their Jamesian mistake of failing to "lead . . . any life at all . . . half the life we might" (I, 156), they too would claim a life in Europe in order to complete and civilize themselves. As always in James, however, their barbarians' claim is ambiguous, and involves their forfeiting, even if temporarily or partially, their identity as American citizens. All the more, then, do they need to "know" everything European: "But there's nothing, however tiny," Maggie Verver tells Amerigo, "that we've missed" (I, 12). The most conscientious of adventurers, they would adorn themselves with the symbols of "civilization condensed" (I, 129). They need decisively to consummate and formalize their enterprise, they would "marry" Europe: "You're at any rate a part of his collection . . . one of the things that can only be got over here. You're a rarity, an object of beauty, an object of price. You're not perhaps absolutely unique, but you're so curious and eminent that there are very few others like you — you belong to a class about which everything is known. You're what they call a *morceau de musée*" (I, 11).

In London on the eve of their international marriage, these pilgrims might be standing before the gates of Rome; strangely enough, this had been Hyacinth Robinson's situation years before. But already they stand in a false position, exoterically, never esoterically, initiated: "It's you yourselves meanwhile," a Roman prince lays down,

> who really know nothing. There are two parts of me . . . One is made up of the history, the doings, the marriages, the crimes, the follies, the boundless *bêtises* of other people . . . Those things are written — literally in rows of volumes, in libraries; are as public as they're abominable. Everybody can get at them, and you've both of you wonderfully looked them in the face. But there's another part, very much smaller doubtless, which, such as it is, represents my single self, the unknown, unimportant — unimportant save to *you* — personal quantity. About this you've found out nothing" (I, 8).

In all innocence the barbarians have embarrassed the civilized, utterly worldly man — perhaps into trying to be something of a divine fool himself, someone improbably good. While they claim him for their own, therefore, he too has to react. The Prince has to insist that he is not for the "knowing." After all, he has actually lent himself to the barbarians, if he has not actually consented to being wrongfooted; and among the Anglo-Saxons, a quintessential Roman can never be quite as essential as he might otherwise have been.

Into this potentially dangerous situation comes a character who suffers the disadvantages of a false position as much as anyone in James, a kind of new Christine Light. Charlotte Stant, we are told, has won no place — has "absolutely failed" (I, 165) to marry, either in America or Europe — above all, in Europe, where, like the newly come Ververs, she can know only what the social aesthete knows: "the Prince in especial wondered at his friend's possession of her London. He had rather prized his own possession . . . When his companion, with the memory of other visits and other rambles, spoke of places he hadn't seen and things he didn't know, he actually felt again — as half the effect — just a shade humiliated . . . It was a fresh light on Charlotte and on her curious world-quality" (I, 89). In fact, unbeknown to Maggie Verver, Charlotte has broken off an affair with the Prince within the year, presumably in part to save herself humiliation, in part perhaps to save Amerigo the awkwardness of having to reject her for her lack of means. It is a Roman prince, princeliness, civilization condensed, to whom Charlotte Stant has been near, yet so far.

But as if absolute failure to live fully were not enough, Charlotte has subsequently had to bear with Maggie Verver's success. Endowed only with her very "small social capital" (I, 49), she herself does not live; rather, Maggie Verver lives, childhood intimate and extraordinary heiress, American "other" who yet seems to have won magnificent European place. It is an unbearable compounding of her situation. Charlotte cannot, one imagines, accept her insufficient self; no more can she forgive the proof of her insufficiency, the galling double. In any case, perhaps, she has in the first place broken off with Amerigo with a view to lying close and keeping herself for another go. All in all, then, Charlotte must claim some redress, she must appear in London on the eve of the international marriage and arrange a meeting with Amerigo of which "absolute secrecy . . . was . . . of the essence" (I, 84). She has been "saving up" (I, 84), she tells Amerigo, "for this . . . To have one hour alone with you" (I, 80). "What I want is that it shall always be with you—so that you'll never be able quite to get rid of it— that I *did*. I won't say that *you* did—you may make as little of that as you like. But that I was here with you where we are and *as* we are—I just saying this" (I, 87-88). This secret hour is to be set subversively against the international marriage. A secret is being set over against it, and certainly for other and deeper reasons than from any considera- tion of tact. Having so weak a sense of identity as to be doomed to con- sciousness of a "reproachful" other self, Charlotte cannot try openly to head Maggie off. Indeed so much does she envy Maggie that that would be to destroy herself; this has been the problem of all James's revengers. If an absolute failure is in any way to *be* the other, it is only on condition of absolute secrecy.

The revenge-feeling which Charlotte has been saving up now finds an ambiguous outlet. During the episode in the antiquarian's shop, Charlotte negotiates an understanding with the Prince that amounts to conspiracy. She refuses "a small ricordo" from the latter on the grounds that "a ricordo from you—from you to me—is a ricordo of nothing. It has no reference." There has been no story, no commitment to speak of, on the Prince's side.

> "You don't refer," she went on to her companion. "*I* refer."
> He had lifted the lid of his little box and he looked into it hard. "Do you mean by that then that you would be free — ?"
> " 'Free' — ?"
> "To offer me something?"
> This gave her a longer pause, and when she spoke again she might have seemed, oddly, to be addressing the dealer. "Would you allow me — ?"
> "No," said the Prince into his little box.
> "You wouldn't accept it from me?"
> "No," he repeated in the same way.
> She exhaled a long breath that was like a guarded sigh. "But you've touched an idea that *has* been mine. It's what I've wanted." Then she added: "It was what I hoped."
> He put down his box — this had drawn his eyes . . . "It won't do, *cara mia.*"
> "It's impossible?"
> "It's impossible." And he took up one of the brooches (I, 97-98).

There has only been an obscure and obscured sacrifice on Charlotte Stant's part. Although she cannot justifiably accept a token from Amerigo, then, Charlotte herself would offer him one — a "box." For this, this Pandora has lain close and kept herself.

It is at this point, when the Prince has in his turn rejected Charlotte's offer, that the antiquarian shopkeeper reveals his golden bowl in its box within a box. Although Charlotte would buy it (obviously more as a symbol of her intimate solidarity with the Prince than as any gift for Maggie), her Epimetheus again backs off, this time for fear of some ominous secret, a concealed "weak place" (I, 104). The upshot is that, while no formal transaction has taken place between the sometime lovers, the golden bowl, "however tiny," has nevertheless come to be an emblem of a mutual knowledge. Almost ceremonially, potential conspirators have adorned themselves with a secret.

What of Amerigo's comparatively defensive part in this community of knowledge? The Prince can never be a barbarian: "He *is* profoundly a Prince" (I, 357). Still, like his forebear the Prince Casamassima, he can be despoiled. He can be, even in England, a social aesthete, for "civilization condensed" in him is refined spirit of place as well as place.[1] As we saw, he is already the social aesthete when he insists, in the face of the Ververs' presumptuous knowledge, on his being-unto-self. Like Charlotte, he has his "weak place." And like Charlotte again, he has already begun to require the compensation of Roman days recollected, what he later thinks of as "something wholly his own" (I, 317): *Charlotte* is his secret. But what if, now, he should in a manner lose even this secret? His social problem is that even while his position steadily if imperceptibly worsens in England, Charlotte in her turn is claimed by Adam Verver. More and more in the hands of the barbarians, the Prince is subtly falsified.

> When she [Charlotte] presently therefore from her vantage saw the Prince come back she had an impression of all the place as higher and wider and more appointed for great moments; with its dome of lustres lifted, its ascents and descents more majestic, its marble tiers more vividly overhung, its numerosity of royalties, foreign and domestic, more unprecedented, its symbolism of "State" hospitality both emphasized and refined. This was doubtless a large consequence of a fairly familiar cause, a considerable inward stir to spring from the mere vision, striking as that might be, of Amerigo in a crowd . . . What did he do when he was away from her that made him always come back only looking, as she would have called it, "more so"? Superior to any shade of *cabotinage*, he yet almost resembled an actor who, between his moments on the stage, revisits his dressing-room, and, before the glass, pressed by his need of effect, retouches his make-up (I, 221-222).

The Prince is theatrical because, as Charlotte tells Fanny Assingham soon after, he has been "placed" (I, 231) on display by the Ververs. That is to say, he has been socially displaced. Time among the Anglo-Saxons has rendered him something of an impostor.

Eventually, even a Roman prince must sue for his sense of social reality. There is nothing, however tiny, that *he* would miss; "This last was after all the point; he really worked, poor young man, for acceptance, since he worked so constantly for comprehension. And how, when you came to that, *could* you know that a horse wouldn't shy at a brass-band, in a country-road, because it didn't shy at a traction-engine?" (I, 140-141). He has been embarrassed by the divine fools into becoming something of a superior fool himself — "saving up, for some very mysterious but very fine eventual purpose, all the wisdom, all the answers to his questions, all the impressions and generalisations

he gathered . . . He wanted first to make sure of the *whole* of the subject that was unrolling itself before him; after which the innumerable
facts he had collected would find their use" (I, 145). The quintessential Roman is a comprehensively rebuffed, light ornamental, ever so
slightly ridiculous man:

> The Prince had the sense, all good-humouredly, of being happily chosen,
> and it wasn't spoiled for him even by another sense that followed in its train
> and with which during his life in England he had more than once had
> reflectively to deal: the state of being reminded how after all, as an out-
> sider, a foreigner, and even as a mere representative husband and son-in-
> law, he was so irrelevant to the working of affairs that he could be bent on
> occasion to uses comparatively trivial. No other of her guests would have
> been thus convenient for their hostess; affairs, of whatever sorts, had
> claimed, by early trains, every active easy smoothly-working man, each in
> his way a lubricated item of the great social political administrative *engren-
> age* . . . If he, the great and clever Roman, on the other hand, had an
> affair, it wasn't of that order; it was of the order verily that he had been
> reduced to as a not quite glorious substitute (I, 316).

Finally the Prince's "saving up" makes a remarkable reactionary of
him. He claims a Charlotte of Roman days in a liaison, a liaison the
value of which lies in its affording "an exquisite sense of complicity" (I,
300). Craving all the time the civil ideal that has led to their displacement, yet also protesting their weak place, the Prince and Charlotte
would provide the official situation, the international marriage, with
its poisoned or left-handed imitation. Ambiguous revengers and
provocateurs, they can perfectly reproduce the Ververs's noble value,
their "superstition of not hurting" (I, 142), even as they determine
obscurely to hurt. It is the knowledge—a "sovereign law" (I, 291) in
their "conscious care" (I, 278)—upon which this community takes its
oath:

> . . . With which, as for the full assurance and the pledge it involved, each
> hand instinctively found the other. "It's all too wonderful."
> Firmly and gravely she kept his hand. "It's too beautiful."
> And so for a minute they stood together as strongly held and as closely
> confronted as any hour of their easier past even had seen them . . . "It's
> sacred," he said at last.
> "It's sacred," she breathed back to him. They vowed it . . . with a vio-

lence that had sighed itself the next moment to the longest and deepest of stillnesses they passionately sealed their pledge (I, 278-279).

The Prince and Charlotte might now be divine fools in reverse, perversions of divine fools, for by this remarkable supplantation or transvaluation they take, in Nietzsche's phrase, "a sublime revenge"—even Charlotte, as deeply mendacious here as any Christine Light and would-be Princess Casamassima, seems quite delivered from conscious hatred. Always ambiguously, the lovers would give the Ververs' quest for civilized identity the lie; they will prevent them from knowing the civil ideal outside its reactionary transformations. And having determined on this, they consummate their community with a voluptuousness that is as much a cherishing or rehearsal of their secret as it is an erotic connoisseurship. " 'If we could but take,' he exhaled, 'the full opportunity! . . . I feel the day like a great gold cup that we must somehow drain together' " (I, 321-322).

The Ververs, then, James's newly come divine fools, have in effect embarrassed the very worldly Amerigo and Charlotte into being or trying to be divine fools themselves. Fanny Assingham does not exaggerate when she says that they have imposed themselves in so improbably good, therefore in so awkward, a way as to render the others "abjectly innocent . . . victims of fate" (I, 350) and as to drive them into perverse community. Together, these characters have entered a cycle that, as Fanny summarizes it, might be the paradigm of all Jamesian compensation cycles:

"Maggie had in the first place to make up to her father for her having suffered herself to become—poor little dear, as she believed—so intensely married. Then she had to make up to her husband for taking so much of the time they might otherwise have spent together to make this reparation to Mr. Verver perfect. And her way to do this, precisely, was by allowing the Prince the use, the enjoyment, whatever you may call it, of Charlotte to cheer his path—by instalments, as it were—in proportion as she herself, making sure her father was all right, might be missed from his side. By so much, at the same time, however," Mrs. Assingham further explained, "by so much as she took her young stepmother, for this purpose, away from Mr. Verver, by just so much did this too strike her as something again to be made up for. It had saddled her, you'll easily see, with a positively new obligation to her father, an obligation created and aggravated by her unfortunate even if quite heroic little sense of justice . . . Before she knew it at any rate her little scruples and her little lucidities, which were really so divinely blind — her feverish little sense of justice, as I say — had brought the two others together as her grossest misconduct couldn't have done (I, 352-354).

Against these divine fools' politics, against their arranging the damnable terms of their reactions, against their subtle barbarization, James now sets his second "half" and Maggie Verver's "general rectification" (II, 62). Let us say that he sets against secret reaction a kind of divine counterreaction. Thus, obscurely hurt, ambiguously given the lie, somehow only for-the-other, Maggie Verver too feels perceptibly theatrical: "she reminded herself of an actress who had been studying a part and rehearsing it, but who suddenly, on the stage, before the footlights, had begun to improvise, to speak lines not in the text" (II, 29). She experiences the fever-chill of the interstice — and the need to protect herself. "She hadn't, so to speak, fallen in; she had had no accident nor got wet; this at any rate was her pretension until after she began a little to wonder if she mightn't, with or without exposure, have taken cold. She could at all events remember no time at which she had felt so excited, and certainly none — which was another special point — that so brought with it as well the necessity for concealing excitement" (II, 6). Indeed, this American girl's second go might be said to be about *her* use of secrecy, a marvellously clement use. Feeling herself known, Maggie would reclaim the secret it would seem that she has forfeited; and then, once she herself knows what Amerigo and Charlotte know, she learns "divinely" to use her knowledge. At the story's great turning point, just after Fanny Assingham has smashed the golden bowl, Maggie tells the Prince that she knows, without telling him what she knows. In this way Maggie coerces Amerigo to break with Charlotte by intimating the possibility of scandal, and also by allowing him some cover for honorable withdrawal. Likewise Maggie trumps Charlotte's knowledge. Having reclaimed her community with the Prince, she secures his agreement not to share his new knowledge with Charlotte. At the same time she refrains from openly humiliating her adversary. Rather than claim her full "rights of resentment" (II, 209), then, Maggie has taken the situation upon herself, asserted, so far as she can, her authentic principle of not hurting, and thus initiated the reversal of a revenge cycle. Of course, the ultimate pressure upon the adulterers lies in her refusing to share with Amerigo the secret of what Adam Verver, his paymaster, knows. Since no one, not even Maggie, either knows or can know this, Verver becomes a kind of unknown master of a conspiratorial society in which there is a "secret behind every face" (II, 207).

By this time James's conspirators have actually entered a further phase in their use of secrecy—it concludes the development between the middle James of *The Portrait of a Lady, The Bostonians,* and *The Princess Casamassima* and the James of the last novels. His international reactionaries not only conspire; as magnificent formalists they now lie and lie ceremonially about their lying. They are high perjurors. This is because a lie has been integral to their situation in the first place. The Ververs themselves have all along occupied the barbarians' false position. And Charlotte in particular seems to have passed beyond the need specifically to lie into a state of "organic mendacity." (Only this paradox can explain her conscious care never to wound even as she dreadfully wounds.) Besides, the adulterers have sealed their liaison-lie with a vow; after this, they live perjuriously, as it were. Their golden bowl itself, concealing as it does a weak place, might be a kind of ceremonial lie.

The ethical problem, therefore, of *The Golden Bowl's* second half goes beyond either renouncing or refusing to renounce the rights of resentment. For Maggie Verver, it is a matter of whether or not ceremonially to give the lie to the liaison and so expose it. In this crisis it is that broker of international marriages Fanny Assingham who shows the way to properly divine counterreaction; Fanny who, when Maggie first opens herself to her denies on oath that she has ever entertained the idea of the liaison. Indeed, far from giving the lie, Fanny would tell a vital or honorable lie on behalf of the gross lie that the situation has become. "Nothing—in spite of everything—*will* happen. Nothing *has* happened. Nothing *is* happening" (I, 357). Sketching out one of her most important scenarios, she tells her husband,

> "We shall have, as I've again and again told you, to lie for her—to lie till we're black in the face."
> "To lie 'for' her?" . . .
> "To lie *to* her, up and down, and in and out—it comes to the same thing. It will consist just as much of lying to the others too: to the Prince about one's belief in *him;* to Charlotte about one's belief in *her;* to Mr. Verver, dear sweet man, about one's belief in everyone. So we've work cut out—with the biggest lie, on top of all, being that we *like* to be there for such a purpose" (II, 108-109).

[*177*]

And just as the reactionaries have pledged themselves from the golden bowl, Fanny would deny that there has ever been a golden bowl. Given the social stakes, she can aptly be said to be telling a "civilized" lie.[2] After such denial, her destruction of the golden bowl in Maggie's presence amounts to a prophetic, and also perfectly perjurious, fiat. It puts the seal upon her energetic quixotry.

But if the ethically negative is upheld by this prophetess as a sacrifice to social duty, it is undertaken by her acolyte "for love"; as we have said, it is in *The Golden Bowl* that the pastoral realm emerges most unequivocally in James. Thus it is for love, love of the others as civil idealists, that Maggie perjures herself when challenged by Charlotte at Fawns:

> It was only a question of not by a hair's breadth deflecting into the truth . . . Charlotte held her a moment longer: she needed — not then to have appeared only tactless — the last word. "It's much more, my dear, than I dreamed of asking. I only wanted your denial."
> "Well then you have it."
> "Upon your honour?"
> "Upon my honour."
> . . . With which she saw soon enough what more was to come. She saw it in Charlotte's face and felt it make between them, in the air, a chill that completed the coldness of their conscious perjury. "Will you kiss me on it then?"
> She couldn't say yes, but she didn't say no (II, 221-222).

Above all, it is for love that Maggie humbugs her father in what is arguably the greatest encounter in James for its range of experience. By the time of this scene at Fawns, the second go version of her original proposal that her father remarry, Maggie is a divine fool well and truly undeceived:

> "Did you think me," she asked with some earnestness — "well, fatuous?"
> " 'Fatuous'?" — he seemed at a loss.
> "I mean sublime in *our* happiness — as if looking down from a height. Or rather sublime in our general position — that's what I mean" (II, 226).

Moreover, always more or less in secret, the two Ververs have recognized the "immorality" (II, 81) or "selfishness" (II, 83) peculiar to their barbarians' divine foolishness. Indeed they recognize that they have provoked the crisis of their lives: and they either claim their rights of resentment and throw up the whole European enterprise as utterly disappointing, or they "love in the most abysmal and unutterable way of all," thus to affirm that, whatever the false position, "you're beyond everything, and nothing can pull you down" (II, 231). It is for abysmal and unutterable love, then, that the Ververs determine to give up the one claim while holding to the higher false position. To this end, they prepare to retrace their own steps, rectify turn by turn their elaborate life-lie. They must as it were revoke their original, divine fools' provocation. They must give up forever their mutual or "married" (I, 154) dependence (which might be the attachment of the American Henry James himself to all his debutante beginners in Europe) in favor of their respective marriages. In effect, therefore, they have to deny their superstition of not hurting and arrange obscurely to do each other and the others a great and obscure hurt. The Ververs must for the first time withhold community and the right to community from one another. They must lie honorably to one another and, as the earnest of their self-sacrifice, absolutely refrain from giving each other the lie.

As Maggie has both consummated and initiated their barbarian pretension by her marriage, so it falls to Maggie both to initiate and conclude the general rectification. She must lie herself, lie about herself. In the knowledge that neither she nor her father have ever been consciously selfish in their design, she nevertheless asserts that "I'm at this very moment . . . frozen stiff with selfishness" (II, 233-234). Thus rather than put responsibility for sacrificing her, and thereby for having to hurt her, upon her father, she offers herself as a paradoxically hurtful scapegoat. Correspondingly, it falls to Adam Verver *not* to claim his right to the truth, not even in the face of the inescapable hurtfulness of his daughter's lie. Further, Adam must efface his own interest to the very last by sacrificing every appearance of sacrificing himself to Maggie and thus contributing to her hurt and hurtfulness. Like his daughter, Adam Verver would take all hurt to the others upon himself and go quietly. In other words, there must seem to be no truth, only the divorce of a lie, between this erstwhile "married" couple. In this way the Ververs make up a kind of sublimely sacrificial and retributive community of knowledge that duplicates, but also transcends and redeems, Amerigo's and Charlotte's sublimely vengeful community:

> He was doing what he had steadily been coming to; he was practically *offering* himself, pressing himself upon her, as a sacrifice — he had read his way so into her best possibility; and where had she already for weeks and days past planted her feet if not on her acceptance of the offer? Cold

indeed, colder and colder she turned as she felt herself suffer this close personal vision of his attitude still not to make her weaken. That was her very certitude, the intensity of his pressure; for if something dreadful hadn't happened there wouldn't for either of them be these dreadful things to do . . .

"Why I sacrifice you simply to everything and to everyone. I take the consequences of your marriage as perfectly natural."

He threw back his head a little, settling with one hand his nippers. "What do you call, my dear, the consequences?"

"Your life as your marriage has made it."

"Well, hasn't it made it exactly what we wanted?"

She just hesitated, then felt herself steady—oh beyond what she had dreamed. "Exactly what *I* wanted—yes."

His eyes, through his straightened glasses, were still on hers, and he might, with his intenser fixed smile, have been knowing she was for herself rightly inspired. "What do you make then of what I wanted?"

"I don't make anything . . . I don't even pretend to concern myself—!"

"To concern yourself—?" He watched her as she faintly faltered, looking about her now so as not to keep always meeting his face.

"With what may have *really* become of you. It's as if we had agreed from the first not to go into that—such an arrangement being of course charming for *me* . . . I never went into anything, and you see I don't; I've continued to adore you—but what's that from a decent daughter to such a father? . . . You don't claim, I suppose, that my natural course, once you had set up for yourself, would have been to ship you back to American City?"

. . . And he waited again while she further got from him the sense of something that had been behind, deeply in the shade, coming cautiously to the front and just feeling its way before presenting itself. "You regularly make me wish I *had* shipped back to American City . . . And if you say much more we *will* ship" (II, 237-239).

But now, having renounced forever their pretenders' pastoral of happiness, the Ververs have reaffirmed a pastoral of prodigious spirit. By virtue of their honorable, civilized lie, all is amazingly true again. Their sacrifice of themselves has brought them into possession of the "sacred." They are irrefutably identifiable.

The sense that he wasn't a failure, and could never be, purged their predicament of every meanness—made it as if they had really emerged, in their transmuted union, to smile almost without pain . . . Oh then . . . she wasn't in that case a failure either—hadn't been, but the contrary; his strength was her strength, her pride was his, and they were decent and competent together. This was all in the answer she finally made him.

"I believe in you more than anyone."

"Than anyone at all?"

She hesitated for all it might mean; but there was—oh a thousand times!—no doubt of it. "Than anyone at all." She kept nothing of it back now, met his eyes over it, let him have the whole of it; after which she went on: "And that's the way, I think, you believe in me."

He looked at her a minute longer, but his tone at last was right. "About the way—yes" (II, 241-242).

Appropriately in a story that might be said to be about a series of embraces—the Prince's and Charlotte's in Portland Place, Fanny's and Maggie's at Portland Place, Maggie's and Charlotte's at Fawns—this utmost transaction and determination is sealed with an embrace "august and almost stern" (II, 242).

After arranging these damnable terms of sacrifice, it remains for Maggie to live out to the end the lie of her selfishness—thus her loving-kindly lie to Charlotte, who rages for an all but unambiguous vengeance for the failure of her dream of European princeliness, and who would now dispossess Maggie of her father and her American patrimony. Before this intimate adversary still "truly . . . believing in her passionate parade" (II, 279), Maggie stands ready to swear that it is she herself who has failed absolutely in the quest for Europe, Charlotte never. Finally, having restored the expelled and infinitely humiliated Charlotte to her best "value" (II, 322), she helps to restore the displaced Amerigo to his "place . . . an attribute somehow indefeasible, unquenchable" (II, 285). All is civilized in this golden cadence, even while all remains openly secret. Like those other improbably good fools in life, Maisie and Strether and Milly Theale, the Ververs have improbably succeeded.

Notes

I. Communities of Knowledge: *Secret Society in Henry James*

1. "Yes; with the examples of all these other novelists in his mind, Henry James was aware that he had much at stake. Not for nothing, in spite of his fears, had he given his own country a 'good trial': all the great novelists had had worlds to interpret, it was necessary to have one's world, and had any one ever heard of a novelist — a serious novelist — whose world was not the matrix of his own inherited instincts? Linger as one might in fancy over this or that alien paradise could one ever be anything else than the child of one's own people, engraft oneself so completely as to assimilate it and live it, and re-live it and create from it? Possibly; conceivably. Still, how much one would have to risk!" *The Pilgrimage of Henry James* (New York, 1925), pp. 49-50.

2. "Social aestheticism" is conceived here as being analogous to what has been called "contemplative aestheticism": "the idea of treating experience 'in the spirit of art,' as material for aesthetic enjoyment." R. V. Johnson, *Aestheticism* (London, 1969), p. 12.

3. See Georg Simmel's very valuable essays, "Types of Social Relationships by Degrees of Reciprocal Knowledge of their Participants," "Secrecy," and "The Secret Society" in *The Sociology of Georg Simmel,* trans. and ed. Kurt Wolff (Glencoe, Illinois, 1950).

4. See Simmel, "Adornment," pp. 338-344. This distinctive Jamesian combination of pilgrim and master is beautifully revealed in a passage on Rome in *William Wetmore Story and His Friends* (Boston, 1904), II, pp. 208-209: "They then, as it were, the good manners, became the form in which the noble influence was best recognized, so that you could fairly trace it from occasion to occasion, from one consenting victim to another. The victims may very well not have been themselves always conscious, but the conscious individual had them all, attentively, imaginatively, at his mercy — drawing precisely from that fact a support in his own submission. He had the rare chance of seeing people kept in order, kept in position before the spectacle, so as to be themselves peculiarly accessible to observation. This faculty had, of course, in the nature of the case, to feed more on their essence and their type than, as it might have done elsewhere, on their extravagance and their overflow; but at least they couldn't elude, impose or deceive, as is always easy in London, Paris or New York, cities in which the spirit of the place has long since (certainly as an insidious spell) lost any advantage it may ever have practised over the spirit of the person. So, at any rate, fanciful as my plea may appear, I recover the

old sense — brave even the imputation of making a mere Rome of words, talking of a Rome of my own which was no Rome of reality. That comes up as exactly the point — that no Rome of reality was concerned in our experience, that the whole thing was a rare state of the imagination, dosed and drugged, as I have already indicated, by the effectual Borgia cup, for the taste of which the simplest as well as the subtlest had a palate." My attention was drawn to this passage by Charles Feidelson.

5. Max Scheler, *Ressentiment* (New York, 1972), p. 78: "He who is 'mendacious' has no need to lie!"

6. There is, one suspects, a good deal of James the expatriate, and probably also of Alice James, in the self-rejecting Rosy. See the *Daisy Miller* preface, where James speaks of how "that confidence in what he may call the *indirect* initiation . . . may even after long years fail an earnest worker in these fields. Conclusive [proof] that, in turn . . . the intending painter of even a few aspects of the life of a great old complex society must either be right or be ridiculous. He has to be, for authority — and on all such ground authority is everything — but continuously and confidently right; to which end, in many a case, if he happens to be but a civil alien, he had best be simply born again — I mean born differently" (xx).

7. See Simmel, "The Secret Society," pp. 345-376 (especially "Ritual," "Degrees of Initiation," "Centralization," "De-Individualization"). James's remarks in the preface ("I recall pulling no wires, etc.") are sometimes used as a basis either for dismissing him as a political novelist or, less often, for taking him seriously as one. But both these ways of taking the novel are somewhat beside the point. The truth is, rather, that James, as a social observer of his time, can imagine a secret society so well that he inevitably borders on the political. For an account of the nineteenth century's obsession with secret societies, see J. M. Roberts, *The Mythology of the Secret Societies* (Frogmore, St. Albans, 1974).

8. Irving Howe makes this point of Conrad, whose reactionary conservatism "reduces history to a cycle of enforced repetition and frees us, conveniently, from the need to study either specific revolutions or their complex consequences. 'All revolutions,' wrote George Orwell, 'are failures, but they are not all the same failure.' Some, I might add, have even been successful, the French Revolution, despite the Terror and Napoleon, having opened Europe to political freedom. Conrad's formula suggests the complacence of a man who fails to see that at times political revolt is the only honorable choice and the skepticism of a man who urges the gesture of moral heroism yet insists that it is ultimately meaningless." *Politics and the Novel* (New York, 1957), p. 90.

9. E.g., Taylor Stoehr, "Words and Deeds in *The Princess Casamassima*," *ELH*, 37 (March, 1970), 95-116.

10. *A Small Boy and Others* (London, 1913), pp. 360-361.
11. *A Small Boy and Others,* pp. 362-363.

II. The Pandora Situation: *Shame, Honor, and Revenge in James*

1. Erik H. Erikson, "Identity and the Life Cycle," in *Psychological Issues,* 1, no.1 (1959), 142: "Shame supposes that one is completely exposed and conscious of being looked at: in one word, self-conscious. One is visible and not ready to be visible; which is why we dream of shame as a situation in which we are stared at in a condition of incomplete dress . . . Doubt is the brother of shame. Where shame is dependent on the consciousness of being upright and exposed, doubt . . . has much to do with a consciousness of having a front and a back — and especially a 'behind.' "

2. Helen Merrell Lynd, *On Shame and the Search for Identity* (London, 1958), p. 17, pp. 204-210.

3. Erikson, "Identity and the Life Cycle," 142: "Shame is early expressed in an impulse to bury one's face, or to sink, right then and there, into the ground. But this, I think, is essentially rage turned against the self. He who is ashamed would like to force the world not to look at him, not to notice his exposure. He would like to destroy the eyes of the world. Instead he must wish for his own invisibility."

4. *The American Scene* (London, 1907), p. 377.

5. *The American Scene,* p. 386. An even more moving example of James's sensibility is his account of the "little old Concord Fight," where he seems half-ashamed for provinciality, but half-ashamed too for the huge expertise history has given him on the cheap:

All the commemorative objects . . . speak to the spirit, no doubt, in one of the subtlest tones of which official history is capable, and yet somehow leave the exquisite melancholy of everything unuttered. It lies too deep, as it always so lies where the ground has borne the weight of the short, simple act, intense and unconscious, that was to determine the event, determine the future in the way we call immortally. For we read into the scene too little of what we may, unless this muffled touch in it somehow reaches us so that we feel the pity and the irony of the *precluded* relation on the part of the fallen defenders. The sense that was theirs and that moved them we know, but we seem to know better still the sense that wasn't and that couldn't, and that forms our luxurious heritage as our eyes, across the gulf, seek to meet their eyes; so that we are almost ashamed of taking so much, such colossal quantity and value, as the equivalent of their dimly-seeing offer. The huge bargain they made for us, in a word, made by the gift of the little all they had — to the modesty of which amount the homely rural facts grouped there together have appeared to go on testifying — this brilliant advantage strikes the imagination that yearns over them as unfairly enjoyed at their cost. Was it delicate, was it decent — that is *would* it have been — to ask the embattled farmers, simple-minded unwitting folk, to make us so inordinate a present with so little of the conscious credit of it? Which all comes indeed, perhaps, simply to the most poignant of all those effects of disinterested sacrifice that the toil and trouble of our forefathers produce for us. The minute-men at the bridge were of course interested intensely, as they believed — but such, too, was the artful manner in which we see *our* latent, lurking, waiting interest, like a Jew in a dusky back-shop, providentially bait the trap (261-262).

6. Saul Rosenzweig's study of the Jamesian ghost still seems to me to be essentially correct. I should myself, however, put a shame interpretation rather than a strictly Freudian one, on his evidence. "The Ghost of Henry James: A Study in Thematic Apperception," *Partisan Review,* 11 (Fall, 1944), 435-455.

7. In the preface to *The Reverberator,* James remarks that "As I read over 'A Passionate Pilgrim' and 'The Madonna of the Future' they become in the highest degree documentary for myself (xxiii). "A Passionate Pilgrim" was of course the title story of James's first book.

8. "The Jolly Corner" was written in August, 1906, during the period when James had begun to be preoccupied with the New York edition of his work. Edel, *The Master, 1901-1916* (London, 1972), pp. 319-332.

9. *William Wetmore Story and His Friends,* II, p. 224.

10. *A Small Boy and Others,* pp. 9-10.

11. Albert J. Guerard, for example, appears to assume that doubling is confined in James to "The Jolly Corner." See *Stories of the Double* (Philadelphia and New York, 1967), pp. 1-14. See also Claire Rosenfield, "The Shadow Within: The Conscious and Unconscious Use of the Double," *Daedalus,* 92 (Spring, 1963), 326-344.

12. *A Small Boy and Others,* pp. 184-185.

13. "The Theme of the Double in Dostoevsky" (trans. René Wellek), in *Dostoevsky: Twentieth Century Views* (Englewood Cliffs, N.J., 1962), pp. 112-129.

14. Otto Rank, *The Double, a Psychoanalytic Study* (Chapel Hill, 1971), p. 85.

15. *The Double,* p. 78. See also "The Double as Immortal Self" in *Beyond Psychology* (New York, 1958), where Rank writes: "Originally conceived of as a guardian angel, assuring immortal survival to the self, the double eventually

appears as precisely the opposite, a reminder of the individual's mortality, indeed, the announcer of death itself" (p. 76).

16. *The Brothers Karamazov,* trans. Constance Garnett (London, 1961), p. 294.

17. See my article "The Consciousness of 'Twin Consciousness': Patrick White's *The Solid Mandala,*" in *Novel,* 2 (Spring, 1969), 241-254.

18. Julian Pitt-Rivers, "Honour and Social Status" in *Honour and Shame: The Values of Mediterranean Society,* ed. J. G. Peristiany (Chicago and London, 1966), pp. 21-22.

19. "Ivan Turgenev's New Novel" (review of *Virgin Soil*), *The Nation,* 24 (1877), 252.

20. *Calderón and the Seizures of Honor* (Cambridge, Mass., 1972), pp. 12-13.

21. Another shame-axis imagination would be the loose and baggy Tolstoy, who might in some ways be James's literary double. See John Bayley's *Tolstoy and the Novel* (London, 1966): "Whereas Dostoevsky's [characters] can live with — and even live *by* — the cracks and contradictions in themselves, to be penetrated by the outside world is for Tolstoy's people the supreme anguish, a catastrophe not to be healed or overcome. In terms of the construction of a novel, the dramatic principle of the *nadryv* [Dostoevsky's term for division or rent] is replaced in Tolstoy by the static principle of the *samodovolnost,* self-sufficiency, or self-esteem. When that is gone, the Tolstoyan character is lost indeed" (p. 43). Yet another shame-axis imagination would be Keats. See Christopher Ricks's study of Keats's letters and early poetry, *Keats and Embarrassment* (Oxford, 1974), especially chapters 1-4.

22. For many of these distinctions I am indebted to Helen Lynd, pp. 13-71.

23. James frequently uses the word confession, but generally with a shame connotation. "He had at that time been trudging . . . and it was no shame to him to confess that he was mortally tired" (*Roderick Hudson*); " 'I'm ashamed,' she still more simply confessed" (*The American*); "There seemed to flash through these words a sort of retrospective confession which told him something that she had never directly told him. She blushed as soon as she had spoken" (*Confidence*); "they had ideas that people in England nowadays were ashamed to confess to" (*The Portrait of a Lady*); "She hesitated a moment, as if there might be something indecent in the confession" (*The Princess Casamassima*); "Doctor Hugh, after a little, was visibly worried, confessing, on enquiry, to a source of embarrassment at home" ("The Middle Years"); "I blush to confess it, but I invited Mr. Paraday that very day to transcribe into the album one of his most characteristic passages" ("The Death of the Lion"); "He told me he didn't esteem them . . . There was a certain shock for Paul Overt in the knowledge that the fine genius they were

talking of had been reduced to so explicit a confession" ("The Lesson of the Master"); "After this she appeared to have regretted her confession, though at the moment she spoke there had been pride in her very embarrassment" ("The Altar of the Dead"); " . . . Americans . . . who confessed brazenly to not being in business" (*The American Scene*); " 'If you really want to know,' the poor man confessed, 'I was a little ashamed of myself' " (*The Sacred Fount*); "I perfectly admit that your smashed cup does come back to me? I frankly confess, now, the occasion" (*The Golden Bowl*).

24. Julian Moynahan, "The Hero's Guilt: The Case of *Great Expectations,*" *Essays in Criticism,* 10 (January, 1960), 60-79; and Taylor Stoehr, *Dickens, The Dreamer's Stance* (Ithaca, N.Y., 1966).

25. *The American Scene,* p. 300.

26. *Ressentiment,* p. 53 and 88-113. Scheler defines *ressentiment* as follows (p. 39): "First of all, *ressentiment* is the repeated experiencing and reliving of a particular emotional response reaction against someone else. The continual reliving of the emotion sinks it more deeply into the center of the personality, but concomitantly removes it from the person's zone of action and expression. It is not a mere intellectual recollection of the emotion and of the events to which it 'responded'—it is a re-experiencing of the emotion itself, a renewal of the original feeling."

27. For a stimulating account of the "secret revenge for secret injury" formula, see Edwin Honig, "Dehumanizing Honor: Secret Vengeance for Secret Insult," in *Calderón,* pp. 37-52.

28. E.g., Charles Thomas Samuels, *The Ambiguity of Henry James* (Urbana, 1971), esp. "The Joys of Renunciation" (pp. 61-68). Samuels' understanding of the Jamesian fine conscience might be represented by the following: "But although James can give society its due, at bottom he is ascetic. His moral opposition to worldliness goes even deeper than his understanding of its advantages. As a result, the ideal Jamesian gesture is renunciation" (p.87).

29. See Mark Spilka's sensible and perceptive essay "Turning the Freudian Screw: How Not To Do It," *Literature and Psychology,* 13 (Fall, 1963), 105-111. Spilka relates "The Turn" to the nineteenth century domestic ideal or ethic.

30. Thea Astley, *The Acolyte* (Sydney and London, 1972), p. 147. As a story of the ambiguous revolt of the servant or slave, "The Turn of the Screw" might be compared with another double fantasy of this period, "The Real Thing." Here James's socially and sexually anxious artist-hero has a choice of two pairs of models, the undistinguished, even epicene Miss Churm and Oronte, and the needy, fallen-genteel Major and Mrs. Monarch. The latter are "the real thing" ("their close union was their main comfort and . . . had no weak spot. It was a real marriage, an encouragement to the hesitating

. . .," 242); but, as they begin to displace him from his false security, they invariably turn out "colossal" (252) in his illustrations. He finds himself, therefore, preferring the *servant* Oronte to the "brawny giants" (244): "He stood his ground, however, not importunately, but with a dumb dog-like fidelity in his eyes that amounted to innocent impudence, the manner of a devoted servant — he might have been in the house for years . . . " (248). Eventually he determines to use this "artful little servant" (254) as a model for a society character, while at the same time he offers "to make use of Major Monarch as the menial" in a scene in which "a footman briefly figured" (254). Later, while he is at work on Oronte, he asks Mrs. Monarch to serve tea: "I know they felt as if they were waiting on my servant, and when the tea was prepared I said: 'He'll have a cup, please — he's tired.' Mrs. Monarch brought him one where he stood, and he took it from her as if he had been a gentleman at a party, squeezing a crush-hat with an elbow" (255). Thus the precluded, servant-like artist revolts, nominally on behalf of actual servants against the masters, the "social people"; making the latter the servants of servants, he imposes their humiliating doubles upon them. As in "The Liar," however, the secretly humiliated hero is taught the lesson of the "real thing" at the very end, when Mrs. Monarch arranges Miss Churm's hair in real humility: "It was one of the most heroic personal services I have ever rendered. Then Mrs. Monarch turned away . . . stooped to the floor with a noble humility and picked up a dirty rag that had dropped out of my paint-box" (257).

31. Leon Edel argues for a strong connection between "The Turn" and James's establishing himself at Lamb House: "James wrote 'The Turn of the Screw' accordingly on a theory of unexplained extrahuman terror, that terror within himself that could not tell him why he had felt a sinking of the heart, at the simple daylight act of providing himself with an anchorage for the rest of his days," *The Treacherous Years, 1895-1901* (London, 1969), p. 203. Edel believes that, by so establishing himself, James was asserting his independence of his family. If this is true, he was also the anxiously honorable, ghost-encumbered civil alien daring at last to claim a palpable *place* of his own in England.

32. A case not at all unlike the episode in Dickens in which Miss Havisham is set on fire. There Pip, who has for years lived on his great expectation of Estella, is at last disenchanted by Miss Havisham. Although profoundly shocked, he nevertheless forgives his tormentor and disclaims any revenge. But then, immediately after forgiving the woman who has wronged him out of her own burning sense of wrong, he re-experiences the murderous fantasy that he has had years before when humiliated by Estella. Like Fleda Vetch, he imagines that "something might happen" with a vengeance, that Miss Havisham is hanging by the neck to a roof beam. Filled suddenly with guilty

anxiety, Pip returns to his tormentor's room to "assure myself that Miss Havisham was as safe and well as I had left her"—only to find her burst immediately into flames under his eyes. This seemingly magical coincidence is completed by Pip's rescuing Miss Havisham after they have been "struggling like desperate enemies" on the floor. See Julian Moynahan, "The Hero's Guilt: The Case of *Great Expectations,*" 74-77.

33. *Notes on Novelists,* p. 246.

34. *Notes on Novelists,* pp. 227-228.

35. *The Notebooks of Henry James,* ed. F. O. Matthiessen and Kenneth B. Murdock (New York, 1955), p. 218. James is speaking of Fleda Vetch's lie to Mrs. Gereth about her feeling for Owen Gereth, a renunciatory lie that she compounds first by asserting that Owen has never even discussed Mona with her, and then by concealing Owen's own love for herself.

Elsewhere, in "Longstaff's Marriage," James speaks of "sublime hypocrisy" (239). An analogy would be the "true lie" in Conrad. See Robert Penn Warren, introduction to *Nostromo* (New York, 1951), p. xxiii: "He has lied, but his lie is a true lie in that it affirms the 'idea,' the 'illusion,' belief and love."

36. Pitt-Rivers, *Honour and Shame,* p. 33.

37. See Stephen Reid's interesting discussion of the Jamesian pledge in "Moral Passion in *The Portrait of a Lady* and *The Spoils of Poynton,*" *Modern Fiction Studies,* 12 (Spring, 1966), 24-43. E.g., "Fleda's commitment *is* now her life; to abandon it would be death" (38). Also Stoehr's excellent discussion of the revolutionary's vow and avowal in "Words and Deeds in *The Princess Casamassima,*" 118-27.

38. Pitt-Rivers, *Honour and Shame,* p. 34.

39. *The Comic Sense of Henry James* (London, 1960), pp. 251-252.

40. *Notebooks,* p. 18.

41. "The ugliest trick it plays at any rate is its effect on that side of the novelist's effort—the side of most difficulty and thereby of most dignity—which consists in giving the sense of duration, of the lapse and accumulation of time," "London Notes" in *Notes on Novelists,* p. 441.

42. In "The Spatial Form of *The Golden Bowl,*" *Modern Fiction Studies,* 12 (Spring, 1966), 103-116, Alan Rose takes spatialism to mean an organization of scenes, symbols, and images by which James achieves, in Coleridge's phrase, "a kind of visual magnitude." See also Austin Warren, "Henry James: Symbolic Imagery in the Later Novels," in *Rage for Order* (Chicago, 1948), pp. 142-161.

43. *Notebooks,* p. 415.

44. I owe the notion of binary form to Joseph H. Friend's "The Structure of *The Portrait of a Lady,*" *Nineteenth-Century Fiction,* 20 (June, 1965), 85-95. J. A. Ward, in *The Search for Form, Studies in the Structure of*

James's Fiction (Chapel Hill, 1967), consistently draws attention to one-two "balance" and "parallelism" in James's fiction, but stops short of my notion of "system."

45. *Aspects of the Novel* (Harmondsworth, 1962), p. 155. Forster would call "system" in the novel "pattern triumphant" (p. 154).

46. Van Wyck Brook's account of James's venture into theater seems essentially correct to me. *The Pilgrimage of Henry James,* pp. 122-124.

47. *Notebooks,* p. 198.

48. *Experiments in Form, Henry James's Novels, 1896-1901* (Cambridge, Mass., 1968), p. 98.

49. *Experiments,* pp. 100-101.

50. *Experiments,* p. 116.

51. *Experiments,* p. 116.

52. *Experiments,* p. 117.

53. *Experiments,* p. 100.

54. Significantly, the earliest unmistakable "sacred fount" in James is the vampirist fantasy "Longstaff's Marriage," the theme of which is the international marriage and its problem of social and sexual aestheticism.

55. Jean Frantz Blackall, *Jamesian Ambiguity and "The Sacred Fount"* (Ithaca, N.Y., 1965), pp. 81-83. "In the course of the novel every other major figure is represented at some point as having his back turned toward the narrator" (p. 81).

56. *Notebooks,* p. 275: "Don't lose sight of the little *concetto* of the note in former vol. that begins with fancy of the young man who marries an old woman and becomes old while she becomes young. Keep my play on idea: the *liaison* that betrays itself by the *transfer* of qualities — qualities to be determined — from one to the other of the parties to it. They *exchange.* I see 2 couples. One is married — this is the *old-young* pair. I watch *their* process, and it gives me my light for the spectacle of the other (covert, obscure, unavowed) pair who are *not* married."

III. Child-Cult and Others

1. See Peter V. Marinelli's very interesting study *Pastoral* (London, 1971), p. 22. Also Renato Poggioli (on whom Marinelli draws) for the distinction between the pastoral of happiness and the pastoral of innocence, "The Oaten Flute" in *The Oaten Flute* (Cambridge, Mass., 1975), pp. 1-41.

2. Marinelli sees true pastoral as conveying always a "sense of preparation" for the world (p. 52).

3. *Stigma: Notes on the Management of Spoiled Identity* (Harmondsworth, 1973), pp. 147-148.

4. *The Treacherous Years,* p. 247.

5. *The Treacherous Years,* p. 248.

6. *Notebooks,* p. 179. This phrase is from the entry for January 23, 1895, just after the *Guy Domville* fiasco, that turning point in James's career: "I take up my *own* pen again—the pen of all my old unforgettable efforts and sacred struggles. To myself—today—I need say no more. Large and full and high the future still opens. It is now indeed that I may do the work of my life. And I will."

7. *The Ambassadors* is as extraordinary a case of system as, say, Spenser's *Epithalamion.* In its original serial form in the *North American Review* its twelve "medallions" each consisted of between twenty-two and twenty-six pages, and averaged about twenty-three. Moreover, the two halves of the novel each ran to one hundred and forty-one pages: the perfect hourglass!

8. See Edel, "The Little Girls," in *The Treacherous Years,* pp. 246-252. Edel's thesis here about James's "education of the emotions" is a variant of Van Wyck Brooks' contention that the American claimant in James projected himself in the guise of beginners-cum-chaperons. "Do we not distinguish, in the continual recurrence of this motif, the vestiges of James's own absorption in the problem of educating himself? These characters are all engaged in remodelling one another, in preparing one another for a career that involves infinite difficulties, a career that is beset with dangers" (pp. 62-63).

9. "It was very probably this sweet-tasting property of the observed thing in itself that was mainly concerned in Ralph's quickly-stirred interest in the advent of a young lady who was evidently not insipid . . . It may be added, in summary fashion, that the imagination of loving—as distinguished from that of being loved—had still a place in his reduced sketch" (*The Portrait of a Lady,* I, 47).

10. F. R. Leavis, *The Great Tradition* (London, 1962), p.158.

11. Christina Stead, *For Love Alone* (Sydney, 1960), p.104.

12. *A World Elsewhere* (London, 1967), p. 136.

IV. For Love

1.Geoffrey Hartman speaks of "something more primitive and essential in James—his refinedly superstitious response to spirit of place. The fact is that there are few neutral places in the world of his novels: place is always impregnate with spirit, and spirit is characterized by intentionality. The displacement of a person, as from America to Europe, is the start of a spiritual adventure involving a gothic traversing of unknown areas of influence—not necessarily forbidden rooms, recesses, and gardens, yet analogous to these. Place has presence or is an extension of a presence: and if people fall under the spell of others, it is because they cannot escape an intentionality that extends to place and haunts imagination like a ghost." *Beyond Formalism* (New Haven and London, 1971), p. 53.

2. Leon Edel, *The Master*, p. 115. Also p. 221: "Many lies have had to be told to save the marriage, but they have been, as in *The Wings of the Dove* and *The Ambassadors,* 'constructive' lies — the lies by which civilization can be held together."

Index